CW00696961

TROILUS AND CRISEYDE
A READER'S GUIDE

Troilus and Criseyde, Geoffrey Chaucer's most substantial completed work, is a long historical romance; its famous tale of love and betrayal in the Trojan War later inspired William Shakespeare. This reader's guide, written specifically for students of medieval literature, provides a scene-by-scene paraphrase and commentary on the whole text. Each section explains matters of meaning, interpretation, plot structure and character development, the role of the first-person narrating voice, Chaucer's use of his source materials and elements of the poem's style. Brief and accessible discussions of key themes and sources (for example the art of love, the holy bond of things, Fortune, and Thebes) are provided in separate textboxes. An ideal starting point for studying the text, this book helps students through the initial language barrier and allows readers to enjoy and understand this medieval masterpiece.

JENNI NUTTALL is College Lecturer in English at St Edmund Hall and a Research Fellow of Wolfson College, University of Oxford. She is the author of *The Creation of Lancastrian Kingship: Literature, Language and Politics in Late Medieval England* (Cambridge, 2007).

TROILUS AND CRISEYDE
A READER'S GUIDE

JENNI NUTTALL

CAMBRIDGE UNIVERSITY PRESS
Cambridge, New York, Melbourne, Madrid, Cape Town,
Singapore, São Paulo, Delhi, Mexico City

Cambridge University Press
32 Avenue of the Americas, New York, NY 10013-2473, USA

www.cambridge.org
Information on this title: www.cambridge.org/9780521138765

First published 2012
Reprinted 2012

Printed and bound by MPG Group, UK

A catalog record for this publication is available from the British Library.

Library of Congress Cataloging in Publication data
Nuttall, Jennifer Anne, 1975–
Troilus and Criseyde : a reader's guide / Jenni Nuttall.
p. cm.
Includes bibliographical references and index.
ISBN 978-0-521-19144-9 (hardback) – ISBN 978-0-521-13876-5 (pbk.)
1. Chaucer, Geoffrey, d. 1400. Troilus and Criseyde. I. Title.
PR1896.N88 2012
821′.1–dc23 2012007355

ISBN 978-0-521-19144-9 Hardback
ISBN 978-0-521-13876-5 Paperback

Contents

Textboxes

Acknowledgements

I started to write this book (though its gestation began much earlier in my academic career) during a period of maternity leave. I have thus had the greatest good fortune to be married to a man with an extraordinary sense of fair play and decency as regards both the ideals and the realities of being both a mother and an author. I would therefore like to thank Jon Abbott with all my heart for helping me to find miraculous amounts of solitary writing time amid the hurry-scurry of one full-time job, one part-time job and the shared business of being parents and spouses. Our daughter Molly Alys has been happily tolerant of those times when I have been *doin' writin'*. I would also like to thank Sharon Preston and her family and Victoria Penny for their parts in our juggling of home and work. Thanks too must go to the staff and owners of the Aston Pottery Café, who made me feel very welcome whilst I nursed endless cups of tea, plugged in my laptop surreptitiously and slowly worked my way through Chaucer's glorious poem in their calm and creative establishment.

I have been teaching *Troilus and Criseyde* as a commentary text to Oxford University undergraduates for nearly ten years. Being on hand as each year-group of students is by turns delighted and frustrated by this poem, seeing it come alive, read and misread and disagreed about, has inspired me to help beginning readers find their way through this work. I therefore humbly dedicate this book to all those students (and especially each courageous cohort of Oxford English Finalists, anxiously overwhelmed but suddenly thirsty for every bit of knowledge and assistance when revising this poem) who are set or set themselves the task of reading and understanding Chaucer's brilliant but challenging work. Professors Lucy Newlyn and Sharon Achinstein have been supportive colleagues at St Edmund Hall. I would also like to thank Professor Ralph Hanna for bracing yet benevolent encouragement which has meant a great deal to me. Professor Nick Havely kindly granted me permission to quote from his translations of the *Roman de Troie* and the *Teseida*. I am also grateful to Linda Bree, Maartje Scheltens and Lucy Edwards of Cambridge University Press for their patience and expert assistance as this reader's guide has taken shape, and to Damian Love for his perceptive and intelligent copy-editing.

Introduction

Geoffrey Chaucer's *Troilus and Criseyde* tells the story of the twin sorrows of Troilus, son of King Priam of Troy. First we are told of the lovesickness (and also great joy) he experienced after falling in love with Criseyde, a Trojan noblewoman, and later we see his despair following her forced departure from Troy and subsequent betrayal of him. Chaucer completed the poem in the early to middle part of the 1380s, when he was about forty years old. By this point in his literary career, he had composed three works in the dream-vision genre, namely the *Book of the Duchess*, the *House of Fame* and the *Parliament of Fowls*. He had also written several of the narratives which he would later incorporate into the *Canterbury Tales* framework. In the early part of the decade, Chaucer translated Boethius's *De consolatione philosophiae* ('the consolation of philosophy') into English prose (for the influence of Boethius's work on *Troilus and Criseyde*, see the textboxes at pp. 87, 98, 112 and 133 below). During this period, he was also experimenting with verse which drew on, translated and adapted works of the Italian scholar and poet Giovanni Boccaccio (1313–75). Whilst *Anelida and Arcite* and the story of Palamon and Arcite (which would later become the *Knight's Tale*) are indebted to Boccaccio's *Teseida* (see textbox at p. 193 below), *Troilus and Criseyde* is an adaptation of his *Il filostrato* ('the one prostrated by love').

SOURCES AND BACKGROUND

The events narrated in *Troilus and Criseyde* are set against the backdrop of the Trojan War. A Greek army besieged the city of Troy for ten years after the abduction of Helen, wife of King Menelaus of Sparta (one of the Greek city-states), by Paris, another of Priam's sons. Following many battles and the deaths of many famous warriors, the city of Troy was destroyed, its citizens killed and its temples desecrated by the avenging Greek army. Whilst Chaucer did not have direct access to the ultimate source for these mythological events of prehistory, Homer's Greek epic, the *Iliad*, he knew the story (and assumed his readers did too) from other subsequent versions of the story of Troy written in Latin and French. Alongside Homer, Chaucer names two other writers as authorities for the story of Troy's fall, Dares the Phrygian and Dictys of Crete, both supposed eyewitnesses of the events of the war (see *TC* 1.146). The texts attributed to these authors in the Middle Ages were Latin translations and adaptations of by then lost Greek originals. The *De excidio Troiae historia* ('a history of the fall of Troy'), purportedly a translation of the account of Dares the Phrygian, dates to the sixth century, whilst the *Ephemeris Belli Troiani* ('a journal of the Trojan War'), supposedly a translation of the account of Dictys of Crete, dates to the fourth century.[1] Chaucer had probably read neither work, but he did consult the *Daretis Phrygii Ylias* ('the *Iliad* of Dares the Phrygian'), a Latin epic poem in six books by the English poet and scholar Joseph of Exeter, completed in the middle of the 1180s.[2] It is based in large part on *De excidio Troiae historia*, though it also draws on the *Ephemeris Belli Troiani*.

These versions of the fall of Troy name most of the characters of Chaucer's poem and give details of their part in the events of the war between the Greeks and Trojans, but they do not narrate Troilus's love affair. The first account of Troilus's love for the daughter of Calchas (here called Briseida), and the subsequent transfer of her affections from Troilus to the Greek Diomedes, appears in *Le Roman de Troie* ('the tale of Troy'), a French verse romance written in the late 1150s by the French poet Benoît of Sainte-Maure.[3] Benoît's poem was translated and adapted by Guido of Colonna, an Italian judge and author, into a Latin prose work, the *Historia destructionis Troiae* ('the history of the destruction of Troy'), completed by November 1287.[4] Both works narrate the history of the siege and fall

[1] For translations of the *De excidio Troiae historia* and the *Ephemeris Belli Troiani*, see *The Trojan War: The Chronicles of Dictys of Crete and Dares the Phrygian*, trans. R. M. Frazer (Bloomington: Indiana University Press, 1966).

[2] For a translation, see Joseph of Exeter, *The Iliad of Dares Phrygius*, trans. G. Roberts (Cape Town: Balkema, 1970).

[3] Appendix B of *Chaucer's Boccaccio: Sources for 'Troilus' and the 'Knight's' and 'Franklin's Tales'*, ed. and trans. N. R. Havely, Chaucer Studies 3 (Cambridge: Brewer, 1980), pp. 167–83, offers a translation of most of the relevant excerpts from the *Roman de Troie*. Extracts are also translated in *The Story of Troilus: As Told by Benoît de Sainte-Maure, Giovanni Boccaccio, Geoffrey Chaucer, Robert Henryson*, trans. R. K. Gordon, paperback edn (New York: Dutton, 1964) but several relevant passages are omitted. For the text of Gordon's omissions, see G. Mieszkowski, 'R. K. Gordon and the *Troilus and Criseyde* Story', *Chaucer Review*, 15 (1980), 127–37.

[4] For a translation, see Guido of Colonna, *Historia destructionis Troiae: Guido delle Colonne*, trans. M. E. Meek (Bloomington: Indiana University Press, 1974).

of Troy, with the story of Troilus, Briseida and Diomedes appearing as interwoven episodes within the larger narrative. Chaucer had read both of these works and uses some details from each of these sources. Yet the main (though unacknowledged) source for *Troilus and Criseyde* is Boccaccio's *Il filostrato*, an Italian poem written around 1335. Boccaccio based his version of the story of Troilus's love and loss on Benoît's *Roman de Troie*, supplementing his reading with a prose redaction of the *Roman de Troie* and other earlier Italian accounts of the history of Troy. He made the love affair between Troilo and Criseida (as these characters are known in the Italian) the focus of his poem, transforming Benoît's interwoven episodes into a unified narrative. While Benoît and Guido concentrated on details of Briseida's betrayal of Troilus after her departure from Troy, Boccaccio added to these earlier versions the details of Troilo's courtship of Criseida and the consummation of their love affair, introducing the character of Pandaro (the equivalent of Chaucer's Pandarus) as a go-between. Chaucer (possibly with the help of a French translation of Boccaccio's poem) freely adapted and altered his Italian source, at times translating closely yet at other times transforming the story radically as the nine books of the *Filostrato* became the five books of his *Troilus*. More than half of the lines of *Troilus and Criseyde* are independent of Boccaccio's work.

HOW TO USE THIS READER'S GUIDE

This reader's guide divides up each book of Chaucer's poem into many shorter sections, providing paraphrase, explanation and commentary on each section in turn. Some of these subdivisions correspond to divisions in the manuscripts, in which for discrete sections of the poem scribes provide the labels *canticus Troili* ('Troilus's song') in Books I, III and V, *proem* or *prohemium* (indicating a separate introductory preface) at the beginning of Books II, III and IV, and *litera Troili* ('Troilus's letter') and *litera Criseydis* ('Criseyde's letter') in Book V. The majority of the subdivisions, however, are my own fragmentation of Chaucer's continuous narrative within each book. Such short sections are intended to allow students and beginning readers of the poem to work through the text in sequence. In order to prevent unnecessary duplication, more general topics which might be touched upon at many different points in the commentary are briefly introduced and discussed separately from the main text in the form of independent textboxes. Two textboxes provide the text in translation of the sources of two of Chaucer's minor borrowings from works other than those dealing with elements of the narrative of Troy's fall. Topics which are discussed in the various textboxes are printed in bold in the main text of the reader's guide.

This reader's guide signals the major changes which Chaucer makes as he translates his main source, *Il filostrato*, and indicates some of the points at which he supplements this source with information from other versions of the story at his disposal. However, a guide of this length cannot fully discuss the similarities and differences which are revealed when *Troilus and Criseyde* is compared to *Il filostrato*. The Norton Critical Edition of *Troilus and Criseyde* edited by Professor Stephen A. Barney provides a translation of Boccaccio's *Filostrato* on facing pages, by means of which student readers can compare Chaucer's poem with its major source in every detail. All quotations from both *Troilus and Criseyde* and the *Filostrato* in this reader's guide are taken from Barney's edition, referenced by book and line number in the case of *Troilus* and book and stanza number in the case of the *Filostrato*. The extensive editorial apparatus of B. A. Windeatt's 1984 edition of *Troilus and Criseyde* (with a facing-page text of Boccaccio's poem in its original Italian) offers a wealth of detailed commentary on the relationship between *Troilus* and the *Filostrato*, as well as evidence of the variant readings of the surviving manuscripts of Chaucer's poem. Windeatt's edition also annotates and comments upon the multitude of direct and indirect borrowings and allusions to other writings which Chaucer adds to his translation of the *Filostrato*, many of which, for reasons of brevity, this reader's guide does not record or comment upon.

As befits its ambition, complexity and sophistication, Chaucer's *Troilus and Criseyde* has been the subject of considerable scholarship and criticism. Each generation of scholars has brought to bear different contexts, approaches and critical theories upon their readings and interpretations of the poem. Chaucer's text itself seems designed to provoke debate, disagreement and questioning. It prompts its readers to examine and re-examine, amongst many other things, received notions of literary authority, the conventions of the art of love and of writings about love, gender identities, roles and relationships, the nature of happiness and virtue, matters of philosophy (especially those of causality, our understanding of the interactions of individual choice, fate, Fortune and chance) and even patterns and processes of human history itself. Student readers of the poem are, in my experience, only too well aware of the importance of such themes. Yet under the weight and pressure of thematic interpretation, the text itself, its literal meanings, local details, likely inferences and implications, its interior logic and particularity, can often get left behind, passed over, trivialized or ignored. The commentary offered here is thus largely self-contained, intended to return students' attention to the first principles of what is thought, said, meant and done in the poem, and the motivations, constraints and circumstances which might plausibly explain those things. By seeing what can be explicated, I hope that student readers will be able to recognize what is genuinely opaque, puzzling, peculiar and paradoxical. In doing so, I am conscious that this is a predominantly literal *explication de texte*, not indicating the full extent of Chaucer's punning, his ambiguities and equivocations of meaning, syntax and tone. Moreover, this reader's guide does not seek to show how the poem might be interpreted as a product of its particular historical moment of composition. It likewise does not attempt to catalogue and reference the extensive history of critical interpretation of this work. The select student bibliography at the end of this volume offers starting points for further such reading. Nevertheless, I have endeavoured throughout to indicate the key points in the narrative at which interpretive choices might be made and where wider thematic or self-reflexive questions are raised. Often such indications take the form of speculations rather than answers, alternatives rather than decisions, paradoxical extremes rather than resolved solutions. By such equivocation, I hope that student readers will be prompted to make their own decisions and construct their own interpretations of this poem.

Student readers of *Troilus and Criseyde* are already well served by Professor Barry Windeatt's magisterial guide to the poem in the Oxford Guides to Chaucer series. It is an unparalleled reference manual, providing students with concise yet detailed introductions to the poem's date, textual tradition, sources, genre affiliations, structure, themes and style. I must here acknowledge my deep indebtedness to Professor Windeatt's scholarship, not only in his guide to *Troilus* and his edition of the poem, but also in his translation of *Troilus and Criseyde* in the Oxford World's Classics series. I have also benefited greatly from the detailed scrutiny of the poem's lexis and intertextual allusion presented in Gerald Morgan's two-volume study, *The Tragic Argument of 'Troilus and Criseyde'*. However, by dint of its very structure and purpose, Windeatt's guide does not navigate the poem in sequence but rather divides up its wealth of relevant information into the categories listed above. This volume, in contrast with Windeatt's guide, is intended primarily to help readers clarify *in situ* matters of meaning and inference, plot development and structure, the purpose and implication of each speech and dialogue, and the role of first-person narratorial interventions in influencing how each episode is interpreted, amongst many other challenges.

Users of this reader's guide should be aware of several important caveats. This commentary subscribes to A. C. Spearing's argument that the narrating 'I' in *Troilus* should not be thought of as a unified, coherent and fully characterized narrator (one who is often described as fallible, biased or only partially competent), a puppet mouthpiece controlled by a more sophisticated poet. Rather what is encoded by Chaucer in the narrative is a 'sequence of narratorial first-persons', at times a self-consciously poetical voice, at times a compiler, translator and organizer of historical and literary sources, at times a commenter on and respondent to his own narrative, at times a voice which addresses an audience or reader in order to engage (and perhaps direct) their attention and reactions – a variety of effects which personalize and subjectivize the narrative in different ways.[5] Hence this commentary refers to a narrating first-person or narrating voice rather than to a Narrator – circumlocutions, however inefficient, which are intended to resist any tendency to synthesize all of these first-person interventions into the putative personality and psyche of a fictionalized individual.

Users of this reader's guide should also be aware that, for reasons of space, it cannot paraphrase and comment upon every line of Chaucer's poem, and hence my commentary on the poem is itself a form of abridgement. Whilst the narrating first-person recounts the events of this story almost entirely in the past tense (though many of his interjections and observations are in the present tense), I here paraphrase the action in the present tense, just as students and tutors alike tend to do when discussing literary texts. The bibliographical policy of this reader's guide has been dictated by a desire to demystify and render accessible the process of learning about the poem. Quotations from and references to Chaucer's borrowings are thus provided *in situ* using, where possible, widely accessible translations. The titles of potentially unfamiliar works in other languages have been translated in parentheses when they are first mentioned in the text (such first mentions can be located via the index). Relevant literary terminology and elements of classical mythology which might not be known to all are explained in brief at the first instance of their use. The names of the main characters in Chaucer's version (Troilus, Criseyde, Pandarus and Diomede) are given as per the main form in which they appear in *Troilus and Criseyde*. Similarly, the names of their equivalent characters (and that of Deiphebus, Troilus's brother) in the earlier versions

[5] A. C. Spearing, *Textual Subjectivity: The Encoding of Subjectivity in Medieval Narratives and Lyrics* (Oxford University Press, 2005), p. 76.

by Benoît of Sainte-Maure, Guido of Colonna and Giovanni Boccaccio are given according to the main forms of their respective texts. The names of other Trojan and Greek figures and the names of figures and places of classical mythology are given in their usual modern spellings. Where the Middle English spelling of such a name is potentially unfamiliar enough to cause confusion, I have indicated the Middle English version of the name in parentheses at the first mention.

Book I

LINES 1 TO 56: THE POEM'S SUBJECT AND PURPOSE, AND PRAYERS

Though they are not formally labelled as a proem (a separate introductory preface), the poem's opening lines establish its subject, purpose and implied audience before the narrating first-person turns to the initial events of the story. He addresses his audience in the second-person plural, ostensibly speaking to a group of lovers who are listening to him recite his poem (5, 30 and 54). He tells them that he will recount the twin sorrows suffered by Troilus, son of King Priam (these being the sorrow experienced after falling in love with Criseyde and the sorrow of being first separated from and then betrayed by her). This will be the story of how Troilus's fortunes changed from sorrow to happiness, before returning once again to sorrow. The narrating voice, who weeps as he composes these lines, prays for help in composing such sorrowful poetry not from a Muse but rather from Tisiphone, one of the Furies, both tormentor and herself tormented. In classical mythology, the three Furies were predominantly agents of vengeance, sent from the underworld to punish wrongdoers, but in some depictions they themselves were also endlessly suffering. Protagonist, narrating voice and presiding deity are united by their shared sorrow.

The narrating first-person prays to Tisiphone because he does not dare appeal directly to **the God of Love** (who might more obviously aid the writing of a love story, though perhaps not one which ends in sorrow) for success in his literary venture. This is because of his own 'unliklynesse' (16), his unworthiness or unsuitability to be either a lover himself or even a writer about love. He identifies himself humbly as someone whose role is secondary and inferior, serving those who themselves serve **the God of Love**. The narrator of Boccaccio's *Il filostrato*, by contrast, begins his story by praying to his own lady, who has become a kind of muse and deity to him. The narrator and his lady are apart and it is the sorrow caused by her absence which provokes Boccaccio's narrator to retell the story of Troilo's sorrows. Whereas Boccaccio's narrator uses the story to give expression to his own troubles, Chaucer's narrating first-person sees himself as the means by which other lovers can lament their own unhappinesses through hearing about Troilus's double sorrows.

Because he dare not address **the God of Love** directly, he now asks those lovers who currently bask in happiness (and are hence in Love's favour) to make various prayers on his behalf. He first evokes their compassion by instructing them to remember their own sorrows and setbacks in love as well as the misfortunes of others. His sequence of imperatives (29, 32, 36, 40, 43) imitates the form of bidding or intercessory prayers in which a priest tells his congregation for whom or what to pray. Just as he has asked lovers to be charitable, so the narrating first-person says that he hopes to best improve the state of his own soul by acting charitably towards lovers. He sees his literary endeavour as something akin to one of the spiritual works of mercy which medieval Christians were expected to perform in their daily lives. Comforting the sorrowful and praying for the living and the dead were two such works.

The final line of this section baldly acknowledges the fact of Criseyde's betrayal of Troilus, reminding readers that this is a story whose conclusion is known in advance. There can be no other outcome, though we may at times forget the inevitability of this ending as we read on.

The God of Love

The God of Love has a number of related identities in *Troilus and Criseyde*. He appears equipped with the arrows which he fires at those he wishes to make fall in love (I.206–10) and is named by Troilus as 'blisful lord Cupide' (V.582). Yet he is more than Venus's 'blynde and wynged sone' (as he is called at III.1808). The God of Love is also a powerful enslaver, taking his revenge on those who mock love by making them lovers in turn. He embodies the natural law of sexual attraction which cannot be easily resisted. Those who fall in love become bound to him, pledged to serve him as serfs do their feudal lord. They become his followers, his subjects and servants. He is also the divinity of **the religion of love**, intervening in human affairs with grace and mercy, converting former sceptics to his faith and granting lovers success or misfortune as he chooses. When the

God of Love is invoked both by the narrating first-person and by individual characters within the narrative, the terms of address used are often applicable both to Cupid (the classical god of love) and to the Christian deity. In his omnipotence, omniscience and providential overview, the God of Love in *Troilus* resembles and perhaps invites association with the Christian deity. Moreover, the God of Love is equated by Troilus with a version of divine love itself. In his praise of love in the consummation scene in Book III, Troilus's address first to 'Love' and 'Charite' (III.1254) who is the son of Venus, and then to 'Benigne Love' (III.1261) associates Cupid, god of love, both with **the holy bond of things** which orders and unites the universe and with the virtue of charity, whether we take that to mean simply reciprocated human affection or a pagan equivalent of the Christian virtue of charity, the love, mercy and benevolence shown by God to mankind and by one Christian to another. Similarly, whilst Troilus's song at the end of Book III is largely a translation of one of the verse sections of **Boethius's *De consolatione philosophiae*** celebrating love abstractly as **the holy bond of things**, Chaucer nevertheless personifies this more abstract love as a masculine figure through the third-person pronouns *he*, *his* and *him*, identifying such sacred love with the God of Love referred to elsewhere in the narrative.

LINES 57 TO 154: CALCHAS, CRISEYDE AND THE FATE OF TROY

The narrating first-person now provides a summary of the historical frame which surrounds his chosen subject. In order to avenge the abduction of Helen (here *Eleyne*), wife of King Menelaus of Sparta, by Paris, Troilus's brother, a Greek army has laid siege to the city of Troy for nearly ten years. Calchas, a famous Trojan prophesier, correctly foretells that the Greek siege will succeed and that Troy will fall. The inevitability of this future destruction seems guaranteed by an ominous echo ('Troie sholde des*troi*ed be', 68, repeated in lines 76–7). Calchas secretly defects to the Greek army and is therefore condemned as a traitor by the citizens of Troy, who desire vengeance on him and his family.

We are told about Calchas's defection to the Greek camp in order to establish the consequences for his daughter Criseyde. She is introduced as vulnerable and fearful, a widow who does not have any confidant.

Yet though she is isolated and afraid, Criseyde nevertheless has ready access to Hector, oldest son of King Priam. She asks Hector for protection and he, moved by her plight and her beauty, guarantees that her father's defection will not endanger or dishonour her. Despite her father's treachery, she therefore remains in Troy, not shamed by his actions but able to live in a manner appropriate to her social status, held in affection and respected by her fellow citizens. The narrating voice claims to be unable to tell us whether Criseyde is a mother as well as a widow because he has not read anywhere about such matters. Chaucer's unacknowledged source is clear at this point that she has not been able to have children (*Fil.* 1.15). In removing the *Filostrato*'s reference to Criseyde's infertility, Chaucer takes away a piece of information which readers might use to make a judgement about her. Moreover, through the narrating voice's claim to be limited to what he finds in his sources, Chaucer draws attention to potential gaps in our knowledge (and hence matters for speculation).

The narrating voice now summarizes the military successes and failures of the Trojan and Greek armies. In an addition to the *Filostrato*, **Fortune** is said to whirl both the Trojans and Greeks around on her wheel, each going up and down in turn. The narrating first-person reminds us that he does not intend to retell the sequence of events leading to Troy's destruction (as his chosen subject is Troilus's twin sorrows). Troy's fall (the epic subject matter of earlier narratives) is here relegated to the status of a lengthy potential digression from his preferred material. These events, says the narrating voice, can be read about in the works of Homer, Dares and Dictys (here *Dite*), authors famed for their accounts of Troy's destruction. Although it keeps the ultimate context of Troilus's private sorrows in mind, such an intervention also emphasizes the innovative nature of the literary project created by Boccaccio and translated and adapted by Chaucer. Boccaccio's and Chaucer's versions of this love affair take what was a minor romantic episode in an epic story and narrate it at much greater length, relocating the events of the fall of Troy from centre stage to background and potential detour.

Despite the siege, the Trojans do not forget their ancient customs and the honouring of their gods. They continue to venerate and place their trust in a sacred object called the Palladium, a statue of the goddess Pallas Athena. This talismanic object is seen by the Trojan citizens as the guarantee of their city's safety. Yet it can also be seen very differently by readers looking forward into Troy's future. In some accounts of Troy's fall, this relic was stolen by the Greeks with the assistance of the Trojan traitor Antenor in order to make a successful attack on the city possible. As well as holding out the possibility of its preservation, the Palladium therefore signals Troy's destruction. These two ways of seeing, one inside the narrative and temporal and one external and atemporal, coexist throughout. The Trojan citizens are blind to their future which, as their fortunes fall and rise on the battlefield, is open and undecided. Yet for Calchas the prophesier, for historians, for the narrating voice and for us his readers, the fate of Troy is predetermined and fixed. Just so the futures of Troilus and Criseyde are hidden from the lovers themselves but are already known to Chaucer and his audience.

LINES 155 TO 357: TROILUS FALLS IN LOVE

(i) Lines 155 to 205: Criseyde and Troilus in the temple

The first set-piece of the narrative now begins, leading up to the moment when Troilus's eyes first alight on Criseyde. The scene starts with descriptions of April's springtime greenery and flowers. Many Trojan citizens visit the temple in order to hear a religious service celebrating the Palladium. The occasion is both a religious and a social one, with the Trojan nobles dressed in their finery in honour both of the occasion and of springtime. The narrative now focuses on Criseyde, dressed in the black clothes of a mourning widow. She is pre-eminent in beauty, just as the letter A is first in the alphabet. The narrative develops an antithesis, which Boccaccio's poem does not emphasize, between the darkness of Criseyde's clothing and the brightness of her beauty, saying that everyone who saw her agreed that there was never so bright a star seen under a black cloud. Although her beauty delights the crowds, Criseyde stands in a humble manner, simply dressed and meek in her appearance, alone, occupying a small space behind other visitors near the door. This is a prudent strategy given her father's treachery and her own fear of being shamed. Yet we are also told that her look and behaviour are self-confident and assured at the same time that she is apprehensive and physically marginalized. She is both a traitor's daughter and an attractive and poised noblewoman.

For Troilus, the festival is predominantly a social occasion. He leads his retinue of young knights and squires around the temple, constantly inspecting all of the Trojan ladies because he is not in love with anyone in particular. He mocks any of his men who show signs of falling in love. As in the *Filostrato*, Troilus's sarcastic comments about love and lovers are reported to us as direct speech. The content of the two speeches varies, however, creating very different back-stories. Boccaccio's Troilo, while he admits that he has experienced the joys of being in love, has been made cynical by his experiences. He blames the fairer sex for this, bitterly describing women's supposed changeability and capricious behaviour. He considers himself well out of the affairs of love, and his scorn and arrogance of course invite **the God of Love** to make him a target for his arrows. Chaucer's Troilus similarly sees love as a foolish, unpredictable, laborious and potentially miserable experience, but this is an observation made at second-hand. Nevertheless, Troilus is certain in his opinions and proud of his mockery. He mocks lovers as silly and blinded by love, but of course it is he who is blind to his imminent fate.

(ii) Lines 206 to 266: an apostrophe

The God of Love, angered by Troilus's mockery, takes his revenge, hitting him with one of his arrows. Yet before we witness the moment at which Troilus, now predisposed to fall in love, encounters Criseyde, the narrating first-person suspends his account for eight stanzas of apostrophe (an exclamatory address to a particular person or thing) and direct address to his audience. At the equivalent point, Boccaccio's narrator pauses for only a single stanza of comment. Prompted by the example of Troilus's imprudent goading of Love, the narrating voice laments the lack of insight or foresight in the human world in general. He laments the world's ignorance and humanity's 'blynde entencioun' (211), our inability to understand what is likely to happen as a result of particular actions or **intention**. He exclaims at how often, as a result of pride and overconfidence, consequences prove to be unfavourable and contrary to what was intended.

Troilus's unsuspecting pride and his sudden chastisement are next compared to that of a cart-horse named Bayard who wanders excitably off-course thanks to his full stomach and is whipped by his driver back towards the right direction. We hear Bayard's solemn thoughts as he plods along after his punishment. He reminds himself that, although he occupies lead position in his team and is a very handsome animal, he is merely a horse and must therefore submit to his fate. Troilus similarly thought that, as a noble prince, nothing could influence his heart against his will, yet the narrating first-person predicts that one look at Criseyde will inflame his heart with love. Troilus, like Bayard, has swiftly gone from being most arrogantly superior to being most controlled by love. In keeping with this fall from authority, Troilus is treated with little respect in this apostrophe, castigated with pithy proverbs and compared at length to a farmyard beast of burden.

The narrating voice then addresses those in his audience who resemble Troilus, being noble and proud and considering themselves wise. They should learn from what happened when Troilus mocked Love and be fully aware of Love's powers. As well as emphasizing Troilus's imprudence, the apostrophe thus also pre-emptively cautions those who might mock Chaucer's own narrative of sorrows in love, just as Troilus himself has shown no respect to **the God of Love**. As the strongest natural force or law, love can dominate and enslave any person. Love demonstrates its power by conquering the strongest and worthiest, and it cannot be resisted or avoided. Yet its effects are nevertheless positive, pleasing, comforting and ennobling. Since it cannot be resisted and is so virtuous in nature, the narrating voice urges his addressees not to refuse to be bound to **the God of Love** just as a serf is bound to his feudal superior. As a sapling which will bow and twist is better off than one that breaks, so they are advised to submit to the power of Love. Yet given that the narrating voice cautions us about deluded understanding in his apostrophe, we might well question his own representation of love. If love is so beneficial, why are its methods of operation so coercive and tyrannical? Will the romance upon which Troilus is about to embark prove to be an example of the virtue of love? Will it prove debasing and enslaving or ennobling and enlightening?

(iii) Lines 267 to 357: Troilus falls in love

As Troilus continues his playful inspection of those in the temple, by chance his gaze pierces through the crowd so far that he sees Criseyde standing at the edge of the room. Having been primed by Love's arrow, he is now transfixed by her. Criseyde's appearance is now described so that we readers see as Troilus sees. Criseyde is the epitome of femininity and her very manner of moving suggests her respectability and nobility. Troilus is enamoured of her rather disdainful manner as she glances to one side as if to say to onlookers 'Can't I stand here?' (this being the hauteur expected of a beautiful and dignified noblewoman). Criseyde's appearance creates such desire and devotion in Troilus that her image becomes deeply rooted in his heart. Echoing the belittling tone of the apostrophe, the narrating first-person now emphasizes how swiftly Troilus's behaviour has changed. Though he had previously gazed everywhere boldly, Troilus is now so overcome that he is happy to shrink back just as a snail withdraws its horns when threatened. Though he considered himself very clever when mocking the suffering of lovers, Troilus is now entirely unaware that **the God of Love** is present in the 'subtile stremes' (305) of Criseyde's eyes. In medieval physiology, the eyes were thought to be active, sending out beams or rays which seized the object at which they looked. Via Criseyde's gaze, Love thus takes hold of Troilus so powerfully that he feels as if his very life force has died. The narrating voice hails **the God of Love** who can, as he has just demonstrated, convert people to **the religion of love** so forcefully.

Though he stands still and gazes at Criseyde, Troilus does not reveal his desire in words or facial expression. According to the conventions of **the art of love**, a lover must keep his desire secret and act with discretion. Throughout the religious ceremony, Troilus thus imitates his former behaviour, glancing away from Criseyde from time to time to look at other things. He continues to mock love as he leaves the temple in order to disguise his new feelings. This charade is developed by Chaucer from a brief summary in the *Filostrato* into three stanzas of direct speech. Troilus mocks **the religion of love** by characterizing it as a faith which is arbitrary yet arduous. He sarcastically says that love's 'ordre' (336) is well ruled, just as an order of monks or friars is governed by a set of regulations. Love's 'observaunces' (337), its duties, rules or rituals, are conducted in a state of uncertainty. Yet no religion requires as much devotion as this 'lay' (340), this creed or set of religious customs, laws or practices.

In this pretence Troilus no longer means what he says, but we may find other types of meaning in his mockery. Given that his own devotion to Criseyde will ultimately be repaid by betrayal, Troilus's words ironically anticipate his own future in ways he cannot now imagine. We see that words can be used to conceal and misdirect, yet the pretence itself may have an element of truth about it. Though the preceding apostrophe warned us that mocking love is foolhardy, this feigned mockery nevertheless prompts readers once again to think of the criticisms which might be levelled at love (yet which do not prevent Troilus from loving). **The God of Love** has, figuratively speaking, covered Troilus's feathers with birdlime, a sticky substance spread upon branches to catch birds.

LINES 358 TO 546: TROILUS PRACTISES THE ART OF LOVE

(i) Lines 358 to 388: Troilus's beginning

Having gained some privacy by retreating to his bedchamber, Troilus can now express his newfound desire. He sighs and groans, thinking about Criseyde so much that, in a kind of waking dream, he sees her in the temple once more. He is certain that it is a piece of very good fortune to fall in love with someone like her and thinks that if he does his best to serve her then he may obtain her favour or at least become one of her servants. Within **the art of love**, devotion to a lover's lady was described as service, just as a serf was bound to serve his feudal superior. The narrating voice points out that Troilus considers all this at the very beginning of his love affair, entirely unaware of the future sorrow to be caused by Criseyde's betrayal. Yet prompted by this comment, we readers contemplate these matters both within the temporality of the narrative and with omniscient foresight. Criseyde's excellence coexists with our knowledge of her future betrayal. We know that Troilus will experience first the happiness of love but later also the pain of betrayal. What sort of fortune, good or bad or both, will his love for Criseyde ultimately prove to be?

Troilus now commits himself to the practice of 'loves craft' (379), **the art of love**. He thus intends to conceal his desire for Criseyde from everybody unless it would benefit him more to reveal it. His love will be hidden as if it were in a secure cage or coop, the mews in which birds of prey were kept while their plumage was shed in the process of moulting. This secrecy seems to him the best course of action, as he remembers the proverbial wisdom that love which is too widely publicized will eventually lead to unpleasant or unwelcome consequences.

The art of love

Romantic love in *Troilus and Criseyde* is more than desire, passion and emotion. It is also described as a craft or an art, a set of conventions and expertise which a lover must learn to manipulate in order to woo his lady successfully. Those inexperienced in love such as Troilus require advice and education on the art of love from those more knowledgeable as regards the art of love's theory and customs. According to the art of love, a lover's feelings for his lady should be kept secret and the lover should act with discretion at all times. Because of this, the lover is archetypally an isolated figure, one who expresses his sorrow in solitary complaint and lamentation. Though a lover burns with desire, it may prove difficult to woo his lady without making his love for her public, and so he is likely to require a go-between who can approach the lady on his behalf. If permitted, the lover becomes the lady's knight and devoted servant, constantly fearing his lady's displeasure and obeying her every instruction. The lover makes extravagant pledges of devotion to his lady and considers her beauty and manners to be beyond compare. Because of the overwhelming intensity of his love and the ever-present fear that he might offend his lady or fail to adhere to the conventions of the art of love, the lover is conventionally portrayed as timid and fearful, bashful and hesitant when in the presence of his lady. Courtships are expected to be lengthy and perilous, demanding great patience and stoicism on the part of the lover. Falling in love thus brings great happiness but also much fear, anxiety and distress. Yet though at times it is presented as a coherent body of expertise, the art of love was not a unified code observed by all classical and medieval lovers both literary and in reality. In the proem to Book II, the narrating first-person points out that even amongst his audience of contemporary lovers, scarcely three of them have behaved the same way when in love (II.43–6). The art of love should be thought of as a mixture of roles, behaviours and poses, as well as a range of styles of speaking and writing about love, which are deployed by lovers and by authors in a variety of ways, sometimes with great sincerity, sometimes cynically, sometimes ironically, sometimes humorously. Many of Troilus's assumptions, anxieties and self-imposed restrictions can be explained with reference to this art of love and he himself takes it very seriously. Yet the events of this particular story also expose some of the potential consequences of these expectations of secrecy and obedience (for example the result of Troilus's decision not to speak during the parliamentary discussion of the proposed exchange or his deferring to Criseyde on the decision not to elope). Similarly, the characteristic behaviour of lovers is both celebrated and mocked in the course of the narrative. The art of love is both accepted and challenged in *Troilus*, its conventions both believed in and questioned.

(ii) Lines 389 to 420: Troilus's song

By giving expression to his feelings in a song, Troilus now starts to overcome his sorrow. The song marks the moment at which Troilus fully commits himself to loving Criseyde. This moment of assent (added by Chaucer to his source) reminds us that Troilus actively and voluntarily commits himself to love, even though love is elsewhere said to constrain and coerce lovers.

Whilst the *Filostrato* simply describes Troilo as singing with joy, the narrating first-person here interjects to tell us that he will give us not merely the gist of Troilus's song but every single word which Troilus sings, just as his supposedly authoritative source written by an author named Lollius does. He will do this as faithfully as he can, notwithstanding the difference between Troilus's native tongue and his own. Due to a misreading of a passage in an epistle by the Roman poet Horace, medieval writers, including Chaucer, may well have believed there was an ancient author called Lollius whose work about Troy had been lost. Chaucer thus has his narrating voice present the poem as a translation of a famed and now purportedly rediscovered work. Chaucer here suppresses his actual source, Boccaccio's *Filostrato* (which, as a near-contemporary poem in a vernacular language, a text probably unknown in England when Chaucer was translating it, did not possess the same authority as an ancient classical work). Chaucer does not in fact invent the text of the song, but, again without acknowledging his borrowing, adapts a sonnet written by another fourteenth-century Italian author, **Francesco Petrarch's sonnet 132**. The song reveals Troilus caught between two sets of emotions. On the one hand he feels that love is beneficial, pleasing and delightful, yet on the other it makes him sorrow and suffer. He therefore both desires love and laments its effects, a paradox which seems to him inexplicable. In the song, Troilus, who formerly mocked love's uncertainties and irrationalities, now commits himself to love by marvelling at love's paradoxes.

Here, as elsewhere, the narrating voice refers to his supposed source at precisely those moments when Chaucer adds material to his sources. Chaucer uses the narrating voice's identification of his source as the lost work of Lollius to camouflage his literary innovations, both the translation and reworking of a near-contemporary Italian narrative and the first translation of a sonnet by Petrarch into English. He thus presents his work (whether playfully or as a matter of expediency) to his initial audience in the terms of classical authority which they would recognize and value. Yet for modern readers of the poem, this substitution paradoxically also highlights an author's freedom to mislead his readers, to invent supposedly authorized details and to present one thing under the guise of another.

Petrarch's sonnet 132

Sonnet 132, beginning 'S'amor non è', which Chaucer here translates as the first of Troilus's songs, comes from a collection of sonnets and other short poems now known as the *Canzoniere* ('the songbook' or 'collection of poems') or *Rerum vulgarium fragmenta* ('fragments of material in the vernacular') by the Italian author Francesco Petrarch

(1304–74). The sequence of lyrics in the *Canzoniere*, written and reworked over a period of about forty years, forms a complex and varied meditation on love inspired by Petrarch's unrequited desire for a woman named Laura. Sonnet 132 begins with a series of anxious questions about the paradoxical (that is, seemingly contradictory or counter-intuitive) relationship between on the one hand what love is and how one falls in love and on the other how a lover is affected by love. The questions are arranged as doubled antitheses: two antithetical possibilities first about the nature of love and then about the lover's volition and consent are in turn paired with two antithetical effects or responses. Love itself is addressed via oxymoron, two seemingly contradictory terms in conjunction:

'If this should not be love, what is it then? But if it is love, God, what can love be? If good, why mortal bitterness to me? If ill, why is it sweetness that torments? If willingly I burn, why these laments? If not my will, what use can weeping be? O living death, delightful agony, how can you do so much without consent? And if I do consent, wrongly I grieve. By such cross winds my fragile bark [a small boat] is blown, I drift unsteered upon the open seas, in wisdom light, with error so weighed down that I myself know not the thing I crave, and burn in winter, and in summer freeze' (Petrarch, *Canzoniere*, trans. Mortimer, p. 69).

Chaucer makes some small alterations in the process of translation. Whereas Petrarch's speaker begins by asking whether or not he himself is in love, Troilus first asks whether love in fact exists. Yet in comparison with Petrarch's speaker, Troilus feels love's effects more strongly as a physical disease, not knowing why he faints when he is not tired and marvelling that he can be both perilously cold when feverish and perilously feverish when cold (410, 420). Chaucer also omits the Petrarchan speaker's admission that (presumably because of the overwhelming effects of love) he is so lacking in wisdom and so burdened with error that he does not have the capacity to understand his own desires. In Chaucer's version, Troilus does not doubt his own ability to understand love but instead is amazed by love (403, 419). Chaucer thus adapts the sonnet to Troilus's particular situation. He omits those lines which hint that love appears paradoxical in part because, in falling in love, the lover himself becomes foolish and incapable of understanding. Troilus, who has only just fallen in love for the first time, has no such insight or scepticism, instead expressing only surprise at the emotional and physical effects of love.

(iii) Lines 421 to 504: the effects of love

Having thus committed himself to love, Troilus now addresses **the God of Love** directly as a servant and a devotee. He pledges his soul to Love and thanks him for this sudden change in fortune. He says he is not sure whether Love wishes him to serve a goddess or a mortal woman (indicating how divine Criseyde's beauty seems), but he nevertheless pledges to serve her. To indicate his sincerity, Troilus formally resigns his royal status into Criseyde's hand and becomes her servant (this being not an actual abdication but part of the tradition of **the art of love**). As the narrating first-person points out, Troilus is not spared the effects of love because of his royal status and chivalric virtue. Love does not respect Troilus's nobility but rather subjugates him as a humble slave. Though a royal prince, by falling in love Troilus paradoxically becomes the servant both of **the God of Love** and of Criseyde.

Love also dominates Troilus in physiological fashion and he thus begins to show the symptoms of **lovesickness**. So much do his private thoughts grow and intensify that he pays no attention to any other concerns. To try to quell love's fires, Troilus strives to see more of Criseyde's beauty but of course this merely inflames his passion for her further. His heart is devoted to Criseyde, whom the narrating first-person calls more beautiful even than Helen of Troy (whose beauty was legendary) or Troilus's sister Polyxena. Troilus has been changed by love: his life is now one of devotion to his lady and only she can prevent him dying from **lovesickness**. Because of this new focus, he is now uninspired by the ferocious attacks which his brothers make on the Greek army. Yet he proves to be the most courageous of the Trojan soldiers, not because of hostility to the Greeks or to save his own city but in order that Criseyde might be better pleased by his renown as a warrior. **Lovesickness** also prevents him sleeping, takes away his appetite and increases his unhappiness, to the point where he pretends he is suffering from another sort of illness, a fever, to conceal the effects of his desire. Discretion in love thus requires deceit and pretence. In the *Filostrato*, Troilo simply disguises his love with smiles and clever speeches, whereas Chaucer has Troilus disguise one disease with the facade of another.

The narrative now turns to Criseyde's possible response to this transformation of Troilus. The narrating first-person cannot say for certain whether Criseyde did not understand that she was the cause of Troilus's **lovesickness** or whether she pretended she did not know. He says that he reads in his sources that Criseyde gave no sign of caring about Troilus and his distress. Troilus is thus caused great pain by fears that she is in love with someone else. These lines emphasize the painful predicament of the lover who must keep his love discreet and also provide the context for Troilus's first solitary complaint, yet they nevertheless also illustrate the initial one-sidedness and potential absurdity of **the art of love**, in which a lady might be expected to perceive distress and take pity on a lover whose love has not yet been revealed.

Lovesickness

At the end of his song in Book 1, Troilus asks himself despairingly 'what is this wondre maladie?' (419), what is this extraordinary disease which now afflicts him? In comparison with his source, Chaucer develops much more extensively the suggestion that, in falling in love, Troilus falls prey to the disease of lovesickness. Lovesickness, also called *amor heroes* (originally a term meaning 'erotic love', but later taking on the meaning 'noble or heroic love'), was treated very seriously by medieval medical authorities. Its symptoms, as Troilus himself demonstrates, include sleeplessness, a lover's desire to be alone, frequent sighs and tears, obsessive thinking and loss of appetite. Thus Troilus's self-confessed pain and suffering must be seen as credible and entirely real, indicative of how excruciatingly his noble nature is afflicted by love. The excessive fears and sorrows prompted by love (such as those which Troilus himself experiences) might lead to melancholy, that is, a depression characterized by fixed and irrational thoughts. Severe melancholy might verge on madness, and, in extreme cases, could lead to death. Chaucer therefore adds to his source references to the possibility that Troilus might die from lovesickness.

Lovesickness was explained by medieval medical authorities as a disease of the brain. A lover becomes preoccupied by his lady and her beauty and disregards all other duties, commitments and sources of happiness. Lovesickness leads the lover to make an error of judgement, valuing his lady above all other things when she is simply another human being. Troilus's love for Criseyde might thus also be seen as a type of folly or an abandonment of reason, in which his rational nature has been dominated by love and through which he becomes wretchedly subject to the wishes of his lady. But if it is in fact a disease, should we not have more sympathy for Troilus and see his experience of love not as foolish and absurd but as inevitable and imperilling (and one which perhaps demands the remedy which Pandarus arranges)? And yet, if it is a form of medical disorder, how can love also be inspiring, ennobling, enlightening and perhaps even part of the divine ordering of the universe?

(iv) Lines 505 to 546: Troilus's complaint

Because he dare not reveal his sorrow to Criseyde in person, Troilus instead makes a complaint in private. He makes an apostrophe to himself, calling himself a fool. He is now caught in Love's snare and can do nothing but gnaw his own chain (that is, to worry away about that which has enslaved him). Since it is his destiny to love, if only, he laments, his heart were set on someone who was aware of his suffering, even if she were without pity for him. Yet Criseyde behaves as coldly towards him as a frosty night under the clear skies of winter, whilst he has been destroyed as quickly as snow melts on the fire. Her indifference moves him from near-fatal **lovesickness** to an active pleading for death. If only he had arrived at his final destination and refuge, the port of death to which his grief is currently leading him.

He asks for God's help and for mercy from the absent Criseyde to save him from death. He tells her many things and calls out her name, yet, as he himself realizes, this is all for nothing because Criseyde cannot hear his complaint. Chaucer adds the detail that Troilus nearly drowns in his own tears and increases the hyperbolical description of his ever-increasing woes at the folly of his situation to a thousandfold from the *Filostrato*'s hundredfold. Love is thus both intensely felt and recognized to be irrational and absurd.

LINES 547 TO 1092: PANDARUS VISITS TROILUS

(i) Lines 547 to 616: the obligations of friendship

Troilus has seemingly become paralysed by sorrow and fear, and thus both he and his narrative require a new momentum. Assistance duly arrives in the form of his friend Pandarus. In the *Filostrato*, Pandaro is described as 'a Trojan youth of noble lineage' (II.1). In Chaucer's version, Pandarus is introduced simply as Troilus's friend, and it is left to the reader to work out what type of person he is from his speech and actions. Chaucer expands the two simple questions asked by Pandaro on his arrival into ten lines of direct speech in which Pandarus suggests reasons for Troilus's distress and a further stanza describing Pandarus's **intention** in saying these words. Pandarus thus speaks with premeditation, not really meaning what he says but saying it for an ulterior, though compassionate, motive. Is Troilus, he asks, so afraid of Greek attacks that he has become thin or feeble? Or has he had an attack of conscience and thus become pious, bemoaning his transgressions and having been frightened into 'attricioun' (557, a type of incomplete contrition in which one is sorry for one's sins not because of love of God but through fear of punishment)? Pandarus, we are told, takes this particular tack with Troilus in order to make him angry because anger will rouse his spirits and temporarily assuage his sorrow.

In reply, Troilus asks wearily what chance or destiny has led Pandarus here to see him suffering. He tries to send Pandarus away because he does not wish his friend to witness his inevitable death. Yet Pandarus's strategy works, as Troilus continues by fiercely rejecting this accusation of cowardice and hinting that there is another cause for the anxiety which so threatens his life. He tells Pandarus that it is best not to reveal this cause. Yet Pandarus reminds Troilus of the obligations of friendship and the extent of their own friendship. These obligations compel Troilus to comply with Pandarus's request. Troilus reveals that he has fallen in love, figuring this as an attack by **the God of Love** by means of so many feelings of despair that he would now welcome death rather than continue to suffer. He tells Pandarus that what he has so far revealed, namely the cause of his woe, must suffice. Convinced that his love must remain secret, he begs Pandarus to conceal his hitherto entirely private sorrow because, he fears, many misfortunes might result if it became known.

(ii) Lines 617 to 760: Pandarus's proverbs and examples

Pandarus is exasperated by his friend's behaviour. Perhaps, he says, Troilus is pining for someone whom Pandarus's advice can help him win very quickly? Troilus is not persuaded by this, pointing out that Pandarus has not himself had any success in matters of the heart. Both Boccaccio and Chaucer indicate that Pandaro/Pandarus is devoted to an unidentified lady but has been unable to win her love (see *Fil.* II.9, 11 and 13, and *TC* I.622, 646–7, 666–7, 711–14, 717–19, II.57–63, IV.484–94). His own unrequited love gives Pandarus compassion for and knowledge of Troilus's predicament. Pandarus says that his advice may be able to help 'us' (620), referring to Troilus and himself together in the first-person plural (see further examples at I.972, 994, II.1319, IV.385, 539). In sharing his friend's sorrow and advising him in how to proceed, Pandarus makes Troilus's love a joint enterprise.

Pandarus now sets out to counter Troilus's pessimism, arguing that his own failures and errors in love will in fact allow him to educate and advise Troilus more expertly. Both Pandaro and Pandarus begin by listing proverbs. Pandarus's speech of persuasion, five stanzas long in the *Filostrato*, is expanded by Chaucer to fourteen stanzas by the addition of further persuasion, proverbs and examples. Pandarus thus has a greater presence in the poem than his equivalent Pandaro. He is more talkative and erudite, presenting his friend with a more extensive range of proverbial wisdom and argument. Pandarus quotes the example of a whetstone which, though it itself is blunt, is nevertheless used to sharpen metal blades, demonstrating that one quality can produce its opposite. By witnessing where Pandarus has gone wrong, Troilus can avoid such errors. Pandarus's argument next becomes one of epistemology, the theoretical study of knowledge, how we know what we know. We can perceive one quality more distinctly if we juxtapose it with its opposite. He illustrates this with a series of oppositions: sweetness/bitterness, joy/sorrow, white/black, honour/shame. From consideration of two opposites, he says, we can derive one lesson or piece of knowledge. Because Pandarus has so often experienced unhappiness, he will therefore be all the more able to advise Troilus about success in love. In this addition, Chaucer not only expands Pandarus's own argument but offers his readers questions which they might ask of the narrative as a whole. What, for example, might we learn from witnessing Troilus's sorrows and their opposite, his joy? Where is the dividing line, for example, between honour and shame in this love story?

Pandarus now further exemplifies his own situation by quoting an example given in a letter written by the shepherdess Oenone to Paris, Troilus's brother, expressing her grief because Paris has abandoned her in favour of Helen of Troy. The example cited recounts how the god Phoebus Apollo could not remedy his own **lovesickness** (considered a disease in classical and medieval medicine) when he had fallen in love with the daughter of Admetus (here *Amete*), king of the Greek kingdom of Thessaly, yet nevertheless it was he who first invented the science of medicine. Just so, Pandarus suffers a great deal for the love of his lady and cannot remedy his own sorrow, yet perhaps (because of his theoretical knowledge of such remedies) he will nevertheless be able to advise Troilus. The source of this example is the fifth letter of Ovid's *Heroides* ('the heroines').[1] The poetic letters in the *Heroides* each purport to be written by a mythological heroine to a lover who has mistreated or betrayed her (accompanied in some cases by a letter from the lover himself). In the letter to which Pandarus alludes, Ovid inhabits the voice of Oenone writing to Paris. Pandarus, living in prehistoric Troy, cannot of course have read a literary letter fabricated by the Roman poet Ovid in the first century BC. For him, Paris's betrayal of Oenone and his abduction of Helen are contemporary reality, the cause of the siege which surrounds his city, and the letter is a real artefact which Troilus may or may not have seen. In Pandarus's example, Chaucer links up the literary fiction with the mythological 'reality' in which it purports to exist. Yet though Pandarus cites this letter for its allusion to the relationship between male **lovesickness** and knowledge of its remedies, he seems uninterested in either female suffering or the disastrous public consequences of male desire.

Pandarus reassures Troilus that he will keep his secret even if tortured. Even if Troilus were in love with Helen of Troy, Pandarus would not prevent him from loving her. Pandarus implies a sequence of betrayals (Paris abandoned Oenone for Helen, Helen might betray Paris for Troilus) which reminds us that Criseyde will ultimately betray Troilus. Once again, Pandarus begs his friend to trust him and reveal the cause of his sorrow. He warns Troilus against adopting an extreme position, either telling no one or telling everyone about his love. Yet he points out that the mid-point between these extremes, namely telling a close friend in order to prove your loyalty to that friend, is not a fault. Pandarus cites a proverb attributed to Solomon, supposed author of some of the books of Wisdom literature in the Old Testament: he that is alone will have sorrow because, if he falls, no one will help him get up. Since Troilus does have a friend to offer assistance, he should take advantage of this opportunity to share his sorrow. Pandarus is certain that weeping and wallowing in grief is not the best way to succeed in love. Pandarus compares Troilus's weeping to that of the mythical Queen Niobe. Niobe was turned to stone as she wept for her children who had been slain by the god Apollo as punishment for the offence given by Niobe to Apollo's mother, the goddess Latona. Yet Niobe's grief was such that even as a stone she continued to weep. Pandarus advises Troilus not to luxuriate in his sorrow: 'Delyte nat in wo thi wo to seche, | As don thise foles that hire sorwes eche | With

[1] *Heroides*, V.151–2, lines which are usually considered by modern editors to be a later interpolation into Ovid's original text.

sorwe' (704–6). The rhyming couplet and repeated nouns here embody the feeling of reaching a stasis within unhappiness.

Pandarus next reminds Troilus of the proverb which says it is a comfort to a miserable person to have a companion in his sorrow. They should both believe in such a maxim because they can be each other's companion in sorrow caused by love. Pandarus confesses that he himself is so grief-stricken in love that there is no more room for any more bad luck to befall him. It can't be the case, speculates Pandarus, that Troilus is afraid that he will steal his lady, because Troilus already knows whom his friend has loved for a long time. Thus (because Troilus should trust him as a friend and not a rival and because he has already shared his friend's sorrow) Pandarus urges him once more to reveal a little about his own sorrow in love.

Troilus lies silent, seemingly talked into a stupor by Pandarus. He comes to with a sigh, listens to Pandarus for a moment, and then his eyeballs roll up as if he has lost consciousness. In comparison with the *Filostrato*, Chaucer makes Troilus's **lovesickness** affect him much more dramatically and Pandarus is thus deeply concerned. He is afraid in case Troilus is about to fall into a fit of madness or even die. He shouts loudly to wake him up. Troilus does not reply because he is determined not to reveal the identity of his lady to anyone. The narrating voice presents further proverbs which would support Troilus's counter-reasoning. It is said that men often make a rod for their own back, particularly by discussing love which ought to remain private. Matters of love are likely of their own accord to become public unless they are carefully controlled. Hence it is a clever strategy to pretend to flee from what you in fact desire.

Despite his apparent stupor, Troilus hears Pandarus trying to rouse him. Grumpily he tells Pandarus that he has indeed heard everything he has said. He is certain that all of Pandarus's proverbs cannot help his situation and thus he commands Pandarus to stop quoting him his ancient examples, such as that of Queen Niobe. Troilus's refusal of Pandarus's advice draws the reader's attention to the value of such exemplification and proverbial illustration. Is Pandarus here knowledgeable and apposite or verbose and pretentious? What sorts of insights can proverbs and examples provide? What is the value of proverbs if one proverb can be set diametrically against another? Do the stories of the classical and mythological figures alluded to throughout the poem match the contexts in which they are cited? Characters cite proverbs and examples in ways which often reveal potential ironies or blindnesses, supplying us with extra questions, different perspectives and alternative meanings which they themselves do not see.

(iii) Lines 761 to 833: Troilus changes his mind

Pandarus briskly refuses Troilus's request that he put an end to his examples and continues to interrogate his friend in an exchange which Chaucer adds to his source. If Troilus revealed the identity of his love, Pandarus asks, would he permit him to whisper his grief in her ear and beg her to have pity on him, given that Troilus dare not speak to her for fear? Troilus swears vehemently that he would not, even if Pandarus did it as earnestly as if his own life depended on it. Troilus here, as elsewhere, calls his friend 'brother' (773), indicating the closeness of their friendship. He is certain that Pandarus cannot help him and that nothing would persuade his lady to be won over to such a wretch as he now feels himself to be. In response, Pandarus laments that Troilus is despairing without having true cause to despair. He asks whether the lady in question is in fact dead (because this is the only situation in which Troilus's hopelessness would make sense). He asks Troilus how he can be sure that he lacks his lady's favour. Troilus should not assume that a remedy is impossible because what will happen in the future is often in doubt. Pandarus tactfully accepts the extent of Troilus's sorrow, comparing his pain to that of Tityus (here *Ticius*, a giant punished in the underworld for the attempted rape of the goddess Latona). Yet he cannot bear to allow Troilus to hold such an irrational opinion as that there can be no remedy for his sorrow.

Pandarus now tries to provoke Troilus into seeing the error of his ways. He demands to know whether what he calls cowardice, anger, suspiciousness and stubbornness will really prevent Troilus from telling him about his sorrow. If Troilus dies of sorrow, his lady will think that he has died from cowardice in the face of the Greek siege because she will not know the real reason. In that case, Troilus will be rewarded by nothing but curses from his lady and from the city of Troy. Pandarus, though he takes **the art of love** very seriously, is also willing to point out the potential absurdities of its conventions and customs. Troilus can, he says, adopt all of the behaviours traditionally associated with lovers (weeping, crying, kneeling), yet if he loves his lady without telling her she will reward his love in ways he will not feel. Pandarus uses negation, particularly *un-* prefixes, to show the absurd non-existence of such love. The lover will remain *un*-known, *un*-kissed, having lost that which is *un*-sought, that which has not been asked for.

Troilus considers these arguments and comes round to Pandarus's point of view, feeling now that his own position is one of foolishness and Pandarus's one of truth. To kill himself because of his despair would be not only fruitless but also a sin and an ignoble act. Troilus now realizes that Criseyde would not be to blame for his death because she knows very little about his sorrow (of course in all likelihood she knows nothing). Troilus therefore asks Pandarus what is the best course of action. Pandarus replies that the best thing Troilus can do is to tell his friend all of his sorrow. He makes Troilus an exuberant pledge: if he does not prove a help to him very quickly, then let him be punished by being first dismembered (by being pulled apart by horses) and then hanged. Pandarus invites not one but two different capital punishments upon himself in a promise which is both extreme and nonsensical in its order.

(iv) Lines 834 to 854: the nature of Fortune

Despite Pandarus's promises, Troilus is certain that he cannot be helped by Pandarus because the goddess **Fortune** is his personal adversary. No living person, whether free man or slave, can withstand the damage done by her wheel. In an exchange added by Chaucer to his source, Pandarus accuses Troilus of blaming **Fortune** in this way because he is fearful or perturbed (and therefore prone to irrational or ill-considered opinion). Doesn't Troilus know, asks Pandarus, that **Fortune** is common to everybody, that her influence applies to all? This should, Pandarus argues, provide comfort for Troilus, because (as **Fortune** unceasingly transfers her influence from person to person) just as good fortune is short-lived so misfortune will likewise be temporary. If her wheel were to stop turning, the goddess would in effect cease to be **Fortune** because her very nature is one of perpetual change. Perhaps **Fortune**'s mutability will bring about exactly the change that Troilus would wish and perhaps she is just about to help Troilus?

(v) Lines 855 to 903: Criseyde's virtues

Given that Troilus's fortunes may soon change, Pandarus once again appeals to Troilus to renounce his suffering. He cites another proverb (again added by Chaucer): whoever wishes to be healed by his doctor must first remove the bandages covering his wound (in order that his physician can make a diagnosis and decide upon the appropriate medicine, so Troilus must reveal whom he has fallen in love with so that Pandarus can provide remedy). Pandarus says that even if it were his own sister for whom Troilus suffered such sorrow, Troilus should have her for his lady if Pandarus's feelings on the matter were taken into account (a promise which reveals Pandarus's loyalty to Troilus but also demonstrates how casually Trojan men offer women to each other). Chaucer adds to his source Pandarus's extravagant promise that he should be perpetually bound to Cerberus (the three-headed dog that guards the entrance to the pagan underworld) if this claim proves untrue. Pandarus demands to know whether he knows the woman in question. By asking this question, Pandarus has hit near the mark and so it is as if Troilus's vein (that is, his heart or blood, the location of his innermost feelings) has been wounded. We will discover at line 975 that Criseyde is Pandarus's niece, yet Chaucer postpones this revelation in contrast with his source, where Criseida is at this point named as Pandaro's cousin (*Fil.* II.20).

In comparison with Chaucer's source, Troilus is much more physically affected by the voicing of Criseyde's name, blushing, trembling as if he were entering hell itself and nearly dying of anxiety. The narrating voice exclaims at how glad Pandarus was to hear this name (presumably, as he is about to explain, this is because of Criseyde's virtue, but we may also retrospectively realize that he is pleased because his friend's lady turns out to be his own niece). Pandarus says that **the God of Love** has treated Troilus well, because Criseyde has much good reputation, wisdom, manners and nobility. Pandarus says that he has never seen someone who was more generous, or more joyful, or friendlier in conversation, or more well-disposed to behave properly, or who had less need to be advised on her actions. Moreover, in matters of honour, a king's heart (that is, the epitome of honour) would seem like that of a wretch in comparison with Criseyde's.

In an addition to the *Filostrato*, Pandarus assures Troilus that loving Criseyde is in fact a piece of good fortune. Troilus should be at peace because, as Pandarus says, it can only be a good thing to 'love wel' (895), that is, to love virtuously or fittingly, and to have set his heart on such a worthy object of affection. Troilus should not think of his love for Criseyde as a chance occurrence but as 'grace' (896), a divine intervention into human affairs by **the God of Love** himself. Yet we readers must square Pandarus's description of Criseyde's virtues and Troilus's good fortune with our foreknowledge of her future betrayal. Will this affair prove to be a piece of good fortune and an example of virtuous or fitting love? Do we agree that it can only be a good thing to love well?

Pandarus tells Troilus that he should also be cheered by the thought that, since Criseyde is entirely virtuous, it follows she will have pity amongst her other virtues (and so she is more likely to be sympathetic to

Troilus's suffering). Yet Pandarus advises him not to ask for any favour which would be contrary to her good reputation, because virtue by definition cannot encompass anything shameful. (Boccaccio's Pandaro, by contrast, worries more candidly that his cousin's chastity may prove a hindrance but is confident that he can find a way to overcome it.) By means of Pandarus's concern for Criseyde's honour (whether genuine or strategic), Chaucer here raises the question of what it is Troilus and Pandarus each intend and whether their **intention** is or can truly be honourable.

(vi) Lines 904 to 1008: Troilus's repentance and Pandarus's advice

Despite being delighted that Troilus has had good fortune, Pandarus nevertheless admits that he had formerly been absolutely certain that such luck in love would never have befallen Troilus. This is because Troilus had previously railed at **the God of Love** so scornfully. Pandarus quotes back to Troilus his earlier derisive comments about love in stanzas which Chaucer adds to his source (once again reminding us of the criticisms which might be levelled at love). Troilus apparently honoured Love sarcastically as Saint Idiot, lord of all of those who behave foolishly in love. He joked that Love's followers are 'Goddes apes' (913), that is, natural-born fools, and mocked their behaviour. Lovers eat alone, lie in bed groaning, suffer a 'blaunche fevere' (916, a type of **lovesickness** which makes the lover shiver with cold), and wish passively for death rather than recovery. Some of them therefore put on unnecessary clothes because they feel the cold so badly. Some of them have fabricated the symptoms of **lovesickness**, pretending that they are suffering from insomnia when they in fact sleep well. They do this in order to put themselves in a favourable position with their lady but are eventually found out and end up worse off. In order to enhance their odds of being successful, they woo many ladies and speak in general terms (thus hedging their bets by not referring to a particular lady). Troilus has thus pointed out how love can be absurd, and lovers can be feeble and perhaps deceptive and insincere, yet he has now consented to love. Because Troilus mocked love so harshly, Pandarus next advises him to confess his sins and repent his behaviour. Pandarus plays the role of priestly confessor within **the religion of love**, encouraging Troilus to beat his breast and pray for grace from **the God of Love**. Troilus plays the role of penitent, praying for forgiveness and promising to avoid future misdeeds. Pandarus evaluates his contrition and acts as the mediator of divine forgiveness.

As well as acting as his confessor, Pandarus continues both to encourage and to advise his friend. He next tells Troilus that he should also be cheered by the fact that Criseyde, now the source of his sorrow, may soon be a source of comfort. Pandarus proves this point by a series of proverbial examples which show that one quality is often found close by or is closely followed by its opposite (namely weeds and medicinal herbs or beautiful flowers, depth and height, darkness and light). Likewise, a period of joy must closely follow the ending of a period of sorrow. He next cautions Troilus that he should behave with temperance, patience, diligence and discretion. He cites the seemingly paradoxical proverb that he who can wait prudently often makes good haste. Thus if Troilus serves his lady cheerfully, generously and with perseverance, Pandarus is confident that all will be well. He reminds his friend of another proverb: he whose attention is distracted and divided is nowhere entirely focused on one aim, and thus it is no surprise if a person so distracted (by different impulses and anxieties) has no luck in love. Pandarus also reminds Troilus that impatience never succeeds, just as if one were to plant a tree or plant and then pull it up the next morning to see how it is growing. Since **the God of Love** has bestowed Troilus's affections on a person whose virtues make her entirely appropriate for someone of Troilus's own merit, he should persevere. Even if his love causes him sorrow, he should remain hopeful, because Pandarus expects to bring about a favourable outcome to this matter unless melancholy or excessive haste (on Troilus's part) ruins their efforts.

In the *Filostrato*, Pandaro here admits that love brought about by the cunning of a go-between is not fitting for an honourable lady and may bring shame on Criseida. Yet he argues that if such love can be kept secret, such shame can be avoided (*Fil.* II.24–5). Chaucer omits this admission of impropriety and instead has Pandarus assert love's naturalness and universality. Pandarus explains that he is not afraid to discuss this matter with Criseyde because, as he has learned from wise and learned people, all men and women are predisposed to experience the ardour of love. Pandarus divides love into two kinds, one heavenly and spiritual and the other earthly and physical. Because of her beauty and youth, it is not fitting that Criseyde love only that which is divine, even though she is sufficiently pious to do so and might (because of her virtue) be that way inclined. As an attractive widow, Pandarus thinks that it is more fitting for her to love and cherish a worthy knight such as Troilus. (These verbs make us think of the vows with which one spouse promises to love another in marriage, though marriage is not envisaged by Troilus or Criseyde at any point in this story.) It is for this reason that he is willing to act as go-between for his friend and niece. Just as Troilus voluntarily consented to love as he began his song (I.391–2), so Pandarus here commits himself to help his friend. Chaucer's readers are likewise invited to consent to Pandarus's defence of earthly love as natural, universal and fitting.

Pandarus ends his advice with a further piece of encouragement which Chaucer adds to his source. Since **the God of Love** has in his mercy converted Troilus from his sinful conduct, Pandarus believes that his friend will become the strongest pillar of Love's church, the most resilient defender of **the religion of love**. In order to support this notion, Pandarus cites the example of those learned scholars who are most heretical in their opinions. Once God converts them to the true faith and away from their wicked deeds, they become the most devout believers whose faith is strongest and who know best how to counter heresy.

The religion of love

In *Troilus and Criseyde*, elements of religious belief, worship and practice are used to describe various aspects and stages of the lovers' experience of love itself. Troilus begins the story as a sceptic or heretic who mocks **the God of Love** and his devotees, but is then converted when, having been hit by Love's arrow, he sees Criseyde in the temple (just as Criseyde becomes partially converted at II.903). Pandarus then acts as a kind of priest-confessor and we see Troilus regret his sins against love and become repentant and fully devoted to this faith. Criseyde's beauty is praised as almost divine, often expressed by comparison with the contemplation of Paradise and heaven. The physical union of the lovers in Book III is represented as the reaching of the bliss of heaven, whilst their separation is imagined as a kind of hell. Death in the service of love would be a kind of martyrdom.

Such analogies are on the one hand potentially solemnizing, indicating the intensity of human erotic love, the bliss it brings about and the belief placed in it in this poem. Yet on the other they are also potentially inappropriate, given that earthly things cannot truly be divine and that romantic love cannot really be a form of religious belief. It is therefore left to us to decide on what grounds to accept such figures or how much to condemn such metaphors as a mistaken mislabelling of one thing in the terms of another. They might be viewed as tongue-in-cheek irreverence on the part of the narrating first-person and his characters, a witty reanimation of a clichéd metaphor of love as a quasi-religious devotion. More sternly we might see them as a kind of blasphemy in which the sacred is profaned or as a kind of idolatry in which human love is worshipped in a way which should be reserved for the divine. Yet what other metaphor might do justice to the extremes of happiness and despair experienced by the poem's characters?

(vii) Lines 1009 to 1092: Troilus's fears and Pandarus's plotting

Having secured his friend's assistance in wooing Criseyde, Troilus becomes untroubled by his sorrow. Yet because his sense of hopelessness has been assuaged, his desire becomes more intense. He asks Pandarus a series of anxious questions about their next steps. Pandarus responds scornfully to Troilus's anxieties, telling him that he is fretting about events as likely to happen as the Man in the Moon falling from his perch. He despises Troilus's foolish worrying and tells him to meddle only in his own business. The wooing of Criseyde therefore becomes Pandarus's occupation which he needs to be left alone to pursue. Troilus agrees to defer to Pandarus, but cautions him that he does not desire anything that might entail sinful or shameful conduct. He would rather die than have Criseyde think he intended anything other than that which is in accordance with virtue. Pandarus laughs at such a request, because to him these worries are entirely unnecessary. With Pandarus as his 'borugh' (1038), his guarantor of discretion, decency and thus success in love, Troilus should be confident. Yet this exchange again prompts us to consider what exactly they each intend and whether their joint **intention** is indeed virtuous. Can a secret love affair be conducted virtuously or is it inevitably shameful and improper?

Pandarus bids Troilus farewell and reassures him with an offer of an arrangement entirely in Troilus's favour. Troilus should confer the responsibility for this task on Pandarus, whilst Pandarus will grant Troilus all the enjoyment of his success. Troilus, now much more buoyant, pours scorn on the Greek army and feels confident that God will help the Trojans to victory. He vows that he will injure some of the Greek soldiers on the battlefield if he can, though he immediately regrets such a boast (as befits the humility of a knight). He places everything, his survival or death, in Pandarus's hands (because he feels his well-being is now entirely contingent on Pandarus's intercession and Criseyde's favour). Pandarus responds by offering Troilus his 'trowthe' (1061) in return, making a solemn promise to act faithfully on his behalf.

The advancement of Troilus's love is now in the hands of his friend. As Pandarus departs, he begins to plan the wooing of his niece. The narrating voice compares this premeditation to that of the house-builder who does not rush to start his construction but instead imagines the entire project in advance, determining his plans using 'his hertes line' (1068), the mental equivalent of the measure used by masons to gauge length or verticality (see also III.530). The source of this stanza is Geoffrey of Vinsauf's *Poetria nova* ('a new poetics'), a Latin poem completed *c.* 1200 which takes as its subject the art of poetry. In the *Poetria nova*, the same simile is used to describe how a poet should meticulously plan his entire project in his mind before beginning to compose his verse.[2] Chaucer's borrowing, as well as proposing an analogy between a go-between's creation of a love affair and the poet's creation of his poem, thus prompts other speculations both about this narrative and about its author. What does Pandarus imagine the end of the love affair will be as he premeditates its construction? What decisions has Chaucer made in advance about his story?

Book I comes to a close with descriptions which indicate how Troilus's despair has been lifted by his friend's intervention. Troilus is no longer prostrate with sorrow, but fights savagely on the battlefield like a lion. Moreover, he has been ennobled by love to the extent that his pleasant manner attracts the commendation and affection of everyone he meets. He becomes superlative, the friendliest, noblest, most generous, honourable and best knight in Troy. His former mockery and harshness, as well as his former arrogance and aloof manner, are dead (that is, they have ceased completely). Every fault has been replaced by a virtue. Yet the narrating voice concludes by reminding us that Troilus's resurgence is merely temporary and partial, contingent on Pandarus's intercession and Criseyde's response. Troilus is compared to an injured man whose pain has been relieved but whose wound is not yet treated or healed. He must now wait like a compliant patient, whilst Pandarus, acting as his doctor, goes in search of a cure for his injury.

[2] Geoffrey of Vinsauf, *Poetria nova*, trans. M. F. Nims, rev. edn, Mediaeval Sources in Translation 49 (Toronto: Pontifical Institute of Mediaeval Studies, 2010), p. 20.

Book II

LINES 1 TO 49: THE PROEM

Book II begins with a proem added by Chaucer to his source. The narrating voice calls for the wind to help him make a metaphorical sea voyage away from Troilus's suffering in Book I. The ship of his literary abilities has been navigating the stormy sea of his turbulent subject matter (namely the severity of Troilus's sorrow in love). His vessel has found this ocean such hard going that the narrating first-person feels he can hardly steer (this admission being testament to how affected he is by Troilus's suffering). Yet (because Pandarus has offered Troilus a way out of his despair) he now feels that the weather of his metaphorical journey has begun to improve and that the calends of hope are beginning. Calends are the first day of each new month (hence *calendar*), so here meaning the first days of a new emotion. The narrating voice next calls on Clio, the Muse of history, for assistance. From this point in the poem onwards, he hopes she will help him to compose his verse successfully. He claims he does not need to employ any other artistic know-how beyond the accuracy of a historian here (because, as he goes on to explain, his task is a limited one). To every lover who might read or hear his poem, he offers the excuse that he is not inspired by personal feelings or experiences to compose his poem (as is Boccaccio's narrator). Instead, he maintains that he is simply translating the story from Latin into English (in keeping with his claim to be translating the work of the famed author Lollius). Thus, as a translator, he does not deserve either praise or criticism for his poem. He asks lovers not to blame him if they find any word of his story faulty, because he claims simply to be repeating what his source says.

The narrating voice next reminds his audience of lovers that ways of speaking have changed considerably over the last thousand years. Those utterances which might now seem foolish or unfamiliar were once prized and de rigueur. Ancient lovers said such things and had as much success in love as today's lovers do with their different conventions. In order to succeed in love in different times and places, different customs must be employed. The narrating first-person therefore says he cannot agree with anyone in his audience of lovers who hears how Troilus gained Criseyde's favour and thinks that he would act differently or who marvels at Troilus's speech or behaviour. He points out that not everyone who travels to Rome (the destination for many travellers going on pilgrimage or papal business in the Middle Ages) follows the same route (and so there are many routes to success in love). **The art of love** is so varied that if in another land a lover behaved as today's lovers do then everything would go wrong for him. It is for this reason that it is said that every country has its own laws (that is, each place, time and occupation has its own particular rules). Moreover, he claims that he could scarcely find three members of his audience who have spoken or acted in love in the same way even in this present age. Having first addressed his audience of lovers in the collective second-person plural, he now speaks to them individually in the second-person singular. What may suit one in love will not suit another, thus he is confident that the subjectivity and cultural specificity of love mean that every type of love-talk occurs. The narrating first-person thus pre-emptively defends himself against those who might respond to his story with surprise or scepticism. Yet of course these attempts to engage and manipulate his audience's responses also suggest the possibility of disagreement whilst asserting that we should be tolerant of any perceived difference. Love is both universal and individual, leaving us unable to do anything but accept Book II on its own terms.

LINES 50 TO 595: PANDARUS VISITS CRISEYDE

(i) Lines 50 to 108: signs and omens

The narrating first-person claims to be following his source as he begins Book II, but in fact the first thirty stanzas have no equivalent in the *Filostrato*. Chaucer adds much preparatory detail before Pandarus begins to steer his conversation with Criseyde to matters of love at line 278. The narrating voice first describes the natural rejuvenation and astrological configuration which occur at the beginning of May, a month conventionally associated with love and lovers. On the third of May, Pandarus, despite his wise words to Troilus and his skills as a preacher of **the religion of love**, is so strongly affected by his own unrequited love that he retires to bed in grief and endures a fitful night's sleep. This opening reminds us that Pandarus empathizes with Troilus's sorrow in love as a result of his own experience (though we may also suspect that his wish to help his friend is a displacement of his own futile desire).

Pandarus is woken by the swallow Procne (here *Proigne*) singing her gruesome story outside his bedchamber. Procne was turned into a swallow and her sister Philomena into a nightingale after the sisters had avenged the rape of Philomena by Procne's husband Tereus by murdering the son born to Philomena as a result of the rape and feeding him to his father. In bird form, the metamorphosed Procne is part of the natural world which surrounds Chaucer's characters, simultaneously both mythic portent and incidental disturbance to Pandarus's sleep. Now awake, Pandarus remembers what he has promised Troilus. He makes an astrological forecast, discovering that the moon is in a favourable position for travelling. The narrating voice asks Janus, god of entrances, to guide Pandarus on this trip. Janus was depicted with two faces looking in opposite directions, a very appropriate allusion given Pandarus's role as go-between, facing both Troilus and Criseyde, simultaneously friend and uncle.

Arriving at his niece's house, Pandarus finds Criseyde and two of her ladies listening to a young girl who reads aloud the story of the siege and subsequent destruction of the Greek city of **Thebes**. Pandarus and Criseyde greet each other courteously. Criseyde says that she has dreamed three times of Pandarus during the previous night and hopes that this will be a sign of good things to come. Pandarus takes this opportunity to offer a brief hint of his news, saying that, God willing, Criseyde's fortunes are likely to improve for the whole year. He apologizes for interrupting their reading, asking what the book is about and whether it is about love (as befits his own identity as an unrequited lover, though also an intimation of what is to come).

Criseyde tells Pandarus that she and her ladies have already heard how King Laius of **Thebes** died at the hands of his son Oedipus (here *Edippus*) and that they have paused at the red letters (the rubric, a chapter heading written in red ink) which introduce the section of the story in which Amphiaraus (here *Amphiorax*) falls through the earth into hell. As they discuss the point at which the reading has been interrupted, uncle and niece perhaps refer to two different versions which would have been known by Chaucer's fourteenth-century audience. Criseyde's 'romaunce' (100) might be something akin either to the *Roman de Thèbes* ('the story of Thebes'), a French mid-twelfth-century verse epic-romance, or to one of the later prose redactions of the *Roman*, whilst Pandarus, in explaining that he knows the whole story from a version in 'bookes twelve' (108), refers to something akin to the *Thebaid*, a twelve-book Latin epic poem written by the Roman poet Statius in the first century AD.[1]

Despite Pandarus's claim to know the whole story, as with Procne's song he does not seem to recognize it as anything other than incidental. Yet the mentions of Procne, Oedipus and Amphiaraus each allude to narratives of familial betrayal and violence. The Theban stories also suggest that fate is inescapable even if one can look into the future through prophecy. Oedipus unwittingly kills his father even though his patricide had been predicted at the moment of his birth and Laius had tried to avert the prophecy by ordering Oedipus's death.[2] Likewise, Amphiaraus prophesies that he will die if he joins the Argive army on their journey to besiege **Thebes**, as well as predicting correctly that the majority of the Argive army will die at the siege, yet the Argive nobles and their allies do not believe him.[3] Amphiaraus hides in order to avoid this fate, but his hiding place is revealed to the Argive army by his wife and he is forced to accompany them, falling into hell when the earth opens up and swallows him on the battlefield before **Thebes**.[4] These allusions are ominous as an uncle sets about the wooing of his niece, steering her inexorably towards a betrayal which we readers can already predict.

(ii) Lines 109 to 207: news of Hector and Troilus

Pandarus urges Criseyde to put aside her solemn reading matter just as she should remove her 'barbe' (110), the cloth covering her neck and bosom which indicates her status as a widow. He suggests that they dance together in celebration of the month of May. Criseyde vociferously rejects Pandarus's proposal to join with him in celebrating the season of love. She considers his suggestion improper because, as a widow, her behaviour is expected to be restrained and pious. Whilst unmarried girls and young wives might dance, she tells him that it would be more fitting for her to withdraw from society in order to pray and read devout material (though

[1] Laius's death is recounted in the first chapter of the *Roman de Thèbes*, whilst the events surrounding Amphiaraus's fall into hell are described in the eighth chapter. Statius begins at a later point in the story and does not recount the events of Oedipus's life. Amphiaraus's fall into hell is described at the end of Book VII and the beginning of Book VIII of the *Thebaid*.

[2] *Le Roman de Thèbes (The Story of Thebes)*, trans. J. Smartt Coley, Garland Library of Medieval Literature 44 (New York: Garland, 1986), pp. 1–5.

[3] Statius, *Thebaid*, II.180–99, in *Silvae, Thebaid, Achilleid*, ed. and trans. D. R. Shackleton Bailey, 3 vols., Loeb Classical Library 206, 207, 498 (Cambridge, MA: Harvard Universiy Press, 2003); *Roman de Thèbes*, trans. Smartt Coley, pp. 48–9.

[4] Statius, *Thebaid*, trans. Shackleton Bailey, II.218–19, III.10–11; *Roman de Thèbes*, trans. Smartt Coley, pp. 113–14.

rather than this ideal of widowhood she has been enjoying the communal reading of a secular epic-romance). Having had his first proposals turned down, Pandarus now begins an unhurried sequence of preparatory hints and suggestions before he divulges his errand to Criseyde at line 316. His strategy is to pique her curiosity by hinting about news which concerns her, trying to guarantee a positive reaction by presenting such news as favourable before specifying what it is.

Criseyde's first thought on hearing of Pandarus's promise of good news is that the siege has been lifted. She also modestly protests that she is too dim-witted to guess successfully what the news might be. Yet she is also perhaps capable of countering Pandarus's strategies with subterfuge of her own. Her protestation of incapacity may be insincere, intended to hasten the revelation of the news by admitting defeat to Pandarus in this game of hints. She partially conceals her curiosity with modest gestures of obedience to her uncle's wishes. Yet though she often defers to her uncle, their relationship also seems to be one of intellectual equals. They talk not only as uncle and niece but as friends, playfully discussing a wide range of topics as well as delving into subjects which are unusual and hard to understand. This shows Criseyde as sophisticated, mature and thoughtful, a good match for Pandarus's conversational skills.

Pandarus bides his time until Criseyde asks for news about Hector (who has personally guaranteed her safety in Troy). He reports that Hector is well apart from a small wound and also takes his chance to draw her attention to Troilus, Hector's brother. He calls Troilus a second Hector, equal to his older brother in every virtue. Criseyde is pleased and wishes both brothers well. She comments that it is a great honour when a royal prince demonstrates both military prowess and good character. She indicates the rarity of this combination with a proverb: great power and moral goodness are seldom seen together in a single person. Picking up on her reference to one individual (and wishing to turn her attention towards Troilus), Pandarus reminds her that King Priam has not one but two sons (in fact he has five sons by Hecuba). Hector is, as everyone knows, the superlative knight. Pandarus says he could say the same thing about Troilus and Criseyde agrees with his verdict. She has first-hand experience of Hector and believes the praise-filled reports she has heard of Troilus.

Pandarus then corroborates such reports by relating Troilus's battlefield exploits on the previous day. In a vivid though traditional comparison, he says that a dense swarm of bees never flew as crowdedly as the Greek army did when fleeing out of Troilus's way. Through Pandarus's echoing words and rhythms ('Ther nas … Ther nas', 'Now here, now there … now hem … and hem', 195–9), Chaucer momentarily evokes the hurrying style of popular romances which narrated tales of warfare and heroism. Yet Pandarus also assures Criseyde that Troilus is not simply a bloodthirsty warrior. He is the friendliest nobleman Pandarus has ever encountered, one who knows how to show the greatest amity to those he thinks should prosper.

(iii) Lines 208 to 252: Pandarus's and Criseyde's confidences

Not wishing to overplay his hand by revealing the matter too quickly or too enthusiastically, Pandarus makes as if he wishes to end his visit. Criseyde delays his departure, saying that he cannot leave before she has asked his advice about the management of her property and her household (though perhaps she also hopes that he will reveal his news in due course if she can detain him further). Her request for advice about administrative and legal matters is a clever choice because it permits them a moment of privacy. Criseyde's attendants, recognizing that confidentiality is required, move further away out of earshot.

Having concluded these discussions, Pandarus once more makes as if he wishes to leave, yet immediately returns to his previous suggestion that Criseyde should do away with the public signs of mourning and grief because of the good fortune which has befallen her. It is clear that Criseyde now recognizes the game of tantalizing insinuations which he is playing. She congratulates him on how well he has thought out the dropping of this latest hint and exclaims in frustration because it is impossible to ignore. He continues to stall, arguing that he would need more time than is available to break the news to her. He also hesitates, he claims, because he would not wish to offend her. In advance of the moment of revelation, when she might take offence at his requests on Troilus's behalf and he might take offence at her responses, uncle and niece remind and reassure each other of their intimacy and good **intention** towards each other.

(iv) Lines 253 to 314: Pandarus's preamble

Pandarus now approaches his revelation by means of a long preamble. He tells Criseyde that even though some speakers delight in embellishing their topics of conversation with inventive verbal artistry, their **intention** nevertheless remains that their speech have some particular communicative purpose. Since the important part of every topic is its 'ende' (260), its intended purpose or the conclusion it offers, and since his news is so opportune, why, he asks, should he speak floridly or prolong his subject matter? Pandarus next gazes at Criseyde's face, hoping that good fortune will be granted to 'swich a mirour' (266), such a model or example of beauty. Here we are given access to Pandarus's inner thoughts during this moment of inspection. Pandarus decides (as he has already told Criseyde) that he will not make a complex or lengthy description or explanation because she would not enjoy this and might be suspicious that such elaboration was intended to deceive (nevertheless making us perhaps more inclined to suspect him). He cites the proverbial wisdom that those with sensitive minds are inclined to suspect everything that they do not understand. Thus he will endeavour to cater to Criseyde's way of thinking as he reveals his news. These two sets of assurances that the matter will not be elaborated or prolonged unnecessarily have the ironic effect of deferring Pandarus's revelation. Moreover, though the terms employed (*tale*, *endite*, *ende*, *matere*) refer here to speech, the same terms can also refer to literary narration. Pandarus's inaccurate self-analysis can therefore also be a moment of authorial self-reflexivity. Does Chaucer elaborate or lengthen the narrative for the sake of verbal invention or for other reasons? What is the ultimate purpose of this story and what conclusion is reached? How are Pandarus's actions as a go-between analogous to those of an author?

Pandarus claims, as he gazes at her, to be considering whether Criseyde is going to be favoured by **Fortune**. He reminds her that everyone is (at some point in their lives) destined to have some good fortune, if they only know how to accept it. Yet if they ignore and deliberately spurn it, then they cannot claim to be misled by chance or **Fortune** but should be blamed for their own negligence and misfortune. Pandarus tells Criseyde that she has found a piece of good fortune without much effort on her part, though it is up to her to capitalize on it. He urges her to seize the opportunity before it has passed. He takes her hand to indicate his sincerity, saying that she is the most fortunate person in the world. He re-emphasizes his good **intention** and his affection for his niece, yet his reassurances end in the threat that he will never see her again if she is angered by the information he brings or if she thinks that he is misleading her. From our position of readerly omniscience, we may be less certain that Pandarus's news is indeed a piece of good fortune for Criseyde. We are also more aware of Pandarus's potential conflict of interests in his loyalties and responsibilities to his friend Troilus and to his niece.

We can infer Criseyde's reaction to his threat because Pandarus tells her not to be afraid and to stop trembling with fear. Although his news is unexpected, he assures her that he has prejudged its propriety and would not bring her news which is improper. As Pandarus forewarns but does not reveal his news, Criseyde is compelled to take the initiative. She confesses that she is both fearful and curious, yet her curiosity wins out. She begs her uncle to tell her, whether the outcome is for better or for worse.

(v) Lines 315 to 406: Pandarus reveals and pressures

Lines 316 to 319 encapsulate Pandarus's delaying and pre-empting in miniature, as Troilus's identity is made known only after a string of commendatory premodifiers. In the *Filostrato*, Pandaro extols Troilo's virtues and advises his cousin to capitalize on this piece of good fortune before finally revealing his identity. In Chaucer's version, Pandarus reveals Troilus's identity straight away but immediately pressurizes his niece with cruel and violent threats before she can respond. Troilus, claims Pandarus, is so in love with her that if she does not help him such unrequited devotion will bring about his death. Furthermore, Criseyde is made responsible not only for Troilus's life and death but for her uncle's welfare, as he threatens that if his friend dies he will also die, even if he has to cut his own throat. He refers deictically to 'this knyf' (325), indicating that he emphasizes his threat to Criseyde by showing her his dagger. He bursts into tears and tells her that if she were to cause their death she would have fished well (meaning ironically that she would have wasted her time), asking bitterly how this might benefit her. Pandarus laments his friend's situation, telling her that Troilus is near to death even though he is still fighting in Troy's cause, doing everything he can to seek out death on the battlefield.

Pandarus also laments Criseyde's beauty. If she were to care about the death of such a noble man as Troilus as little as she might care about the death of some insignificant person, her beauty would not be sufficient to make up for such an act of callousness. His point emphasized by anaphora (the repetition of the same word or phrase at the beginning of successive sentences, phrases or clauses), he curses those things which are beautiful but not also beneficial, such as a gemstone which does not have a talismanic power or a plant which has no medicinal qualities. Damningly, he concludes that if she does not have compassion then it is a shame that she is alive, even though she is the 'crop and roote' of beauty (348), meaning idiomatically the entirety, from top to bottom. Pandarus goes on to assure Criseyde that his news is not intended to deceive her (by disguising improper desires with the pretence of true love). He would rather the three of them were all publicly executed than act as Troilus's 'baude' (353), that is, someone who procures sexual partners for other men (though he later implies that this is indeed what he has done at III.253–6). As her uncle, it would shame him as well as her if he agreed that Troilus should, with his assistance, destroy her reputation for virtue. Pandarus assures her that he is not asking her to pledge herself to Troilus with a formal promise to be his lady but merely to be more friendly to him so that he does not die of despair. Pandarus swears that this is the limit of their **intention** and that he does not mean anything else. Given that we know in advance that Troilus and Criseyde will become lovers, we see here the ingenuity (but also the duplicity) of Pandarus's strategy – not a single request for favour but the first of a series of small concessions.

Pandarus now puts forward worst-case scenarios in order to refute them. Yet his hypotheses assume more than a change of demeanour on Criseyde's part. Presuming that Troilus will visit her in person, Pandarus reassures her that anyone who observes him coming or going will consider his visits to be those of friendship rather than of romantic love. Moreover, social visiting and affectionate friendship are so prevalent in Troy that Pandarus advises Criseyde to disguise Troilus's visits as social ones. If it can be disguised as social friendship, then Pandarus's ultimate **intention** requires more than friendliness from his niece. Criseyde likewise decides to sound out more about their **intention**, asking her uncle how she should respond (in order that he reveal more). Pandarus now asks for reciprocity, that Criseyde should match Troilus's devotion with love of her own. Pandarus applies one last form of pressure before allowing Criseyde to respond. Speaking proverbially, he says that ageing consumes part of a woman's beauty every hour, so Pandarus urges her to leave her mourning and return to the world of romantic affairs before she becomes too old to attract a suitor. Two linked proverbs illustrate his argument through the action of personified abstractions. Beauty cries out 'I realized too late' once her beauty has passed, whilst Old Age overpowers *Daunger* (the resistance or reluctance to love which a lover's lady might express in the form of disdain or diffidence towards him) in the end (because, as a woman ages and her youthful beauty fades, she may have to be more flirtatious and less haughty in order to attract a suitor).

(vi) Lines 407 to 497: Criseyde's response

Pandarus now hangs his head and Criseyde immediately bursts into tears. She wishes she were dead, because, she says, all fidelity must have vanished from the world (if her uncle can so betray her). She asks what strangers might do to her given that he whom she believed to be her best friend advises her to love a suitor when he should caution her against loving (because love might endanger her honour). If she had fallen in love with Troilus, or his brother Hector, or even the Greek warrior Achilles or anyone else, she says she would have expected Pandarus to have admonished her robustly. She asks despairingly who can therefore place any trust in this illusory and deceptive world (in which a seemingly trusted uncle can suddenly act in such an unexpected manner). Criseyde sarcastically pinpoints several of Pandarus's previous comments and questions their aptness. Was all of his specious argument intended for such a purpose? Criseyde feels that the situation which has befallen her is not fortunate and happy but frightening and perilous. In the *Filostrato*, Criseida's objections are more concrete: she is still in mourning for her husband, and Troilo (who unlike Troilus is experienced in love) is prone to brief fancies, thus she prefers to remain chaste.

Hearing Criseyde's intense disapproval, Pandarus threatens that he will not visit her again this week (a comically indignant yet minimal threat) because he is so mistrusted. He concludes that she does not care about the possibility of their deaths. He invokes the punishment of the violent and ruthless god Mars and of the Furies, whom he calls upon to smite him down if his **intention** in making this request was in any way immoral or improper. Since Criseyde's response will ensure (according to Pandarus) that both Troilus and he will die, he dramatically claims to make his confession before supposedly imminent death, though all he confesses is that it is Criseyde who acts wickedly by causing their deaths. Since Criseyde seemingly wishes him to die and because he intends to die alongside his friend, he swears by the sea god Neptune that he will starve himself until he sees his own lifeblood (signalling his death).

Pandarus gets up to leave, but Criseyde prevents his departure. The narrating first-person, who calls Criseyde the most fearful person who could be, says that she was nearly dying of fear at this moment. Whatever we might think of Pandarus's tactics, to the narrating voice and to Criseyde they demonstrates his 'sorwful ernest' (452), his distress and the seriousness with which he makes this request. In the *Filostrato*, it is Pandaro who makes to leave and then stops himself in order to persuade Criseida further, but in Chaucer's version the change of heart is Criseyde's, brought about by Pandarus's extreme threats and Criseyde's fear of public humiliation. We hear the string of thoughts which passes through her mind. She now sees nothing improper in Pandarus's entreaty and is more afraid of the harm and public shame which might occur if she rejects Troilus. Romantic love often leads to calamity, men who are lovesick often act destructively towards themselves, Troilus might commit suicide in front of her, she cannot conceive what sort of rumours would arise if that happened. She resolves that she must therefore act cautiously and carefully.

Criseyde next makes clear to Pandarus her limited room for manoeuvre in stanzas which have no parallel in the *Filostrato*. For Criseyde, Troilus's love is not the promising opportunity which Pandarus claims, but rather a stroke of bad luck. It places her social and moral standing at risk and puts her uncle's life in danger. Caught between these two perils, Criseyde decides that she must choose the less serious one. She will accede to their request and treat Troilus affectionately as long as her honour – her good reputation and moral decency – remains safeguarded. She checks anxiously that they will not ask anything more of her and Pandarus confirms their limited request. Thus reassured, she makes her first concession, agreeing to treat Troilus not as a stranger but as a friend. Criseyde declares that she will endeavour to treat Troilus kindly, yet she will do this by compelling her heart to act in opposition to her own feelings. This limited kindness is not designed simply to keep him in suspense before eventually becoming his lover because she does not love him and cannot make herself love him. She admits that it was only imagined fears which prevented her from agreeing to such respectable friendship. Quoting a proverb, she says that if the cause of an illness disappears, the disease must inevitably stop (implying that Pandarus has assured her that what he is asking is proper and therefore she feels she has nothing to fear). Nevertheless, she emphasizes the limits she places on her actions by making a formal declaration of her wishes to Pandarus. She warns that if they go further, she will not correspondingly take further pity on Troilus by granting him further favours, even if both her uncle and his friend die and the whole world turns against her. Pandarus accepts her declaration, guaranteeing that they will stick to her terms but also taking the opportunity to demand that she will keep her side of the agreement so that he will not find fault with her or have to lecture her on how to behave. We readers know that both sides will change this agreement: Pandarus and Troilus will indeed ask for more and Criseyde will concede more. Yet, given that we cannot truly know a person's inner **intention** (and perhaps they do not know or are not honest about it to themselves), we cannot know for certain how sincere these limited requests and concessions are.

(vii) Lines 498 to 595: Troilus overheard

In the *Filostrato*, it is Pandaro's account of Troilo's overheard complaint to **the God of Love** which instigates Criseida's change of heart (see *Fil.* II.65–6). In Chaucer's version, however, the narration of this scene occurs *after* Criseyde has agreed to treat Troilus with affection. Criseyde asks Pandarus to describe how he first became aware of Troilus's love for her (suggesting, despite her misgivings, that she is flattered by this news and wishes to hear more). Pandarus now describes how he and Troilus supposedly met in the garden of the royal palace in order to discuss a particular military strategy by which they might check the advances of the Greek army. Troilus then pretended to sleep (though of course **lovesickness** prevented him from sleeping). Pandarus thus wandered about the garden, returning to eavesdrop once Troilus was lost in his own thoughts. The narrative has not previously featured such a scene, so we, like Criseyde, have to trust Pandarus (or not, given his subsequent fabrication of various pretexts for events) that these events occurred as he describes.

In the *Filostrato*, Troilo declares the intensity of his passion to **the God of Love** and prays for help in revealing his love to Criseida. He asks Love to make her fall in love with him so that his love will be reciprocated. In Chaucer's version, Troilus once again repents his former mockery of **the religion of love**. He asks **the God of Love** to have pity on his suffering even though he was once rebellious in his opinions. He is now contrite, being sorry for his former sins and accepting his guilt by exclaiming 'mea culpa' (525, 'the fault is mine'), a phrase from the prayer used in confession. Troilus also addresses Love as the divinity who, through his ordaining power, controls the ultimate destiny of everyone through even-handed providence. He begs him to accept his humble confession and send him whatever penance he likes, yet he asks him to prevent him from succumbing to despair or hopelessness (the spiritual state in which a believer feels that salvation is impossible, perhaps leading, as Troilus fears, to his soul becoming alienated from his new god). He testifies that the look from Criseyde's eyes has wounded him so deeply that it has penetrated to the very bottom of his heart. He feels he will inevitably die from unreciprocated devotion because he dare not reveal his love. He illustrates this proverbially: just as when desire is concealed it becomes stronger, so hot coals are covered with ash in order to intensify their heat.

Pandarus conceals his eavesdropping from his friend and later finds Troilus lamenting alone in his chamber, a situation which gives him the necessary privacy to question Troilus about this new love. This conversation has already been narrated, so it is here summarized for Criseyde. Pandarus offers the excuse that if he were to repeat it word-for-word he would faint with emotion, so moving is Troilus's suffering. He emphasizes the severity of Troilus's case, the seriousness of his response and the extreme secrecy and discretion which Troilus demanded. Once again, Pandarus stresses that Criseyde must act only to save the life of her uncle and his friend. Their **intention** is 'cleene' (580), it is respectable and proper, and Pandarus does not intend anything sinful or improper to occur. Yet he adds one further comment which brings their **intention** into question. These parting words are drawn from advice given much earlier in the scene in the *Filostrato* (*Fil.* II.43). Pandarus reiterates that what has happened is a piece of good fortune because Troilus is such a good catch, even if Criseyde did not set out to net herself a new lover. Yet he goes a step further by speculating on just how well matched they might be in the future. Two people, he says, would be never as well joined together as when Criseyde and Troilus fully possess each other. Criseyde recognizes this sexual innuendo but does not dismiss the future possibility or retract her promise of affection now Pandarus has, in hypothetical form, let slip a different **intention**, implying perhaps that she is, despite her protestations, open to the prospect of a love affair. Laughing awkwardly, she says that she has not given her consent to anything of that nature and accuses Pandarus of spoiling everything (suggesting perhaps that she wishes to enjoy the experience of courtship in the form of a series of less morally troubling concessions). Pandarus hurriedly assures her that whatever he said it was meant well. He begs her not to be angry, once again emphasizing their kinship, and she forgives him.

LINES 596 TO 931: CRISEYDE FALLS IN LOVE

(i) Lines 596 to 686: the first coincidence: Troilus rides by

Pandarus bids Criseyde farewell and returns home in good spirits. She retreats into the privacy of her bedchamber in order to replay in her mind every part of their conversation. She is somewhat astonished by this unexpected turn of events but, once she has thought everything through, feels that there is nothing to fear. She reasons that even though a man might love a woman so deeply that his heart might break, such love would only be reciprocated if the woman were also willing. Yet despite these feelings of control, the first of two coincidences added by Chaucer to his source now predisposes Criseyde to fall in love with Troilus in return.

As she sits alone in her chamber, reports of a skirmish outside the walls of the city cause excitement among the Trojan citizens. Outside in the street, passers-by call out the news that Troilus has just chased part of the Greek army from the battlefield. Criseyde's servants realize that he will ride past her house as he returns to the royal palace because there is no other way to get there from the Gate of Dardanas, the one gateway into the city whose metal chain (used to close off entrances to traffic) is currently open. They shout to the porter to open the gates of her property so that they can see Troilus as he passes by. The narrating voice draws attention to this coincidence, commenting that it is as if it were Troilus's lucky day. This fortunate coincidence, so he says, demonstrates the often-observed truism that those future events which must necessarily occur cannot be stopped from happening. Though Pandarus has already manipulated his niece's feelings to some degree, the bringing about of the lovers' relationship also depends on the chance coincidences and changes of **Fortune** by which the divine providential plan for the whole of human history is unfolded in time as a series of fated events.

Criseyde now observes for herself the man who has fallen in love with her. The damage to Troilus's military trappings bears witness to the violence of the battle which has just occurred. To look at Troilus, says the narrating first-person extravagantly, is more like gazing at the epitome of the chivalric warrior than if one were to look at Mars, the god of war. The narrating voice comments upon Troilus's youth and strength in terms which convey both military prowess and sexual potency. He feels it was 'an heven' (637) to gaze at him, an utterly blissful experience, encouraging us likewise to swoon at his masculinity. Troilus's head is bare and thus Criseyde can see his modest gaze and blushes when he is publicly acclaimed by the Trojan citizens. The citizens hail Troilus as their source of joy and, second only to his brother Hector, the defender of their city.

Criseyde lets the sight of Troilus sink tenderly into her heart. She feels intoxicated or refreshed by this, asking wonderingly who has given her such a powerful drink. She blushes as she remembers that this is the man whom her uncle swears will die unless she has mercy and pity on him. She is so ashamed that she quickly moves away from the window. Yet despite her embarrassment, she nevertheless carefully considers Troilus's qualities in a sequence of coordinate nouns (660–2). She is most influenced by the flattering fact that it is she who is the cause of his distress. She thinks that if he has good **intention**s in love (again raising the questions of what Troilus's **intention** in fact is and whether it is virtuous) it would be a pity to kill such a man (by refusing to reciprocate his affection). Here she begins to envision more than the limited love of friendship to which she has already agreed.

The narrating first-person interposes a comment here, speculating that a mean-spirited person might consider that Criseyde has fallen in love with Troilus very easily and at first sight (even though Criseyde has merely begun to think about taking pity on his suffering). The narrating voice defends his heroine from this accusation, countering that everything has a beginning, a point of origin, and that in this scene we witness just the beginning of her love. She does not give her heart to him suddenly at this moment but rather she becomes disposed to like him. From this point onwards, his manliness and suffering make love begin to tunnel within or beneath her. This metaphor figures Criseyde as a walled city like Troy itself and love as a besieging force which attacks the city by tunnelling underneath the walls in order to gain entry to the city or to destabilize the fortifications themselves. Yet despite his assurances about the unhurried progression of her love, the first-person interjection paradoxically creates the suspicion that Criseyde's love *is* too sudden and therefore perhaps built on unstable, undermined foundations (and will be destroyed just as Troy will fall). Given that we know her love for Troilus will not last, such qualms, even when countered, seem to predict her ultimate betrayal.

(ii) Lines 687 to 812: Criseyde contemplates the matter

Criseyde now contemplates what she will resolve to do if Pandarus continues to pressure her to accept Troilus's love (showing how, following the coincidence of his ride past her window, her inclinations and suspicions can now conceive of a love affair with Troilus). These stanzas are more extensive and differ in emphasis from the equivalent passage in the *Filostrato*. Criseyde thinks so intensely that it is as if she pleats the subject up into many folds. Her thought turns first one way and then another and becomes jam-packed, just as fabric or paper is folded alternately and becomes compressed when it is gathered into pleats.

Criseyde first reminds herself that she knows Troilus's appearance and nobility by sight (even if she has not had direct dealings with him). Although it would be improper to love him in return, Criseyde thinks that it would bring honour on herself, as well as averting his suffering, to behave in friendly yet proper fashion towards Troilus. Moreover, because of his royal power and influence, she would be in a very perilous position if she tried to avoid his love by fleeing out of his sight and he then became resentful. She poses herself a rhetorical question: would she be wise to gain his hatred when she could instead gain his favour? Thinking proverbially, she reminds herself that there is moderation in everything, a middle way between two extremes. For example, though drunkenness might be forbidden, such a prohibition would not mean that drinking in moderation is also banned (and hence there must be a middle way between snubbing him or reciprocating his love). Next she reminds herself of Troilus's morals and good sense. He is not foolish or an 'avantour' (724), a man who brags publicly about his successes in love, though (she reassures herself) she would never treat him so affectionately as to give him cause to boast about anything. In the *Filostrato*, Criseida thinks much more candidly about the prospect of a love affair, arguing that time is passing and that she knows of no other woman who has not already taken a lover. She notes Troilo's virtues and eminence and believes that a secret affair will surpass the joys of marital love. Criseyde, in contrast, is motivated both by possible social advantage and by fear of social humiliation, neither fully accepting nor fully resisting the possibility of a love affair.

Criseyde now sets out the worst-case scenario. If it became public knowledge that Troilus loved her, this would not bring dishonour on her because she could not be held responsible for his love or be expected to prevent him from loving her. Next she thinks how, as a royal prince, Troilus is able to choose the most respected woman to be his love because he is the worthiest Trojan knight, second only to his brother Hector. She is thus flattered that it is she who controls his fate. We are given access to Criseyde's most private feelings, the moment of self-regard that she would prefer that no one else knew. It is not surprising, she thinks, that he has fallen in love with her because she is one of the most beautiful women in Troy according to public opinion (and hence not her own estimation).

Yet, as Criseida does in the *Filostrato*, Criseyde acknowledges the factors which make her reluctant to accept a lover. Being a widow with her own independent wealth, she is her own woman rather than living under the control of a husband. She compares herself to a grazing animal able to go wherever it likes in a 'lusty leese' (752), a pleasant and fruitful pasture. She has no husband to act jealously, to quarrel with her or to say checkmate to her because he has outwitted her or restricted her freedom. Yet she asks herself what purpose there might be in continuing to live according to the expectations of widowhood. She is not 'religious' (759, that is, she is not vowed to remain chaste). She convinces herself that it cannot shame her to set her heart on this most worthy knight and at the same time to preserve her honour and reputation (though readers may wonder whether these two impulses are truly compatible). Criseyde's question here raises further questions for readers. Is earthly love the purpose of Criseyde's life (and indeed of all our lives) or are chastity and piety a more worthy purpose?

The narrative now describes how doubts overcome her conviction just as the sun is often quickly covered by a cloud during March's changeable springtime weather. Chaucer extends the figure from the comparative simile of his source into direct metaphor: a cloudy thought passes through Criseyde's mind and overshadows her formerly brighter thoughts. In *Il filostrato*, Criseida likewise thinks about the suffering caused by love. She fears that Troilo will soon tire of her and take another lover, or that even if their love lasts it will become public and her good reputation will be lost. Criseyde shares these doubts and also has other anxieties about love. Her widowhood gives her a type of freedom, and to fall in love would jeopardize this state of contented security. Her liberty would become enslaved, and she would suffer the same pain and distress which she has seen endured by other lovers, in particular the oxymoronic 'dredfull joye' (776), happiness which is nevertheless filled with anxiety. Criseyde here carries on the weather metaphors first used in narrative description. Being in love is, she thinks, 'the mooste stormy lyf' (778), the most turbulent type of existence in which the sun (that is, moments of happiness) is covered by clouds of mistrust or absurd quarrels.

Criseyde now describes how women fare particularly badly in love because their role is more passive. When they are made unhappy by love, women can do nothing to remedy the situation but cry and brood over the matter. Moreover, women are more likely to be gossiped about. Once men's lust has been satisfied, they are likely to transfer their affections to another. Though men claim to love very intensely at first, such an acute beginning often comes to a sudden stop, yet the hurt caused by such a shift in affections still remains. Criseyde exclaims how frequently it is observed that women are betrayed in love by men whose love proves to be temporary. She cannot see what the purpose of such fragile love is and comments mockingly that no one knows what becomes of such love and nobody trips over it. It must have been non-existent to begin with to evaporate into nothingness. Criseyde's comments invite wider application to the impending love affair between herself and Troilus, a love which ultimately proves to be fragile. To what 'fyn' (794, a word which can mean ending, purpose or result) is a love which proves to be temporary? Does it still have a value or is it inevitably rendered ironic (or even effectively non-existent)? Is it possible to celebrate and idealize such love *in situ* or is it always compromised by its wider context (both the lovers' separation and Criseyde's betrayal and also the moral judgements suggested to us at the end of the poem)? To what different ends will this love lead Troilus and Criseyde respectively?

Finally, she thinks that if she loves Troilus, she will also have to curry favour with those people who gossip about love so that they do not spread stories about her. Here Criseyde gives voice to the criticisms which might be levelled at love from a woman's perspective, making us more alert to the manner in which the roles of lover and lady within **the art of love** coerce men and women into particular subject positions and behaviours. Yet from the reader's perspective, her words are also ironic because it is she, not Troilus, who will be the betrayer in love.

Chaucer signals the end of this section with another change in Criseyde's metaphorical internal weather. Her negative thoughts begin to clear just as the weather improves when clouds clear away. She encourages herself with a version of the proverb 'nothing ventured, nothing gained'. Yet she remains poised between hope and fear, between warm optimism and cold apprehension, just as she was at the start of this scene.

(iii) Lines 813 to 903: the second coincidence: Antigone's song

In a scene added by Chaucer to his source, Criseyde now leaves her room in order to entertain herself with other members of her household. She walks in her garden with her three nieces, followed at a distance by a group of her servants. Her niece Antigone entertains the ladies by singing a Trojan song. This song takes the form of a first-person address of thanks, made by a female speaker, to **the God of Love** whose humble and sincere subject she is. She pledges to give her heart's desire to **the God of Love** as a tribute because he has bestowed on her such favour. The love which he has arranged for her has brought about a life of joy and stability. No one could imagine a better existence because, without jealousy or quarrelling, she loves a man who is most earnestly devoted to her and is least sullied with sinful **intention**. She celebrates her lover's qualities in lines whose two repeating syntactical patterns (*the x of y*, *of y [the] x*) emphasize her certainty that he is the source or epitome of each virtue (841–4). She loves him best just as he loves her. She can therefore do nothing but thank Love for the happiness in which she basks.

The speaker is confident that being in love is 'the righte lif' (851), the most perfect life, one which drives away sin and makes her daily more virtuous. She dismisses those who criticize love as immoral or enslaving. Such people slander **the God of Love** but have never truly experienced love. With a sequence of questions and proverbs the song argues that such criticisms of love indicate the weaknesses of those who hold those views rather than denigrating love itself. Should the sun be thought of as in some way innately inadequate because men's eyes are too weak to look directly at its full brightness? Is love therefore deficient because some people complain about it? The song challenges those who would criticize love (and by extension those who might criticize Chaucer's own love story and the actions of its participants) to examine their own reasons for doing so. Yet it also reminds us that love can be criticized in those terms. Should love be immune from criticism or are those who celebrate it equally blinded in some way?

The song concludes with a stanza showing the reciprocal devotion of the lovers. The lady will love her knight, whom she calls her own dear heart, with all her heart and ability until her last breath. It is as if their hearts have been exchanged, his living in her body and hers in his. The repetition of the word *heart* in varying contexts in this stanza, in combination with the recurrence of the phrase *al my(n)* and of first-person pronouns (the subject pronoun *I*, the object *me* and the possessives *my* and *myn*), represents the intensity of their mutual love and of her wholehearted devotion. The song counters many of the doubts about love which Criseyde has just rehearsed in private. Love is not perilous but secure, not stormy but perfect, not shameful but ennobling, and men are not capricious but devoted. Antigone's choice of song is thus a second coincidence which predisposes Criseyde to fall in love with Troilus.

Criseyde asks Antigone who composed this song with such a commendable meaning. Antigone replies that it was composed by the most praiseworthy maiden of highest social rank in all of Troy, one who lives her life most honourably and happily. Criseyde agrees that the subject matter of her song suggests such a person (yet we might wonder if such an unmarried maiden can fully understand love in all its forms). Criseyde wonders out loud how happy lovers must be to sing such beautiful songs. Antigone agrees, but warns that the supreme joy of love is an exclusive experience which is not understood by everyone. One cannot understand something which one has not yet experienced, just as in order to know what heaven and hell are like we would have to ask saints and devils because no mortal man has experienced these places. In order to conceal her own feelings, Criseyde pretends that she is no longer interested in the matter by changing the subject. Yet Antigone's song has deeply affected her and she imprints every word in her heart. She is now less frightened by love and it sinks deep into the seat of her emotions. She now grows able to 'converte' (903) to **the religion of love**, to change from someone who resists into someone who is devoted to **the God of Love**.

(iv) Lines 904 to 931: Criseyde's dream

Mirroring some elements of the day's beginning, the narrating voice now signals the ending of the day which began with Pandarus being awakened by Procne the swallow. May's rejuvenation is paralleled here by descriptions of the setting sun (given three metaphorical epithets in self-consciously poetic style by the narrating first-person who then glosses his own rhetoric) and the fading light of dusk. Visitors to Criseyde's house take their leave and she is readied for bed by her servants. Once at rest, she continues to mull over all the events of the day. A nightingale sings loudly next to the wall of her bedchamber. The narrating voice tells us that perhaps the song was a song about love. Criseyde is invigorated by the song and sent into a deep and restorative sleep after very willingly listening to it for a long time (indicating her new predisposition to love).

Once asleep, Criseyde dreams that a white eagle tears out her heart and places his own heart in her breast, yet she does not shudder with fear or suffer any pain. The narrative does not interpret the dream and we are left to decide its significance for ourselves. The exchange of hearts appears as a motif in Antigone's song (871–3) and the noble bird of prey might thus symbolize Troilus, a royal prince, with whom Criseyde will exchange hearts. Alternatively, the dream might indicate that Criseyde's fearful nature has been replaced by a more courageous one. It may signal that Criseyde has accepted Troilus into her own heart, a process which paradoxically is both violent and painless.

LINES 932 TO 1302: AN EXCHANGE OF LETTERS

(i) Lines 932 to 1001: Pandarus reports back

Uniting himself and his audience with first-person plurals (932), the narrating voice steers his narrative away from Criseyde and back to Troilus, just as Pandarus goes back and forth between the two characters. Troilus has returned to his palace and waits whilst not one but two or three messengers (indicating his impatience) are sent in search of Pandarus. Pandarus arrives and comes bounding into the room. In order to gain privacy, Pandarus suggests they go to supper and then retire to bed. (As a close friend, Pandarus is granted the privilege of sleeping in the head of the household's bedchamber.) Once they are alone, Troilus asks Pandarus whether he has cause to celebrate or lament his fortunes in love. Pandarus responds in brusque fashion, indicating his businesslike confidence in his own abilities. Troilus, he says, should lie still and go to sleep because matters with Criseyde have been successfully advanced. He can celebrate in any way he likes, because Criseyde will do her utmost to help allay his suffering and will love him best, unless sluggishness on Troilus's part causes the love affair to falter. Pandarus explains how he has already obtained from Criseyde the promise of love of friendship. Troilus is so relieved and grateful for this news that he praises the power of Venus, goddess of love. Chaucer draws from the *Filostrato* the image of Troilus looking up to the heavens in praise like rows of flowers whose heads first droop with closed petals during the cold night and then open up and turn upwards towards the sun in the morning. Troilus also praises and thanks Pandarus because he feels healed from his **lovesickness**. He expresses his gratitude by offering everything he owns to his friend. Even if he (Troilus) were given a thousand Troys, he says that he could not be happier.

Troilus now worries about what he should do next, when he will see Criseyde, and how he can pass the time until Pandarus visits her again. Pandarus advises him not to rush matters because, proverbially speaking, everything has its moment. Troilus will only have to wait until night-time has ended because Pandarus will visit his niece again early in the morning at prime (the first time-division of the day running from 6 to 9 a.m.). Pandarus reminds Troilus of his dedication to this task so far and presents him with an ultimatum. If he follows his instructions, he will succeed; if he does not, he should blame himself for all his troubles because Pandarus will take no responsibility for them (as they will not be his fault).

(ii) Lines 1002 to 1092: Troilus's letter

Though he flatters Troilus by telling him that he is a thousand times wiser than he himself is (hyperbolically increased from the *Filostrato* where Troilo is six times wiser), it is Pandarus who now suggests their next move. If Pandarus were in Troilus's position, he would write to his lady describing his suffering and asking for pity. The letter should be written by Troilus himself (that is, not by a secretary). Pandarus will take the letter to Criseyde and, whilst he is with her, Troilus should ride on his warhorse past her house dressed in his finest armour. If he can, Pandarus will contrive to have Criseyde sitting near a window looking out into the street at the moment when Troilus rides past. He cautions Troilus to behave with dignity when he sees Criseyde. Troilus should greet them formally with a wave or salute and then look directly at him rather than gazing too eagerly at his lady. He should not stay too long and should remain in control of his emotions. Pandarus will then take this opportunity to speak to Criseyde once more. In the *Filostrato*, a scene in which Troilo and Pandaro go to look at Criseida (who has positioned herself at her window in the expectation that they will visit) comes after Pandaro's reporting back of his success but precedes the writing of Troilo's first letter. It is thus the cause both of Troilo's increased desire and of Criseida's falling in love. In Chaucer's version, Troilus has already ridden past Criseyde's window by coincidence and been seen by her, a viewing which caused her feelings for Troilus to intensify. Thus Pandarus here plans to restage an event which, unbeknownst to them, has already occurred.

Pandarus next gives Troilus detailed advice on the way in which he should write to Criseyde. He is sure that Troilus will not write in too grand a manner, nor show off with lots of complex arguments, nor write too artily or like a scrivener (a professional letter-writer). He should allow his tears to drop onto the paper, demonstrating the strength of his suffering as he writes, yet he should not repeat too often his most tender and lovely phrases. Pandarus substantiates his advice by way of an example. If the best harp-player simply played one string over and over again or played just one tune, even on the most melodious harp, every listener would become tired of such music. Yet though Pandarus argues for variety, he cautions against jumbling different types of language together, such as medical terms mixed in with love-talk. Troilus should maintain the style expected in a love letter and keep things consistent because mixed-up styles cannot be taken seriously. For example, if an artist painted a picture of a type of fish called a pike, but gave it a donkey's feet and a monkey's head, then such a painting would only be suitable to be a joke and not a serious piece of art. This stylistic advice, which sounds as relevant for a poem as it does for a love letter, echoes the opening of the *Ars poetica* ('the art of poetry') by the Roman author Horace (65–8 BC), a treatise on poetics which itself takes the form of a Latin poem.[5] This allusion, as well as proposing an analogy between the writing of poetry and the writing of love letters, self-reflexively prompts further speculations about Chaucer's own project. Should the wide range of registers employed in *Troilus and Criseyde* be considered as suitable variety or a discordant jumble or an inevitably humorous composite? What happens when things which are unlike each other (such as philosophy and romantic love) are combined?

[5] Horace, *Ars poetica*, in *Satires, Epistles, Ars poetica*, ed. and trans. H. R. Fairclough, Loeb Classical Library 194 (London: Heinemann, 1952), p. 451.

How much licence does Chaucer have to create such a mixture before the results become frivolously ludicrous?

Troilus welcomes Pandarus's advice, but remains fearful about writing in case his lack of experience in love causes him to write inappropriately. If Criseyde will not accept the letter he thinks he will certainly die of grief. Pandarus reassures him by reminding him that he will deliver the letter personally and endeavour to bring him a letter from Criseyde in return. Troilus now sits down to write. Chaucer gives a summary of the letter rather than presenting the text of the letter verbatim as Boccaccio does. This allows the narrating voice's commentary to be interspersed with the content of the letter. Troilus begins by naming Criseyde as his true lady and other epithets which the narrating first-person tells us are the conventional terms used by lovers. He commends himself to her, entrusting himself to her mercy because his fate lies in her hands. He asks her to forgive the fact that he has written to her (when she has not agreed to receive a letter) and says that it was his love and suffering which forced him to write. He belittles his own worth and competence as a lover (though the narrating voice says he lies in doing so) and then recounts the extent of his suffering (the narrating voice drolly interjects that this account was endless). Troilus then folds the letter up, dipping the carved ruby in his signet ring in his own tears before pressing the ring into wax to seal the letter. He kisses the letter seemingly a thousand times and tells it that a blissful future is predestined for it because it will soon see Criseyde.

(iii) Lines 1093 to 1179: Pandarus delivers the letter

Early the following morning, Pandarus hurries to Criseyde's palace. He insists that the last hour of prime (see p. 55) has passed (suggesting that he knows he has in fact arrived *before* a socially acceptable time). He entertains Criseyde's household by speaking jokingly, explaining his early arrival as a result of his love for his own lady. He can never sleep in on May mornings because of his **lovesickness** which causes a mixture of pleasure and pain (here expressed by two oxymorons combining an adjective of pleasure and a noun of suffering). Criseyde knows the likely reasons for his early arrival and asks why he has come to visit. She is both fearful and curious, though she keeps up a public show of joking. So as to get a moment of privacy with his niece, Pandarus now invents a plausible reason for his visit. He says that a spy has arrived in the city with news from the Greek army's camp which he must pass on to her. (This is a credible story given Calchas's defection to the Greek camp, as the spy's news may concern Criseyde's father.)

Uncle and niece descend from the house into the garden and walk out of earshot of her servants. Pandarus presents the letter, demanding that she provide a kind response because if she does not it is likely that Troilus will die from **lovesickness**. Criseyde, just as Criseida does in the *Filostrato*, believes it would be improper to accept such a love letter. Criseida rejects the letter tactfully, but Criseyde is extremely indignant. She imperiously instructs Pandarus to bring no such letter to her and to pay more attention to her reputation than to his friend's desires. She chastises him harshly, asking him to consider whether this is fitting behaviour on his part and whether it would be appropriate for a woman in her position to accept the letter or to show pity on Troilus in this way, when it might damage her standing or provoke condemnation. Pandarus is equally indignant at her reaction, telling her to stop what he considers to be foolish behaviour. He is amazed, saying that this is the strangest occurrence that he has ever witnessed. He invites the gods to strike him dead with a thunderbolt if the letter is in any way harmful to her reputation. He claims Criseyde's response exemplifies the supposed callousness of all women, who care nothing for the man who is most devoted to them.

In the *Filostrato*, Criseida relents quickly and, taking the letter from Pandaro, hides it down the front of her dress. In Chaucer's version, Pandarus forcefully and intimately thrusts the letter into his niece's bosom. He then challenges her to make a fuss and to throw the letter to the ground so that her servants notice and stare at them. At this challenge, Criseyde's initial indignation subsides very quickly. Is this because she does not wish to attract the attention of her household or because her initial reluctance and indignation were partly for show? She says that she can wait to do this until any observers have gone (signalling that she will in fact accept the letter and will wait until she has the necessary privacy to read it). She now smiles, asking her uncle to provide the answer himself because she will not write a letter. Answering as if she means that she will not physically write a reply, Pandarus says that he will act as her scribe if she dictates the letter to him. Criseyde laughs at this neat reply and ends discussion for the moment by inviting him to join her household for the first main meal of the day. Before dinner is served, Criseyde retreats to her private chamber, giving her the opportunity to inspect the letter without being observed. Having considered every aspect of it, every word in every line, she finds nothing missing and judges that Troilus knows what is right and proper in such a matter. She hides the letter once more and joins the rest of her household in the main hall.

(iv) Lines 1180 to 1246: Criseyde writes a reply

Criseyde finds Pandarus apparently lost in his thoughts in a 'studye' (1180), a moment of deep concentration. She approaches him unnoticed and takes hold of his hood, pointing out to him that she has caught hold of him before he realized what was going on. Pandarus admits that she has seemingly outwitted him and says that as his forfeit she can now do what she likes (yet of course it is Criseyde who is now manoeuvred into position by her uncle). After dinner, Pandarus looks out of one of the windows, asking who has decorated a particular house opposite her own property. Criseyde joins him in order to identify which house he is asking about. They sit in the bay-window and talk about various inconsequential topics. Pandarus waits until Criseyde's servants have retreated out of earshot and then takes his opportunity to ask what she thinks of Troilus's letter. He asks if it demonstrates that Troilus knows about **the art of love.** Criseyde blushes and murmurs, saying that she believes that he shows skill in the letter. Pandarus urges her to respond in kind and offers to sew up the letter for her. (Rather than being placed in an envelope, letters written on parchment were folded and then sewn shut to keep the contents private.) Thinking out loud, Criseyde says that she could indeed write a reply herself, but yet she doesn't know what to say (in the following stanza she says that this is the first letter which she has ever composed without assistance). Pandarus suggests that she at least thank Troilus for his friendliness and write nothing which might cause him to die of sorrow. He draws on her love for him as an obedient niece to beg her not to refuse.

Criseyde retires alone to a small private chamber in order to write her letter. In the act of writing, we are told, she begins to release her heart just a little from Disdain's prison (that is, she allows her feelings to be less constrained by the reserved behaviour expected from noble ladies). Rather than giving us the text of the letter (as Boccaccio's narrator does), the narrating first-person says that he intends to briefly summarize its essence. In the letter, Criseyde thanks Troilus for his good **intention**, but does not offer him false hopes or enslave herself to love like a serf bound to serve his lord. Yet she now concedes a little more and offers Troilus sisterly love in order to help his heartache. Prompted by her first view of Troilus riding past and by his letter, Criseyde now grants him love and affection equivalent to familial intimacy. She returns to Pandarus who has remained seated in the bay-window. Giving him the folded letter, she says that composing it was the most arduous thing she has ever done.

Pandarus, always keen to push Criseyde a little further than she is willing to go, says that Troilus should be thankful that she has proved hard to win over (here assuming that Troilus has indeed gained her love). Two complementary proverbs enclose and justify this observation. Firstly, an undertaking which is begun unwillingly will often end well. Secondly, impressions, whether physical or mental, which are shallow (and therefore easily created) rather than deeply imprinted are usually instantly ready to escape (that is, they will fade away very quickly). Yet our readerly foresight makes us aware that these proverbs apply in ways which Pandarus cannot yet realize. Matters will not end well, and Criseyde's love is unwillingly begun and, ultimately, perhaps shallow.

Pandarus tells his niece that she has now played the part of a tyrant for too long (that is, she has behaved towards Troilus just as a cruel and domineering ruler behaves towards his subjects) and it has proved hard to engrave Troilus's love into her heart. She should now stop resisting his affections, although Pandarus expects that she will maintain an outward show of *daunger* (see p. 43). She should now hurry to make Troilus happy because, Pandarus warns, stubborn resistance maintained for too long will cause distress and therefore resentment.

(v) Lines 1247 to 1302: Troilus rides by again

Just at this moment, Troilus, accompanied by a party of ten men, comes round the corner towards Criseyde's window because, says the narrating voice, this is the route to his palace (though we know that he must be making a circular trip rather than returning from elsewhere). Pandarus points him out and cautions her not to retreat away from the window in case Troilus thinks that she shuns him. Troilus salutes her meekly with an anxious expression. The colour of his complexion changes frequently (presumably between the paleness of fear and the blushes of embarrassment). He gazes up at the window meekly and nods to Pandarus as he passes by.

The narrating voice declares that only God knows for certain whether Troilus behaves appropriately, looks attractive and presents a manly sight at this particular moment (with the implication that these things are of course true). He asks why he should delay the action of his narrative by describing his armour and weaponry (leaving us to supply the answer that it would be unnecessary because of the earlier detailed description of Troilus's perhaps more manly appearance when he came straight from the battlefield). Nevertheless, he lists the aspects of Troilus's appearance which please Criseyde, so many that they spill abundantly over the end of one stanza and into the next. Though this pre-arranged ride-past duplicates the earlier coincidental one, Criseyde is now even more predisposed to love as a result of Antigone's song and Troilus's letter. She is so pleased by Troilus's virtues that she feels pity for his suffering as never before. The narrating voice hopes that love for Troilus is now embedded within her heart like a thorn or splinter which she could not pull out even if she tried for a week.

Pandarus seizes this moment to encourage Criseyde to make further concessions. He asks whether it would be right for a pitiless woman to cause an innocent man's death by making him suffer in love. Criseyde fervently says it would not be right and Pandarus agrees. He demands that she stop her resistance, which he characterizes not as caution or propriety but as immature silliness, and agree to speak to Troilus in person in order to assuage his suffering. Yet Criseyde is not as malleable as Pandarus thinks. Before a meeting can be arranged, the narrating voice comments that there was still much to do and 'to heven' (1289, i.e., to struggle with just as one would labour to lift up a heavy object) before Criseyde would agree to this. The narrative contrasts their different **intention**s at this moment. Criseyde fears malicious gossip and also feels it is too soon to grant Troilus the privilege of speaking with her in private. She intends to love him without her love becoming known in any way and hence to reward his devotion not with a meeting but only by allowing him to look upon her from a distance. Yet Pandarus intends to change her mind. He vows that she will not maintain this stance for two whole years (the conventional period of time which a widow spent in mourning after the death of her husband), implying that Criseyde will soon put aside her widow's weeds and become Troilus's lover.

LINES 1303 TO 1351: TROILUS'S DESIRE GROWS

His heart dancing with joy at his success as a go-between, Pandarus now returns to Troilus's palace in order to deliver Criseyde's reply. Troilus is alone in his bedchamber, paralysed by the effects of his emotions which swing between hope and gloomy despair. Troilus, Pandarus says, should not be thus prostrate with sorrow but should get up and inspect the letter, which Pandarus figures as a magic spell sent to his friend to cure this attack of **lovesickness**. Troilus says he will do so with God's help and Pandarus replies that God has indeed helped them, as he will see if he takes the candle which he offers and inspects the black ink of the letter.

This brief section of the poem is marked by opposites: hope and despair, happiness and sorrow, disease and cure, and light and dark. Troilus's emotions remain in flux as he reads the letter, pleased and fearful by turns according to whether Criseyde's words give him cause for hope or fear. He construes the letter as favourable to his situation, finding some parts of it which calm his emotions, even though those encouraging words are hidden by Criseyde under a shield of circumspect language. The hope provided by the letter leads him to put aside the majority of his suffering in favour of greater optimism. Yet although his suffering is momentarily alleviated by the letter, his love once more intensifies. Criseyde's letter, because it gives Troilus cause to hope, therefore increases his desire and renews his suffering. Acting in accordance with Pandarus's advice, he strives to push matters on, writing to her again about his painful sorrows. He never lets things grow cool (that is, he never lets the intensity of his wooing slacken), using Pandarus to pass on a letter or a message every day. He performs all the duties expected of a lover and either celebrates or laments depending on Criseyde's replies.

LINES 1352 TO 1757: THE MEETING AT DEIPHEBUS'S PALACE

(i) Lines 1352 to 1393: Pandarus suggests a meeting

As his desire for Criseyde increases, Troilus turns continually to his friend Pandarus for help. Pandarus nearly dies out of sympathy for his pain and quickly makes plans to reduce Troilus's sorrow as best he can. He promises to arrange matters so that Troilus can meet Criseyde in person in order to beg her for 'grace' (1365), for her goodwill, kindness and love (and, presumably, even greater concessions). Perhaps anticipating Troilus's fearful objections to such a meeting, Pandarus goes on to justify his proposal. Those who are expert on matters of love declare that the opportunity to speak to one's lady in person, in a private place where the lover can communicate his suffering openly to her, is one of the things which will most advance his cause. Witnessing the sight and sound of a lover's distress in person will inevitably evoke pity from a lady whose heart is not cruel or pitiless.

Pandarus then voices the objections which Troilus might make. He depicts Troilus's fears about Criseyde's possible response as a struggle between different parts of her make-up. Even though 'Kynde' (1374), her human nature with its instinctive compassion, might make Criseyde pity him to some degree, *Daunger* (see p. 43, here personified as a speaking character) might override this pity and say 'No, you shall never win me over.' Troilus might thus fear that there is no point in appealing to Criseyde in person because her 'hertes gost' (1377), her spiritual true self, controls her actions so strongly that, even though she might be swayed by his suffering, she would never love him completely because of her innate honour. It would be as if she were a tree which bends in the wind but whose roots remain firmly embedded in the earth and hence does not fall.

Pandarus counters these hypothetical doubts with a number of proverbs and examples. Momentum, he says, causes a large oak tree to fall very quickly once it has been struck with the stroke which succeeds in felling it, just as large rocks or millstones roll quickly when their tipping-point has been reached because heavy things fall down more rapidly than light things. Conversely, something as insubstantial and flexible as a reed is blown over by every gust of wind, but stands up again when the wind stops. (By this he implies that Criseyde's sturdy resistance to love, though it may be very difficult to overcome, will eventually give way rapidly and decisively.) A significant and difficult undertaking will be greatly celebrated when it is successfully achieved even if it has required much time and effort, so Troilus should not fear but rather welcome the task of overcoming Criseyde's reluctance. This proverbial imagery, though it is intended to persuade, might nevertheless also invite us to question whether Criseyde's resistance is truly sturdy or whether it is in fact already undermined.

(ii) Lines 1394 to 1491: Pandarus visits Deiphebus and Criseyde

Pandarus now begins to make plans for a rendezvous at which Troilus can speak to Criseyde in person. This initial meeting has no parallel in Chaucer's source in which Troilo and Criseida consummate their love at their first meeting. Pandarus asks Troilus to tell him, in strictest confidence, to which of his brothers he is closest. Troilus replies that it is Deiphebus (the third of King Priam's five sons by Hecuba, of whom Troilus is the youngest). Pandarus promises Troilus that within two hours Deiphebus will unwittingly help to arrange such a meeting. Pandarus visits Deiphebus whom we are told has always been, except for Troilus, Pandarus's most beloved lord and great friend (indicating Pandarus's close relationship with the Trojan royal family). Pandarus asks Deiphebus to assist in a matter of legal controversy. Deiphebus reassures Pandarus that he would do more for him than anyone, except for the man he most loves, his brother Troilus. Pandarus invents a story that he and his niece Criseyde supposedly require his help because a group of men who wish to harm Criseyde have illegally seized some of her property. Pandarus makes this request very formally and, in order to show deference to his social superior, does not make assumptions about Deiphebus's knowledge of his family. Deiphebus graciously says that there is no need to speak of Criseyde as if she were a stranger because she is already his friend. As such, he would act as her champion if needed, defending her honour in physical combat.

Deiphebus next asks Pandarus, since he knows everything about this matter, what would be most helpful. Pandarus suggests that Deiphebus invite Criseyde to visit him tomorrow so that she can outline her grievances in person. Moreover, he asks whether some of Deiphebus's brothers, who could also offer help to Criseyde, might also be present at the same time. Such direct access to the ear of the leading Trojan princes, in combination with the guidance of other influential friends, will scare off her enemies and give her all the help she could possibly require. Deiphebus agrees to this proposal and offers a further suggestion that he also invite his sister-in-law, Helen, wife of his brother Paris, because of the influence she has over her husband. He says that he will not ask his older brother Hector because his respect for Criseyde is such that they can take his support for granted. Finally, Deiphebus asks Pandarus to invite Troilus to join them for a meal at which Criseyde's supposed troubles will be discussed.

Pandarus here relies on courtesy and tact, allowing Deiphebus to request and then expand on his suggestion rather than raising suspicion by putting forward his own plan too enthusiastically. He does not mention Troilus directly, for example, but rather relies on the fact that their close relationship will in all likelihood lead Deiphebus to invite him to attend the dinner. He skilfully exploits pre-existing relationships and events in order to create a respectable pretext for a meeting. He next goes to Criseyde, emphasizing how he has arrived in haste in order to ask her if she has heard the news that a man named Poliphete intends to recommence his legal action and put forward new petitions against her in court. Pandarus must thus be reviving a previous legal dispute in order to create a suitable pretext. Criseyde is undoubtedly scared by this renewed threat. It is the fact that Poliphete is in alliance with two prominent Trojan citizens, Antenor and Aeneas, which makes Criseyde fear him. (In medieval versions of the story of Troy, these two figures go on to betray the city, so here Chaucer exploits their later reputation in order to characterize the threat Criseyde supposedly faces.) Criseyde proposes to appease Poliphete by handing over all her property except that which she needs to support her household. Pandarus says that this will not be necessary because he has secured the support of Deiphebus, Hector and other Trojan nobles, turning them against Poliphete so that his legal action will not succeed. As they plan what to do, Deiphebus arrives to ask Criseyde to dine at his palace the following day. Criseyde of course cannot refuse such a request made by a Trojan prince in person.

(iii) Lines 1492 to 1554: preparing Troilus

Pandarus now returns to tell Troilus how he has misled Deiphebus. The dynamism of Pandarus's actions as a go-between contrasts with the inertia of Troilus as a lover paralysed by anxiety. Pandarus explains what has been arranged and how Deiphebus has been deceived, giving voice to Troilus's fears once again. Troilus is wondering how he can speak to Criseyde, because those present will observe his expressions and gestures and will instantly realize that he suffers because of unrequited love for her. He would rather die of sorrow without anyone knowing the reason why than have his love for Criseyde made public.

Pandarus reassures him that he has devised a plan which they can use to conceal everything. His plan is that Troilus should go almost immediately to Deiphebus's house, arriving that same evening rather than just in time for the meal which has been arranged for the following day. He should arrive early, pretending to wish to enjoy an evening of recreation in order to ward off an illness from which he is currently suffering. Troilus, Pandarus says, does indeed look ill because of his **lovesickness**. Once there, he should retire to bed early, claiming that he is too ill to remain up on his feet. He can make the illness more plausible by saying that it is a fever which takes hold of him at the same time each evening and lasts until the following morning. Sorrow does indeed cause a kind of sickness, Pandarus says, so Troilus will be able to pretend to be ill very successfully. If Venus, goddess of love, is present as a favourable sponsor and if Troilus sticks to the plan, Pandarus is confident that Criseyde will unconditionally guarantee him his 'grace' (1526), the mercy and favour which will save him from sorrow (a euphemism for further concessions on her part). Troilus replies that he is 'sik in ernest' (1529), he is genuinely suffering from **lovesickness**, and therefore he does not need Pandarus to advise him to feign illness. Pandarus observes that Troilus will therefore be able to complain about his disease more authentically and have less need to counterfeit, to make a false pretence of sickness.

The narrating voice now asks why he would need to tell us every detail of the events of Troilus's arrival at Deiphebus's palace (though he does recount them in summary) because we have already heard Pandarus prescribe what will happen. Such a comment highlights how Pandarus, in his stage-managing of events, acts rather like an author or a narrator. Before Troilus retires to bed, Deiphebus asks him to act as Criseyde's supporter. Troilus of course quickly agrees to be her true friend. The narrating voice observes that this request is entirely unnecessary (because Troilus wishes to be her friend and much more, though Deiphebus cannot know it), just as it is unnecessary to ask a mad man to run about madly because his insanity will cause him to do this.

(iv) Lines 1555 to 1596: dinner at Deiphebus's palace

The following morning, those invited to Deiphebus's palace arrive in time for dinner, the first main meal of the day at about 10 o'clock. Helen of Troy (here named as queen because of her first marriage to King Menelaus) does not wish to break her promise to Deiphebus and therefore arrives promptly and 'homly' (1559), without ceremony, visiting in her private role of sister-in-law. The narrating voice comments that only God and Pandarus are fully aware of what all of this meant. Pandarus's manipulation of events gives him a God-like omniscience as regards the true purpose of this dinner (though not of all future events, as we shall see in Book IV). In contrast, other guests such as Helen of Troy visit in 'pleyne entente' (1560), with the sincere **intention** of honouring Deiphebus and helping Criseyde, but without any understanding of the real purpose of the occasion. Criseyde, who arrives accompanied by her nieces, is similarly unaware. The narrating voice makes a show of hurrying himself and his readers towards the reason why this occasion has been arranged, urging us to skip over (that is, to allow him to skip over) their formal speeches of greeting to each other. Pandarus's plan means of course that there are two reasons why, the public pretext and the private **intention**. Like God and Pandarus, the narrating first-person and we his readers also understand this scene omnisciently. We know what is camouflage and what is its true purpose.

Deiphebus, though he acts as a good host, repeatedly exclaims 'allas', explaining that his brother Troilus remains confined to bed by illness while they dine. Helen too laments his illness, and every guest acts like a doctor, offering cures for his fever. We are told that there is one guest (whom we know to be Criseyde) who, though she does not put herself forward to propose a remedy, nevertheless thinks silently that she is best placed to cure Troilus's **lovesickness**. The guests then begin to praise Troilus lavishly. Criseyde's face does not betray her emotions but inwardly her heart laughs for joy and pride. The narrating voice presents this pride as understandable rather than conceited, asking who would not likewise feel proud if they had the power to make such a noteworthy knight live or die.

(v) Lines 1597 to 1666: Pandarus takes charge

Pandarus interrupts the after-dinner conversation by asking Deiphebus's permission to begin the discussion of Criseyde's 'nedes' (1603), the difficult situation in which she supposedly finds herself. Deiphebus asks Pandarus to explain the details of the case and he duly gives an explanation of events. The accusations he makes are so terrible that we are told that anyone who heard them might spit (to show their loathing of Poliphete and his tactics). Chaucer evocatively captures the group dynamic of a social occasion such as this. Just as everyone praised Troilus and offered a cure for his sickness, here each guest replies to Pandarus's account 'werse' (1618, that is, each denounces Poliphete more emphatically than the previous speaker). Helen asks whether Hector and Troilus know about Poliphete's supposed machinations. Pandarus takes this opportunity to offer the opinion that it would be advantageous for Criseyde to tell Troilus about the problem in person before she leaves. He says he will quickly go into the bedchamber in which Troilus lies to find out whether he is sleeping and whether he wishes to be told of Criseyde's troubles. He dashes into the room and whispers a lewd innuendo in his friend's ear. The joke is that Troilus is nearly dead with **lovesickness** and so Pandarus commends his soul to God and says that he has brought his bier (insinuating that he will soon lie upon Criseyde just as a corpse is placed upon a bier at a funeral). Troilus's smile makes clear his complicity. There is no question that he, like Pandarus, intends something different from their earlier claims of limited and honourable requests.

Pandarus returns to the main hall and tells Helen and Deiphebus that Troilus wishes the two of them to bring Criseyde to his bedchamber. Troilus will listen to her problems for as long as his sickness allows him. As he takes charge of matters, Pandarus nonetheless makes a continual show of deference and cautious permission-seeking. He warns them that it is only a small room and even the presence of just a few people will make it warm, which would be dangerous for someone with a fever. In order not to seem suspiciously keen, he pretends to ask for advice as to whether Criseyde should wait till another time as he does not wish to do anything which would worsen Troilus's condition. Without waiting for their reply, he suggests that Deiphebus and Helen enter along with himself because he can explain Criseyde's problem most quickly. After that, Criseyde should make a brief visit to Troilus's chamber in order to make a single request that he act as her patron and protector. Her visit must be brief because Troilus will have to forgo his rest and relaxation in her presence because she is 'straunge' (1660), not a member of his family as Helen and Deiphebus are. Pandarus also claims that Troilus wishes to tell them secrets which will aid their besieged city (presumably some piece of intelligence from the Greek camp). Once again, we are reminded that Pandarus has entirely deceived his royal superiors as to his true **intention**. Troy's perilous state as a city under siege appears here tangentially, a piece of camouflage for Pandarus's true purpose.

(vi) Lines 1667 to 1708: Helen and Deiphebus visit Troilus

Deiphebus, Helen and Pandarus now enter the chamber in which Troilus lies supposedly recovering from his fever. Chaucer presents Helen as a model of queenly virtues, not aloof but kind, unpretentious and tactile. On behalf of herself, Deiphebus and Pandarus, she asks Troilus to be a friend and patron to Criseyde, inviting Pandarus to explain his niece's troubles. Once his friend has outlined the case, Troilus pledges to become one of those who will support Criseyde in her case against Poliphete.

Pandarus now asks if Criseyde may be permitted to say farewell to Troilus before she leaves Deiphebus's palace. Troilus agrees if Criseyde herself consents to visit him. He now plays his part in Pandarus's plan, telling Deiphebus and Helen that he must discuss a particular subject with them in order to benefit from their advice. We are now told that Troilus then found by his bedhead, by chance, a letter and a document sent to him by Hector (papers which in all likelihood Troilus and Pandarus have brought with them by way of a diversion). In the letter, Hector writes to Troilus asking for his advice as to whether some unnamed man deserves to die. The 'tretys' (1697) is presumably a memorandum supplying the relevant evidence in this man's case, about which Troilus gravely consults Deiphebus and Helen. Pandarus and Troilus again exploit public matters in order to further private ends. Deiphebus and Helen must read through these papers, and so they leave the bedchamber by an external staircase in order to walk outside in a leafy pleasure garden. Such an enclosed space provides the privacy necessary to acquaint themselves with such a sensitive matter. We are told that it takes them the space of an hour to read through the papers, a time-marker which tells us that the imminent meeting between Criseyde and Troilus will not be the brief farewell which Pandarus earlier described.

(vii) Lines 1709 to 1757: Criseyde enters the bedchamber

Pandarus now returns to the main hall of Deiphebus's palace in order to fetch Criseyde. He salutes all those present and, having thus attracted their attention, he instructs Criseyde to hurry because Helen and her two brothers-in-law are waiting for her. As Deiphebus and Helen are no longer in the bedchamber, Pandarus now openly deceives the guests. He aims to make it seem entirely proper that Criseyde should enter Troilus's bedchamber without any attendants to act as chaperones. First he seems insouciantly unconcerned as to who attends her, telling Criseyde to bring her niece Antigone with her or whichever lady-in-waiting she prefers. He continues the ploy that Deiphebus and Helen have remained, warning Criseyde to thank *all three of them* and to take her leave of *them* when she sees the earliest possible moment at which to make a polite exit. Criseyde, the narrating voice says, is therefore quite unaware of Pandarus's **intention** to allow Troilus to speak to her entirely in private about his love (a comment which inevitably makes us wonder whether Criseyde is as unsuspecting as is suggested). Then Pandarus makes a show of worrying that the room should not become too crowded, asking all of the guests very earnestly to wait outside and quietly amuse themselves. He urges them to remember who is within the chamber (supposedly three members of the Trojan royal family to whom formality and respect should be granted) and what a predicament one of them is in (i.e., Troilus's supposed fever).

Pandarus succeeds in his plan to allow Criseyde to enter unaccompanied. As he escorts her into the bedchamber, Pandarus takes advantage of this last opportunity to influence her behaviour towards Troilus. He urges her to begin her conversation very gently and orders her very solemnly not to kill Troilus by rejecting his love. He commands her to do this on behalf of him who gives us each a soul (a periphrastic name for the supreme deity) and by the power of 'corones tweyne' (1735), perhaps two crowning virtues such as pity and kindness or justice and mercy. She should remember what sort of person Troilus is and his particular predicament, both of which should make her sympathetic to his pleas. She should remember that wasted time cannot be regained, a proverb which, Pandarus claims, both she and Troilus will agree with when they are united in love (again Pandarus betrays his ultimate **intention**). Pandarus mocks the fearful attitude of those who will not seize the day, those lovers who procrastinate by hesitating, by endless 'pursuyte' (1744, that is, by petitioning their lady for favour), and other delays. While they procrastinate, they have time to see bad omens everywhere, even in something as insignificant as the waving of a blade of straw. Such lovers wish to have a happy ending, but do not dare act to bring this about. Why might they do this, he asks? He scornfully repeats their answer: their paranoia is caused by what she said and how he looked (the third-person pronouns used with demonstrative force to indicate the different individuals suspected of gossiping and spying on a lover's actions). Pandarus himself would dare not have anything to do with wasting time in this way. He therefore hurries Criseyde forward in order to return his friend to full health.

The narrating first-person ends Book II not at a point of conclusion but at a point of nervous anticipation. He asks the lovers in his audience whether Troilus isn't indeed in a 'kankedort' (1752), an unknown word which from the context must mean something like a fix or predicament. Troilus hears Pandarus and Criseyde approach and feels that this is the arrival of his destiny because he will either die if she rejects him or be cured if she accepts his love. The narrating voice leaves us in no doubt as to the significance of the first meeting between the lovers, asking the all-powerful God what Troilus should say as he requests Criseyde's love in person for the first time (the use of the present tense here giving a dramatic sense of events about to happen).

Book III

LINES 1 TO 49: THE PROEM

The proem takes the form of an invocation to Venus, goddess of love (though she is not named directly but via a cluster of astrological and mythological epithets). As the source of this proem, Chaucer adapts part of the joyful song sung to Pandaro by Troilo in the days following the consummation of his affair with Criseida (see *Fil.* III.74–9). The narrating voice invokes Venus as the blessed light whose shining beams decorate the third celestial sphere (see p. 191). He calls her the sun's beloved (because the planet Venus appears close to the sun in the morning and evening) and the daughter of Jove (another name for Jupiter, supreme deity in the classical pantheon). He celebrates her as one who is graciously kind and always ready to return to noble hearts. (The implication is that Venus's proper home, to which she is always keen to return, is the hearts of those noble enough to experience love.) He also calls Venus the true cause of prosperity and joy. He praises her power and her favourable influence on the world which is felt everywhere, in heaven and hell, on sea and on land. All of nature at different times experiences Venus's eternal influence (the ever-present way in which the planets were thought in medieval astrology to affect worldly matters). Indeed, God himself loves and will deny nothing to love (that is, He does not hinder or resist Venus's effects in any way). There is no living creature in the world who is of any value without love or who can endure without love.

The rest of the proem comprises a sequence of five stanzas, each beginning with the pronoun 'Ye' as the narrating voice addresses Venus directly. Two stanzas recount Venus's power to influence not only humankind but also other mythological deities. The narrating first-person reminds Venus that it was she who first incited Jove to the fortunate actions through which all things were created (a pagan version of the way in which God's love, in the form of the Holy Spirit, brought the universe to life). Venus also made Jove fall in love with mortal women and gave him success or misfortune in love. It was she who sent him down to Earth in a thousand forms and whomever she chose for him to desire, he seized (this refers to the various myths in which Jupiter assumed different physical forms in order to rape mortal women). Venus's effects are beneficial and procreative, yet they also provoke lust and sexual violence. The narrating voice next reminds Venus that she placated the anger of Mars, the fierce god of war. (Venus does this both in astrological terms, because the propitious planet Venus counteracts the malign influence of Mars, and in mythological terms, because Mars was said to have fallen in love with Venus.)

The narrating first-person now turns to Venus's influence on human affairs. Just as she pleases, she makes hearts noble, or at least the hearts of those whom she wishes to inflame with love. Such people, once they are in love, fear disgrace and leave behind their vices. Venus makes them courteous, cheerful and gracious. Moreover, it is her influence which grants an individual any happiness that he experiences. She maintains the unity of kingdoms and families and she is also the true cause of friendship between individuals. She knows all those hidden properties of things about which people are so curious. Chaucer here gives an illustration (added to his source) of the matters on which people speculate. They are curious when they cannot understand how it may occur that she loves him or why he loves her (the anonymous third-person pronouns giving a sense of gossipy exchanges about various acquaintances). People struggle to understand this just as we cannot know why this fish and not that one reaches the fish-trap at the weir (this simile invites us to consider whether love itself is a kind of trap). Finally, the narrating voice tells Venus that, because she has established a universal law for humankind (and thus because her power is unassailable), whoever rebels against her comes off worst. He himself does not have first-hand experience of this law but has learned about it from those who are lovers.

The narrating voice now asks Venus for assistance as he begins Book III. He asks her, in honour of those lovers who serve her (and for whom he acts as 'clerc', 41, that is, a record-keeper or scribe), to teach him how to narrate some part of the joy which lovers experience in her service. He asks her to pour emotion into his bare heart (bare because he does not have personal experience on which to draw) and to make him able to demonstrate her delightfulness and benevolence. He also calls on Calliope, the Muse of epic poetry, considered the superlative poetic mode, to ensure that her voice is also present. He tells her that there is now need for her help and asks whether she cannot see his distress, caused by the fact that in praise of Venus he must now relate Troilus's joy (making us wonder whether it is his own jealousy which causes him such anguish in the narration of such joy or some other reason). He concludes with a brief prayer asking God to bring whoever has need of it to similar happiness. This celebration of Venus emphasizes the benevolent effects of love, anticipating the joy which Troilus and Criseyde will soon experience, yet the invocation of Calliope reminds us that the happiness of Book III is set within wider contexts, not only of double sorrow and personal loss and betrayal, but also within the subject matter of epic rather than love poetry, the destruction of Troy resulting from Paris's desire for Helen.

LINES 50 TO 231: THE MEETING AT DEIPHEBUS'S PALACE (CONTINUED)

(i) Lines 50 to 190: the first meeting

Book III begins *in medias res*, at the moment at which Troilus waits nervously for Pandarus and Criseyde to enter the bedchamber at Deiphebus's palace. He lies in bed rehearsing his plan of action and the different parts of the speech he intends to make. Pandarus leads Criseyde into the room by a hem or fold of her clothes, bringing the two lovers together by direct physical manoeuvring. He peeks in through the curtained canopy which surrounds Troilus's bed, praying that God give remedy to all sick people (and thus insinuating that Criseyde should provide some cure for Troilus). He introduces Criseyde as the person who is to blame for Troilus's death, almost seeming to weep with sympathy for his suffering. Troilus can barely speak, his first utterance being an interjection expressing the strength of his emotion. He asks who approaches because, he claims, he cannot see clearly. It is left to the reader to decide whether this incapacity is the authentic debility of **lovesickness** or a feigned symptom of his fever. Criseyde by contrast seems self-assured, announcing their identities succinctly. Troilus tries to sit up in bed, apologizing that he cannot kneel before her to show his devotion. Criseyde prevents him from trying to get up, urging him not to do so on her account. She explains the reason for her visit very briefly. Troilus is so overwhelmed that Criseyde asks him for protection (rather than treating him with the haughtiness expected of a lover's lady) that he swoons. In contrast with Troilus's inexperience as a lover, Criseyde demonstrates the maturity of an experienced widow, observing his embarrassment patiently and sympathetically.

The narrating first-person next promises that he will relate Troilus's speeches to Criseyde exactly as he finds them in his historical sources (yet the rendezvous at Deiphebus's palace is Chaucer's own invention). He tells us that Troilus's voice has been changed by fear and shakes, and he looks down humbly, his face blushing and blanching with nerves. The series of descriptive clauses in lines 92–6 stutter their way towards the main clause in lines 97–8, imitating Troilus's own nervousness. Troilus's first words are a simple plea for mercy. Then, after a pause, he tells Criseyde of his devotion and acknowledges that he neither dares nor is able to make a proper complaint (that is, a formal expression of his sorrow). If he offends her in any way, he threatens to avenge her displeasure upon his own life, killing himself if this will in some way appease her anger. Throughout this scene, Chaucer has the narrating voice seek to manipulate our response to Troilus's embarrassment just as Pandarus's words and gestures try to influence Criseyde's reaction. The narrating voice sees Troilus's nerves as indicative of his 'manly sorwe' (113), emotion which is not unbefitting of a Trojan prince but masculine and noble. He urges us to respond in the same way, commenting that even someone with a heart of stone might feel pity at witnessing Troilus's suffering. Pandarus is equally moved, weeping so copiously that it seems as though he will turn entirely into water. He prods his niece both physically and verbally to pity Troilus. Yet such exhortations also simultaneously might make us suspicious, more conscious of Troilus's perhaps unmanly helplessness and Pandarus's interference.

Indicating how this conversation is not a two-way tête-à-tête but rather a three-way exchange, Criseyde swears that she has no idea what Pandarus wishes her to say in response (implying her surprise at Troilus's declaration of devotion). Pandarus mockingly repeats her interjections (120, 122), bluntly supplying her with the response which they have been requesting all along, namely that she have pity on Troilus and save him from death. Yet Criseyde knows that such requests for pity are euphemisms which do not define how far the relationship will ultimately progress. Speaking to Pandarus, she says that Troilus should tell her the intended outcome of his desire, because even now she does not fully understand his **intention**. Troilus now clarifies what he is asking of Criseyde. He begs her to look on him occasionally in a friendly fashion and allow him to become her devoted servant, to formalize their relationship into the roles of lady and knight. As her servant, she can reward or punish him with friendliness or disdain depending on his good service or his transgressions, even bring about his death if he disobeys one of her commandments. He pledges to be hers and to be humble, loyal, diligent, discreet and patient. Once again, Pandarus endorses Troilus's speech with his own comments. This is, he thinks, an appropriate request, a hard one to refuse. He dramatically threatens that if he were a god, he would kill Criseyde quickly because she does not immediately pity Troilus and accept his honourable proposal.

Criseyde now looks at Troilus gently and modestly, taking time to consider her reply which she makes in a quiet and measured fashion (again indicating her greater composure). She will accept Troilus as her servant in the manner he has just outlined and thus become his lady, provided that her honour is preserved. Such a proviso might make us wonder which actions would be honourable and which would not in a secret love affair such as this. Do such ideals remain intact given the means by which such love is brought about or do they become a type of face-saving concern with public reputation? Criseyde now implores Troilus that just as she means him well, he will likewise mean well to her. If she can make him happy from now on, she will not hold back. She thus urges him to be healed and to complain no longer. Yet even though he is a member of the royal family, he will not have undue 'sovereignete' (171) over her in love (that is, she will not submit to his authority as a wife promises to obey a husband). But as well as these warnings, she also commits herself to love him. If it is she who can make him joyful, for every sorrow he has endured she tells him he will now be compensated with a moment of happiness. Once more offering an immediate commentary, Pandarus announces that Cupid should boast and Venus make music to celebrate this newly established love. Such a union is a kind of miracle, illustrating the power of love to overcome all obstacles. He claims to hear every bell in Troy ringing spontaneously by itself, a miraculous event marking the joy of this moment.

(ii) Lines 191 to 231: the meeting ends

Pandarus now hears Deiphebus and Helen returning from the garden where they have been reading the letter and document sent by Hector. Thinking ahead to the lovers' next meeting, Pandarus urges Troilus and Criseyde each to come to his house when he sends them a signal. He says, laughing, that they will there have plenty of opportunity to talk (his laughter hinting that they will have opportunity for more than mere talking). As Deiphebus and Helen enter, Troilus begins to groan as if he is still in pain. He thus hides what has just occurred from his brother and sister-in-law by continuing the pretence that he is ill with fever. Troilus, though he looks briefly at Hector's letter in order to keep up appearances, wishes to be alone and so tells Deiphebus and Helen that he wishes to rest in order to recover from these conversations. The dinner guests return to their homes and Pandarus returns to keep Troilus company, spending the night sleeping beside Troilus's bed on a straw mattress.

LINES 232 TO 420: PANDARUS AND TROILUS DISCUSS DISCRETION

(i) Lines 232 to 343: Pandarus's fears

Once Troilus's servants have left his bedchamber and the doors have been secured for the night, Pandarus takes advantage of this privacy in order to speak to Troilus about his own role in this love affair and about the need for discretion. The source of this scene is a similar exchange between Troilo and Pandaro in the *Filostrato* which occurs before the lovers meet for the first time (*Fil.* III.4–19). Pandarus sits beside Troilus and speaks in a serious fashion. He reviews his actions so far, earnestly reminding his friend that he has acted because of pity for his suffering and not because of greedy desire for a reward. He acknowledges that he has put Troilus on the right path to success in love, but he does not say this in order to boast of his triumph. He could not in fact boast of this success because he is ashamed to say what he has done. He is ashamed because, he confesses, he has become the sort of intermediary who brings women to men, a *baude* or procurer who supplies women for sex. He is reluctant to name himself as *baude*, but says that even if he says nothing more, Troilus will know exactly what he means. He says that he has become an intermediary 'Bitwixen game and ernest' (254). By this expression, Pandarus might mean that he makes this confession half seriously and half jokingly, or that he has acted as a *baude* partly playfully, as a joke or amusement, and partly in all seriousness, or perhaps it is a variation on the expression *in game and in earnest*, meaning 'in any case', 'under any circumstance'. Whatever his motivation, Pandarus admits that he has made Criseyde trust so completely in Troilus's nobility of character that he can now do exactly as he wishes. Pandarus begs him not to exploit her trust, and to behave in such a way that her good reputation is preserved. He reminds Troilus that Criseyde's name is currently honoured by the Trojan people just as the name of a deity or saint is treated with great respect. As her uncle he should protect her but he has in fact betrayed her. If it were public knowledge that he had persuaded Criseyde to become Troilus's lover, the whole world would say that this was the worst kind of treachery an uncle might do, that Criseyde's good name was completely lost and that rather than winning her love, Troilus had gained nothing at all because it was gained so sordidly. Pandarus presents his actions as shameful in order to swear Troilus to secrecy and urge him not to boast publicly that Criseyde has become his lady. His speech reveals a perplexing situation in which a love affair can be thought of as virtuous, yet, if the means needed to bring such a clandestine affair were made public, it would be perceived as sordid shamefulness. Moreover his comments also invite wider consideration of his actions. Do we agree with him that he has become a *baude*? Is he really concerned with Criseyde's reputation or merely with the consequences for himself if the affair is made public? Do we disapprove just as he predicts the Trojan public would? What exactly are Pandarus's motivations for bringing together his friend and niece? Does he act sincerely to help his friend and to advance his niece's fortunes or is this a more amoral type of self-amusement by which he can vicariously enjoy their love affair and demonstrate his own ingenuity?

This request for secrecy prompts Pandarus to make a longer sermon on the dangers of boasting, a speech which Chaucer adds to his source. He begins by urging Troilus to remember the pain and misfortune which has been caused by lovers' boasting. This is why wise scholars have said in a proverb that the first and therefore most important virtue is to hold your tongue, to remain discreet and not to boast. Were it not for the fact that he wishes to be succinct (an ironic wish given Chaucer's additions and his own prolixity), Pandarus claims he could cite a thousand stories of women who were unjustly disgraced by lies and by boasts made by ignorant people. He is certain that Troilus himself knows too many such proverbs and examples to be a boaster. Pandarus seeks to prove by deduction that a boaster is exactly the same as a liar. He *poses* (that is, he puts forward) the following hypothetical situation. If a woman granted him her love exclusively and swore him to secrecy and then he told two or three others about this love, then he would be both a boaster and a liar because he had lied in promising secrecy to his lady. He exhorts Troilus to consider how blameworthy is the type of person who makes untrue boasts.

Pandarus ends his sermon and returns to the main subject of their discussion. He will now arrange matters exactly as Troilus would wish. Criseyde has, Pandarus reminds him, granted him the privilege of becoming her knight, and thus a day has been chosen on which they will draw up the charters (that is, Pandarus will arrange another meeting at which they will figuratively draw up, sign and seal the documents which confirm their love).

(ii) Lines 344 to 420: Troilus responds

In order to convey the inexpressible extent of Troilus's happiness, the narrating voice now asks who could possibly be able to relate even half of the joy and celebration felt by Troilus's soul when he heard the intended outcome of Pandarus's promise (that is, a meeting at which he and Criseyde will confirm their love). It is as if Troilus's former sorrow is dissolved and completely melted away by joy and his formerly abundant supply of anguished sighs has suddenly vanished. Just as woods and hedgerows which were dead and dry in winter re-clothe themselves with green leaves in May, so Troilus suddenly becomes full of joy, the happiest man in Troy.

Responding to Pandarus's request for secrecy, Troilus reminds him how long it took to reveal his love for Criseyde. He found it difficult to tell Pandarus, the man he trusts most, and thus he would dare not tell anyone else. He swears that if he made these matters public he would prefer to end his days shackled in wretched conditions in a filthy and vermin-infested prison as one of the prisoners of King Agamemnon (the leader of the Greek army besieging Troy). If he lies in making this promise, he prays that Achilles (the foremost Greek warrior) will split his heart in two with his spear on the battlefield. Chaucer adds the reference to Achilles to his source material and in doing so creates a moment of dramatic irony. Troilus's prayer has much more significance than he himself can know, as he will indeed be killed by Achilles at the end of the story (see v.1806). Troilus also offers to swear secrecy in the name of all of the gods in Troy's temples. He acknowledges his deep indebtedness, saying that he could never deserve such assistance even if he died for Pandarus a thousand times a day.

Now he turns his attention to Pandarus's shame and his self-identification as a *baude*. It seems to Troilus that Pandarus speaks as if Troilus might think the bringing together of the lovers is a kind of 'bauderye' (397), the actions of a *baude*. To think in such a way would be madness, Troilus says, and he is not mad even if he is ignorant in matters of love. In a stanza added by Chaucer to his source, Troilus says that Pandarus can call someone who undertakes such a mission in order to gain gold or riches any shameful name he likes, but what Pandarus himself has done should be called the product of nobility, compassion, friendship and loyalty. These two different motivations for acting as a go-between should be carefully set apart, because distinctions must be made in order to discriminate between similar things. Yet despite Troilus's conclusion, the nature of Pandarus's actions remains open to question. Is Pandarus motivated by the virtues which Troilus lists or by other, less honourable impulses? Can similar actions really be differentiated by their motivation, by the **intention** which lies behind them? Are Pandarus's interventions *bauderye* or is he simply acting as a go-between in an honourable love affair? What distinctions are revealed by these two alternative representations of his actions?

Troilus next seeks to prove that what Pandarus is doing is not shameful or immoral by offering to do the same thing himself, to act as go-between in order to persuade one of his sisters, Polyxena or Cassandra, or his brother Paris's wife Helen, or anyone else, to become Pandarus's lover. Yet the casual manner in which Troilus offers these women to his friend may not validate Pandarus's actions but rather confirm to us their dishonourable nature. Troilus is nevertheless certain that Pandarus has acted not for reward but to save his friend's life. There is nothing to fear because Troilus sees no shame in Pandarus's actions. He will obey all of Pandarus's commands, especially his request for secrecy.

LINES 421 TO 504: A KNIGHT AND HIS LADY

The next section of the poem summarizes the interlude between the lovers' first meeting at Deiphebus's palace and their second rendezvous at Pandarus's house. These stanzas have no equivalent in the *Filostrato*, where the action moves promptly from the two friends' discussion about secrecy to the lovers' first meeting. Troilus, though he burns as hot as a fire with acutely felt desire and expectation, continues to maintain his self-control when in public. By day on the battlefield, Troilus devotes himself to the service of Mars, god of war, and at night he lies awake thinking how he can best serve his lady. In describing Troilus's sleepless nights, the narrating first-person relates his behaviour via negation and hypothesis rather than by more straightforwardly indicative statements. Such ostentatious caution highlights the obvious: Troilus is stricken by the insomnia of **lovesickness** and cannot yet possess his lady. The narrating voice is nevertheless certain, because it is written in his supposed source (though not in the *Filostrato*), that Troilus occasionally sees Criseyde from afar and that they speak when Criseyde dares to or wishes to. They discuss what they should do next, but these discussions are so brief and conducted with such caution and fear of discovery that they are unsatisfactory. More than anything, therefore, more desirable even than the world itself says the narrating voice, would be an opportunity, sent to them by

Cupid's grace (but of course brought about by Pandarus), to conclude their planning and meet once more in private. Nevertheless, in these brief meetings, Troilus's prudent nature allows him to pay such close attention to Criseyde's desires and fears that he seems to know what she is thinking without her having to say. His service pleases her so much that she thinks that love, like a gatekeeper, has opened the route to every happiness for her. Troilus fashions his words and deeds so well that he always enjoys Criseyde's favour and she thanks God twenty thousand times for her good fortune. Troilus is so discreet and obeys her wishes so fully that she feels he is a wall of steel and a shield from every trouble. He is so prudent that she is no longer afraid to be subject to his guidance, at least, the narrating voice adds, as far as ought to be required in such matters. Pandarus likewise plays his part as go-between. He is always ready and eager to fan the fire of their passion in order to help his friend. He is sent back and forth between the lovers, delivering messages when Troilus is absent from the city on military offensives.

The narrating first-person here speculates that some readers or listeners might expect him to make mention of every aspect of Troilus's service. This would not only make the story very long, he argues, but it would also be impossible because neither he nor any of his audience could find such details already set down in prior versions of this story (yet of course Chaucer is here making the lovers' affair seem less hasty by adding this interlude to his unacknowledged source). The narrating voice claims that the author of his supposed source makes mention of a lengthy letter sent between the two lovers but declines to write about it. He therefore asks how he could write even a single line of such a letter if his source does not supply it. Once again, the narrating voice's claim of limited authorization, intended to reassure his readers about the timely progression of his narrative as the consummation scene approaches, nevertheless has the paradoxical effect of drawing attention to potential gaps and matters for speculation. What might such a letter have said? Is the lovers' affair (and the narrative which describes it) progressing hastily or too cautiously?

LINES 505 TO 938: ARRANGING A MEETING

(i) Lines 505 to 593: Criseyde agrees to visit

In the *Filostrato*, once Pandaro has convinced her to accept Troilo's love, Criseida then takes the initiative. She suggests an occasion on which they might meet at her house and calls Pandaro to her in order to explain her plan (*Fil.* II.143 and III.21). Troilo enters her house by a secret passage and hides. Once the rest of the household is asleep, Criseida goes to fetch him from his hiding-place and they kiss before going to her bedroom. The initiative in Chaucer's version is taken by Pandarus. He intends to bring the lovers together overnight at his house so that they might have the opportunity to consummate what the narrating voice approvingly calls all of this noble matter concerning their love (thus challenging us to decide what we might think of it). We are told that if Troilus and Criseyde wish to come to Pandarus's house, nothing would be found lacking. Pandarus is certain that it would not be possible for their meeting to become public knowledge. His plan is downwind of every magpie (a nickname for an informer) and spoilsport who might gossip or interfere and therefore no traces of it can be detected. All is well, because the world cannot see what Pandarus has planned. It is as if the wood is cut and drilled, ready to be assembled into the framework of a house (see also the earlier comparison at I.1065–71). The narrating voice unites all those in the know with first-person plural pronouns. All that remains to for us to know is the particular day on which Criseyde will visit Pandarus's house.

Troilus, for his part, has also made preparations, fabricating a pretext to explain his absence if he is missed whilst at Pandarus's house. He lets it be known that he plans to make sacrifices to the god Apollo in order to receive a prophecy which will reveal exactly when the Greek army will next retreat from the battlefield. He must therefore keep vigil all alone at a temple in order to be the first to see the sacred laurel tree planted there shake to indicate Apollo's presence before the god himself speaks as if hidden within the tree's branches. On his character's behalf (and seeming to repeat Troilus's instructions to those he deceives), the narrating voice warns everyone not to hinder him and also to pray to Apollo to help during this perilous time for the city of Troy. Once again, weighty public matters, as well as sacred prophecy, are used as camouflage for private pleasure.

On a day very shortly after the new moon when the nights are very dark without moonlight and rain is expected, Pandarus goes to invite Criseyde to come to his house for supper, the last meal of the day. Criseyde meets this invitation with laughter (perhaps expressing her surprise that Pandarus might invite her on such an inclement evening or perhaps nervous laughter because of fear of what he might be planning). She declines the invitation because it is about to rain. Yet Pandarus prevails, the narrating voice saying that either they agreed she would come, or else that Pandarus once more threatened her (leaving the reader to decide which was more likely). Criseyde clearly suspects her uncle's motives and asks in a whisper whether Troilus will be there. Pandarus lies and tells her that he is outside the town walls on military business. Yet he also says that if Troilus *were* there, Criseyde should not fear because he would rather die than let anyone see that Troilus was at his house. Pandarus conceals the truth but then immediately hints at it via this hypothetical reassurance. Chaucer thus makes it a matter of speculation as to whether Criseyde goes to Pandarus's house in the expectation that Troilus will be there. The narrating first-person says that his supposed source does not wish to resolve this issue fully (though this passage has no equivalent in the *Filostrato*), thus raising the very same question in the minds of his audience. He claims that his source merely says that Criseyde agreed to accompany Pandarus to his house because he asked her to and because she obeyed her uncle as she should. We suspect that she does indeed expect Troilus to be present, because, even though there is supposedly nothing at risk in such a visit, she pleads with her uncle to beware of the gossip of people as silly and noisy as a group of geese. She defers to Pandarus, telling him to do as he wishes. Pandarus swears he will by the wooden and stone statues that pagans were thought to worship. He illustrates the unlikelihood of any flaw in his plan by extravagantly claiming that if all is not well he would happily accept the punishment meted out to Tantalus, a figure punished deep in the underworld for his crimes by being eternally hungry and thirsty, with food and drink close by but always out of reach.

(ii) Lines 594 to 693: the rainstorm

Criseyde goes to Pandarus's house for supper, accompanied by a large retinue of servants. Her arrival is witnessed by Troilus, who has been concealed by Pandarus in a 'stewe' (601), a small room often heated by a fireplace, since midnight of the previous night when he entered the house under the cover of darkness so that he would be observed by no one. The supper Pandarus hosts for Criseyde is a pleasant occasion, in keeping with their close and friendly relationship. After supper, Pandarus and his household do everything they can to entertain Criseyde. With third-person pronouns used with demonstrative force (i.e., *he* or *she* for 'that man' or 'this woman'), the narrative describes how one man sings, a woman makes jokes or perhaps plays music, and another man entertains the company with a tale about Wade (a legendary hero whose story is now lost).

At the end of the evening, Criseyde makes her farewells and prepares to depart. The narrating voice interrupts his own narration of events in order to make an address to **Fortune**. This apostrophe to **Fortune** is prompted by the conflict between Criseyde's **intention** and **Fortune**'s own purpose. Criseyde wishes to return home but in fact she will stay at Pandarus's house because a different future has been put into effect by **Fortune**, the goddess who personifies the seemingly haphazard changes and coincidences by which the divine providential plan is unfolded in time as a series of fated events. By pausing for such comment, the narrating voice turns our attention to the complex causes of Criseyde's overnight stay with Pandarus. In this case, **Fortune** operates via a particular astrological configuration which causes a particular type of weather. The conjunction of the crescent moon and the planets Saturn and Jupiter in the astrological house of Cancer causes a powerful rainstorm. Yet it is not solely **Fortune**'s doing as Pandarus has arranged matters in order to take advantage of this natural phenomenon (which he has predicted through his knowledge of the moon's cycle and through his observations of the weather in lines 547–53).

All of the women present are afraid of the rain, which is so misty and murky that it resembles smoke. Pandarus laughs at how this changes Criseyde's plans, saying ironically that now would indeed be the right moment to leave. He then asks her to stay overnight, to treat his house as her own house because their relationship is so close. We are told that Criseyde's good sense leads her to think she should stay overnight with good grace rather than grumble, as going home is now impossible. She saves face, saying that it is fitting to stay if it pleases him and that she only said she would leave as a joke. The evening's entertainments begin again, but we are told that Pandarus, if he could have done so with propriety, would have hurried Criseyde straight off to bed for the night. Pandarus encourages the household to turn in by explaining the sleeping arrangements for his guests, arrangements which will allow him to bring Criseyde and Troilus together in secret. In order supposedly that uncle and niece will not be far apart and so that she will not be disturbed by the storm, Criseyde's bed will be made up in one of the small private rooms off the main hall. The hall will be divided in two by the 'travers' (674), a curtain or screen used to divide a large room. Criseyde's ladies will sleep in the part of the hall nearest to her room, and Pandarus will act as their guardian by sleeping alone in the portion of the hall further away. All those not assigned beds in the hall leave and the storm continues to rage loudly outside. Pandarus escorts Criseyde into her chamber and wishes her goodnight with a bow, reassuring her that her servants are close at hand.

(iii) Lines 694 to 742: Troilus's invocations

Whilst everyone else sleeps, Pandarus begins the work of bringing the lovers together. We are told that Pandarus is experienced in every detail of the 'olde daunce' (695), the timeless and ancient game of love. Pandarus leaves his bed in the outer portion of the hall and by some unspecified route reaches the door of the *stewe* in which Troilus has been waiting. He unlatches the door quietly and sits down beside Troilus. He quickly tells Troilus what has occurred and instructs him to prepare himself because he will soon enter the bliss of heaven (as such happiness might be described within **the religion of love**). Troilus prays to Venus, goddess of love, for assistance, saying that he has never before needed such help or been so afraid. Pandarus tells him not to fear because he will either make things go well, just as Troilus wishes, or he will figuratively throw all the porridge in the fire (that is, that he will make a mess of everything). There will be no half measures: Pandarus will either succeed or fail and he is in control of everything.

Yet despite Pandarus's pledge, Troilus now makes a series of invocations to pagan deities. He prays that if, at the moment of his birth, he had any malign influences in his horoscope from the position of the planets Mars or Saturn, or if the good influences of Venus were burned up by being positioned too close to the sun in the heavens or obstructed in some other way so that his horoscope predisposed him to be unlucky in love, that Venus ask her father Jupiter to prevent the harmful effects of such a horoscope from occurring. He begs her to do this in the name of her lover, the beautiful youth Adonis (here *Adoun*), killed by a boar because of divine jealousy or anger. Following this pattern, he asks for help from each deity in the name of one of their lovers. He prays to Jove in the name of Europa, a Phoenician princess abducted and seduced by him in the form of a white bull, and to Mars for love of 'Cipris' (725, another name for Venus). He begs Phoebus Apollo to help in the name of his love for Daphne (here *Dane*), a nymph whom he loved but who ran away from him, wishing to remain a virgin forever. To escape Apollo's pursuit, Daphne is transformed into a laurel tree. Troilus next asks Mercury for help in the name of his love for Herse (though Chaucer here mistakenly adds that the goddess Pallas Athena was angry with Herse's sister Aglauros because of this love). In these invocations, Troilus alludes to instances wherein the gods experienced love themselves (and perhaps, so reminded, they might be thus more likely to aid Troilus at this moment). Yet the stories of the lovers named are of sexual violence, reluctance and metamorphosis, offering gloomy omens about the consequences of love. Troilus also asks Diana, the moon goddess, not to be displeased with his venture (though as the goddess of chastity it does not seem likely that she will approve). Finally, he asks for help from the three Fates. In classical mythology, the three Fates (here called sisters) determined the course of each individual human life, Clotho spinning the thread of life, Lachesis measuring it (to determine the length of a life) and Atropos cutting it (that is, choosing the manner of death and enacting it).

Pandarus is unimpressed, his pragmatic reply undercutting Troilus's elaborate invocations (and expressing his own confidence that they do not need divine intervention). He tells him pithily that he is a coward, like the wretched heart of a feeble mouse. He commands him to put on a warm cloak and to follow him, though to lag behind a little to allow him to speak to Criseyde first. He undoes a trapdoor, the entrance to a secret passageway that runs between the *stewe* and the bedchamber in which Criseyde sleeps, and leads Troilus through the passage by the hem of his clothes.

(iv) Lines 743 to 798: Troilus's supposed jealousy of Horaste

The sound of Troilus and Pandarus moving along the passageway is disguised by the noise of the strong wind blowing outside the house. Pandarus (who has emerged from the passageway into the bedchamber) goes to the doorway between the bedchamber and the part of the main hall in which Criseyde's ladies are sleeping. He shuts the door so that they cannot be overheard. Criseyde awakes and Pandarus identifies himself, cautioning her to be quiet. He explains that he has entered the room unobserved via the secret passageway which he points out to her. He dissuades her from calling one of her attendants, saying that this might lead them to suspect something which they had never before considered (presumably some shameful action on her part or on his). Pandarus promises that he will leave undetected by the secret passageway once he has finished speaking.

Pandarus reveals the supposed reason for his visit in a characteristically roundabout way. Criseyde, he says, must understand that for a woman to lead a man on falsely or to deceive him by calling him her lover whilst she loves another man is a shame and a deceit. He reminds her of this because she has granted her love to Troilus and should not be unfaithful to him unless he were at fault in some way. Troilus, Pandarus lies, has just arrived at the house in the middle of the rainstorm and has gained access to the room in which Pandarus was sleeping by means of a 'goter' (787, a window opening onto one of the house's gutters) and by negotiating a secret passage. Pandarus swears that Troilus has arrived undetected. He has arrived in pain and distress and at the point of death. According to Pandarus, the cause of this sudden visit is that one of Troilus's friends has told him that Criseyde loves a man named Horaste. The whole story is of course invented by Pandarus in order to persuade Criseyde to meet Troilus. The lovers are thus brought together by lies and manipulation. Do the ends justify the means, especially given the lovers' fears and constraints, or does such trickery taint and render dubious the love it brings about?

(v) Lines 799 to 840: Criseyde's lament on worldly happiness

As she hears this astonishing news, Criseyde's heart grows cold with fear. Her response is one of lament and anguish. She expresses her surprise that Troilus would believe that she could so easily be unfaithful. She swears that she does not know Horaste and tells her uncle that she will meet Troilus in the morning and prove herself innocent of such an accusation. This sudden change in the lovers' relationship from harmony and peace to jealousy and misunderstanding emphasizes to Criseyde the precariousness of all such moments of joy. Her despair prompts a short monologue on the nature of human happiness. Criseyde notes that human happiness is called false **felicity** by scholars and is infused with many bitternesses and sorrows. Such happiness is illusory either because joys don't come together (a man possesses one type of happiness but lacks another) or because they come to an end. Criseyde addresses human happiness directly as a personification, 'thow, joie' (822), characterizing it as uncertain and unstable. Whichever person it currently accompanies and however it acts towards him, such a person either knows or does not know that human happiness is changeable rather than permanent. If he does not know this, he cannot truly say that he is happy because his happiness is experienced in the figurative darkness of ignorance. If he does understand that human happiness is inevitably transitory, then he cannot truly experience happiness, because his happiness will always be tempered by the thought of its loss. If he doesn't care even a small amount about losing a particular source of joy, then the joy itself cannot be very significant. Criseyde concludes that there is no true joy in the temporal world.

Her speech ends with an apostrophe to Jealousy, addressed as a wicked serpent and a mistaken and hostile madness or stupidity. Criseyde asks

Jealousy why it has made Troilus distrust her when she has done nothing wrong. Criseyde's monologue cautions us to remember that moments of happiness (such as the blissful night which the lovers are about to spend together) are short-lived (although as they, and we, enjoy their night of happiness, such cautions are soon forgotten). It prompts us to consider whether the lovers' incipient happiness is in some way false, vain or illusory, being perhaps incomplete and prone to change, or enjoyed in blind ignorance of its true nature. This monologue also becomes ironic when considered in the light of the eventual outcome of this story. The lovers' joy, just as Criseyde here theorizes, will indeed prove transitory and will be ended by her exchange with Antenor and by her own betrayal of Troilus.

Felicity

Both the narrating first-person and the characters of *Troilus and Criseyde* describe the joy of reciprocated love by reference to *felicite*, that is, a source of great happiness, and *suffisaunce*, namely a source of contentment, a state of sufficiency where nothing is lacking or imperfect. At the moment when their love is consummated, Criseyde welcomes Troilus as her 'suffisaunce' (III.1309; see also III.1716 and V.763). The narrating voice extravagantly describes the lovers' joy at the end of Book III as even surpassing that perfect happiness described by scholars (III.1691–2) and names Criseyde as the only source of Troilus's joy (V.25–6). Yet, when she fears that her own happiness will be compromised by Troilus's supposed jealousy of Horaste, Criseyde makes a lament which sets out the limited and imperfect nature of human happiness (III.813–36). Human happiness is not true felicity but rather a false or illusory imitation. At the end of the poem, Troilus sees the human world (including presumably his own love for Criseyde) as entirely worthless when compared to the 'pleyn felicite | That is in hevene above' (V.1818–19), the perfect happiness of heaven.

Criseyde's lament on worldly happiness is based on the teaching of Lady Philosophy in ***De consolatione philosophiae***, in which she consoles Boethius on the loss of his prosperity and success by explaining how bittersweet and imperfect is all human happiness (Book II, *prosa* 4). By contrast, perfect blissfulness is described in *De consolatione* as being a state of such happiness and contentment wherein nothing else is desired (Book III, *prosae* 2, 9). Anything which can be lost, that is, any temporary good fortune or happiness, cannot therefore truly be a source of contentment and happiness (Book II, *prosa* 4). Lady Philosophy examines the different routes by which humanity strives for happiness, namely riches, power, fame and physical pleasure (Book III, *prosae* 3–8). Whilst all of them are of value to some degree, nevertheless they are all ultimately found wanting, not providing true sufficiency and contentment but creating dependencies and anxieties of their own. Instead, Lady Philosophy insists that true happiness can only be found in God, the supreme good (Book III, *prosa* 10). Prompted by Criseyde's lament and these references to *felicite* and *suffisaunce*, we might evaluate the characters' sense of their own happiness, and the narrative's descriptions of such joy, in the light of the discussions between Boethius and Lady Philosophy on the subject of true and false happiness. On the one hand, the short-lived nature of their happiness proves Lady Philosophy's teaching (and indeed Criseyde's own lament) to be correct. Yet on the other, how else might the supreme blissfulness of reciprocated love be conveyed? Does happiness lead lovers towards truth and towards the supreme good, being ennobling and inspiring, praised in relation to love which is universal and sacred? Or is such happiness a form of deception, leading lovers into blindness and folly and away from the divine?

(vi) Lines 841 to 938: Pandarus urges haste

Pandarus deflects Criseyde's further questions about Troilus's jealousy of Horaste. He tells his niece that she has the power to put an end to this matter and should do so at once. Criseyde replies that she intends to do so in the morning, but Pandarus feigns dismay at this plan and encourages her to act immediately by citing the proverbs that procrastination leads to perilous situations and that there is a right moment for everything. For example, when a room or hall is on fire, it is more important to save it from burning down than to argue with each other or to investigate how the fire started. If she allows Troilus to remain in such a state of misery for the whole night, she is acting as if she has never cared for him. Pandarus tries to flatter her into agreeing with him by saying that he is sure she is too wise to behave with such stupidity as to put Troilus's life in jeopardy for the entire night.

In disbelief, Criseyde angrily repeats his accusation that in refusing to see Troilus immediately it is as if she has never cared for him. Repeating

Pandarus's own words but in altered order, she accuses him in turn of never caring for anything as much as this (that is, putting this desire for her to see Troilus immediately before any other previous concern or obligation). Pandarus replies that he will indeed demonstrate his care for his friend. Since Criseyde makes an example of Pandarus in this way (that is, since she so derides his love for Troilus), he will now demonstrate the extent of his concern. He says that if he were to let his friend suffer all night, even if he received all the treasure in Troy as recompense, he would feel so guilty that he would nonetheless pray that he never again be happy. Bluntly, he tells her that if she allows him to remain in distress, she acts neither with kindness nor with graciousness.

Pandarus's vehement reply convinces Criseyde to reconsider. She now suggests that Pandarus take Troilus one of her rings, a ring with a blue stone (blue being traditionally a symbol of faithfulness). This token of her fidelity will, she thinks, please him better than anything except a visit from herself. Pandarus should tell him that his despair is without foundation and that Troilus will see this for himself when she talks with him in the morning. Pandarus is equally dismissive of this second suggestion. He says sarcastically this idea would only work if she had a ring whose stone had the magical power to bring dead men back to life (that is, if it could save Troilus from the peril which might result if she does not see him now). Doesn't she understand, he asks, that someone like Troilus who has a noble and honourable heart wouldn't despair for an insignificant reason or be reassured by something as small as a ring? If Troilus were a fool who had got into a jealous rage, Pandarus wouldn't care at all but would instead 'feffe hym with a fewe wordes white' (901), that is, buy him off with a few fair-seeming but specious words in due course. But this is an entirely different circumstance, one which requires swift action. Troilus is so noble and so easily moved that he is likely to get his own back on his own sorrows by dying. Yet however pained he is, he will not confront Criseyde with angry or suspicious words (supposedly because he is so sensitive but in reality because Pandarus has invented this jealousy). She should therefore meet him in person because she can guide his heart back to happiness with a single word.

Criseyde now relents and begins to concede to her uncle's request. The narrative indicates her change of heart in a stanza (918–24) which seems to combine narratorial observations with what sound like Criseyde's own elliptical thoughts. The events (which Pandarus has invented) are so affecting to hear about and sound so like the truth at first sight (a reassurance which contains more than a hint of doubt). Troilus is so dear to her, he has arrived so secretly and their meeting place is so safe. Once all this is considered, it is no surprise that she grants him the favour of a meeting since she tries to do everything for the best. She swears that she does indeed pity him and wishes to do the right thing if she can. Yet unless God sends her more insight or intellect to decide what she should do, she feels that she has reached a 'dulcarnoun' (931). *Dulcarnon* is the name for one of the geometrical diagrams put forward for discussion and solution in the *Stoicheia* ('the elements'), a treatise on geometry and mathematics written by the Greek mathematician Euclid and used in schools as a textbook. Criseyde thus means that she has been stumped by something which is very difficult to understand. She is at her wits' end and cannot resolve the dilemma of how both to help Troilus and to protect her honour. Pandarus replies that this particular diagram is nicknamed 'the banishment of idlers' (though he or Chaucer in fact wrongly refers to the nickname of one of Euclid's other propositions). It is so called because it seems hard and drives away lazy students who, through laziness or other obstinate vices, won't take the time and effort to understand it. Pandarus reassures Criseyde that she is not in fact stumped, because, unlike these lazy students, she is astute and the dilemma is neither too hard to solve, nor is it reasonable to avoid trying to solve it.

LINES 939 TO 1582: THE MEETING AT PANDARUS'S HOUSE

(i) Lines 939 to 980: Pandarus fetches Troilus

Criseyde now places her trust in Pandarus, asking him to proceed so discreetly that Troilus is restored to happiness but yet her own honour is preserved. She says that she will get up before Troilus enters the room, but Pandarus (keen to promote intimacy between the lovers) commands her to remain in bed. As he leaves to fetch Troilus, Pandarus prays that each of them will ease the other's painful sorrows. Including himself in the outcome of the love affair, he praises Venus, goddess of love, and hopes that the three of them will all soon be made merry.

Troilus kneels by the head of Criseyde's bed, greeting her as best he can. Criseyde blushes and suddenly is too overcome with emotion to reply. Pandarus steps in to speak where she cannot, encouraging her to observe how humbly Troilus, a Trojan noble, kneels before her. To emphasize the respect Troilus deserves (and also to indicate how comically Pandarus fusses over every detail of the action), we are told how Pandarus rushes to fetch a cushion to protect Troilus's knees from the hard floor. Here the narrating voice interjects, once more claiming that he cannot supply details which are not present in his source (though all of this scene is Chaucer's invention). He cannot say why Criseyde did not command Troilus to stand up (the expected response to Troilus's courteous obeisance). He is not sure whether it was because her distress made her forget conventional expectations or because she felt that Troilus should indeed kneel before her as her servant in love. Yet he claims that his source does say that she greeted Troilus with a kiss and asked him to sit down. This claim to be limited by his source emphasizes how the emotions and expectations of **the art of love** clash at times with usual social relationships. It also reminds us that some motives remain unknowable (but yet a matter of speculation) whilst some actions speak for themselves.

Pandarus urges Criseyde to allow Troilus to sit on the side of her bed, within the canopy of curtains which surrounds it, supposedly so that they can hear each other better (but also to create yet more intimacy). He then retreats to the fireplace, finding a candle and pretending to read an 'old romaunce' (980). This pose as the reader of an antique love story reflects our own position as readers, he and we being voyeurs of this scene. However intimate and private the meeting between the lovers is, it is observed by Pandarus and also as it were by the narrating subject and his readers.

(ii) Lines 981 to 1057: Criseyde speaks about jealousy

Criseyde now speaks to Troilus about the jealousy which has supposedly brought him to her in such distress. We are told that Criseyde is indeed Troilus's faithful lady at this moment and that her position is one of certainty in her own blamelessness. Although she knows that Troilus has no reason to suspect her of unfaithfulness, she decides to tackle the subject with him because of his obvious distress. Her monologue is carefully worded and tender, addressing Troilus with epithets of endearment but tactfully yet forcefully making her point. She begins by reviewing the reasons why she took pity on his suffering and agreed to be his lady. She thanks him for the integrity which she has witnessed in his actions so far. She fervently pledges that she has been true to him and wholly his, as far as she could and despite the anxiety she feels. She is confident that her loyalty will be proved in due course.

She next says that she intends to speak out about his jealousy in order to put an end to the suffering which currently keeps both their hearts in a state of grief, even if this means that she will have to criticize him in person. She laments the fact that even a small sliver of jealousy should have found a place of sanctuary in so noble a place as Troilus's heart. She prays that Jove will soon tear out such jealousy from his heart. Her appeal next prompts a complaint to the same god. She questions why Jove allows innocent people such as herself to suffer injury as a result of jealousy whilst guilty people go entirely unpunished.

She also criticizes the fact that jealousy is widely tolerated rather than condemned. It is generally seen as evidence of love, and therefore people excuse a 'busshel venym' (1025), a quantity of malice equal to the capacity of a bushel (a large vessel used to measure wheat), even if just one small grain of love were shoved into it. She admits that some types of jealousy (such as jealous delusions which a lover so nobly and stoically suppresses that they cause hardly any problems) seem more excusable than others, whilst some jealousy, conversely, is so malevolent that it cannot be so suppressed. She tells Troilus that thankfully he is not in the latter state of furious distrust. She attributes his jealousy to nothing more than a delusion caused by the intensity of his love and the anxious diligence with which he serves her. She is thus not angry with him but rather regrets his distress. Finally, she offers to prove her faithfulness by any means. In tears, she ends her speech by taking God as her witness that she was 'nevere yet' (1054) unfaithful to Troilus in word or deed. Criseyde's pledge is heartfelt as at this moment she is and intends to remain entirely loyal to Troilus. Yet for the reader who knows there will come a point in the future at which she is unfaithful, such a pledge also highlights both the fallibility of her good **intention** and Criseyde's blindness about her own future actions.

(iii) Lines 1058 to 1141: Troilus faints

As Criseyde concludes her speech, the narrating voice appeals to God for his assistance in assuaging all of this sorrow (both Criseyde's dismay at the accusations against her and Troilus's response to her speech on jealousy). The narrating first-person is hopeful that things will soon take a turn for the better and cites proverbial observations in support of this hope. Troilus is so pained by Criseyde's distress that as each tear flows from her eyes, he feels the agony of death creep around his heart and constrict it. Inwardly, he curses his decision to visit Pandarus's house because he fears that things are going from bad to worse. He feels that all of Pandarus's stratagems and his own labour have been wasted. We are told that he hangs his head, falls once more onto his knees and sighs sorrowfully. Troilus feels as if he were dead because Criseyde, who should bring him joy, is in fact angry with him. Given that he does not know the cause of Criseyde's dismay, all Troilus can say is that God knows he is not responsible for any part of this occurrence.

Troilus's sorrow provokes a dramatic physical response which the narrative recounts in physiological detail. Sorrow so shuts off Troilus's heart from emotion that he cannot even cry. Similarly, the force of his sorrow restricts the usual vitality of his natural, animal and vital spirits (the fluids which were thought to control different physiological functions in medieval physiology), so that it is as if they are deadened or stopped from functioning. He therefore becomes insensible, not aware of his fear or his sorrow or any other emotion. Then, very suddenly, he faints. Pandarus (who has been pretending to read by the fireside) quickly seizes the opportunity to make the situation yet more intimate. He quickly warns Criseyde to be quiet (in case she were to cry out for assistance from her household and thus reveal Troilus's presence), throws Troilus's inert body onto Criseyde's bed and takes off all of his outer layers of clothing. He tells Criseyde that she must help or else Troilus will die. She must pull out the thorn which is wedged in his heart (that is, she must remove the cause of his pain) by saying that she forgives him for his accusations. Criseyde does this, swearing that she is not angry, but Troilus does not awaken from his faint. Uncle and niece do everything they can think of to revive him. Criseyde kisses him and, finally, he comes to with a gasp of breath. Such desperate actions are dramatic, but they are also so exaggerated as to verge on the farcical, alerting us to the potential comedy and absurdity of this scene.

As Troilus comes to his senses, he is confused and embarrassed. Rebuking him, Criseyde (perhaps more tenderly than disparagingly) questions whether this (meaning perhaps both his supposed jealousy and his faint) constitutes manly behaviour. She embraces him, forgives him and kisses him, cheering and comforting him. Criseyde is thus tolerant of Troilus's behaviour but her question may nevertheless prompt readerly speculation about what manly behaviour should be. Troilus's swoon demonstrates his aristocratic delicacy and the strength of his love for Criseyde, but it also renders him entirely passive and in need of much assistance. It is thus Pandarus who physically places him in bed and Criseyde who in comparison seems more self-possessed. Pandarus now withdraws, saying that he can see no purpose here either for himself or for the light which he brought from the fireplace. He justifies his departure with reference to Troilus's **lovesickness,** saying that such light is not beneficial for the eyes of invalids. He carries the candle to the fireplace, remaining in the room so he can continue to keep an eye on the lovers.

(iv) Lines 1142 to 1190: the lovers reconciled

We are next told that, though there is no need to make Troilus pledge further oaths of devotion, Criseyde nevertheless demands such oaths. Once they are made, she feels there is nothing to fear and no reason to ask him to leave her bed. The narrating first-person comments that in many cases less solemn promises than formal oaths are needed, since everyone that loves virtuously, he supposes, intends to do nothing but noble actions (once again raising the questions of whether this love is virtuous and whether the lovers' **intention**s and actions are indeed honourable). Criseyde now wishes to get to the bottom of Troilus's supposed jealousy, asking him for specific details of the evidence which prompted his suspicions.

Troilus may be somewhat confused at this point, as the story of his jealousy is Pandarus's fabrication. As her knight, he must obey his lady's command and therefore he has to find some answer to her questions. Thinking on his feet, Troilus therefore invents a piece of evidence, saying that at such and such a religious festival Criseyde might have at least looked at him (implying that she ignored him or that her attention was given to someone else). The narrative's vagueness indicates the feebleness of Troilus's story. The narrating voice gives up on repeating it, saying that he doesn't know what Troilus said and that it was entirely trivial. Criseyde replies that even if this were the case, what harm could it cause given that she did not intend anything wicked by it and, she swears, her **intention** is 'cleene' (1166) in all things, it is pure and decent. She tells Troilus that his assertions are worthless. So chastised, Troilus appeals to her for mercy and forgiveness. Criseyde grants him this and warns him not to transgress again. She in turn asks him to forgive her for any pain that she has caused him. Troilus is so overcome with happiness that he forcefully takes her in his arms and embraces her. Seeing this, Pandarus very cheerfully goes to bed in some unspecified spot. It seems likely that he sleeps in the outer part of the hall from where he returns at line 1555, though Chaucer's imprecision might sustain the impression that Pandarus, like the narrating subject and us his readers, remains voyeuristically present throughout the lovers' tryst.

(v) Lines 1191 to 1253: their happiness

The narrating voice now interjects, asking what a defenceless lark can say when a powerful hawk has it in its claws. This rhetorical question seeks to persuade us that Criseyde can do nothing to resist or object to Troilus's sudden embrace (though Troilus has not always seemed formidably powerful and predatory in this scene). The narrating first-person prepares himself for the delicate task of describing the lovers' delight in each other's arms. He insists that whether the story tastes like sugar or soot (that is, whether it pleases his readers by reminding them of their own joys or makes them bitterly contrast their own sorrows), he must follow his source in describing their happiness in as much detail as he previously gave to their sorrows (though in reality this description is much expanded by Chaucer in comparison with the relevant passage of the *Filostrato*, III.30–1).

We are told that Criseyde begins to shake like an aspen leaf, a proverbial simile which compares her trembling to a type of poplar tree whose small light leaves frequently flutter in the breeze. Troilus, in contrast, is not afraid or distressed but entirely healed of his former sorrows. He gives thanks to the seven planetary gods (to whom he earlier appealed for assistance in lines 712–35). Troilus tells Criseyde that she is now captured and, as they are alone, she must surrender to his will because there is no way to escape. Criseyde replies that if she had not previously been made to yield (perhaps to love itself rather than to his desire or to the will of Troilus and Pandarus), then she would certainly not now be here in his arms (and hence he does not need now to demand submission). This lovers' talk plays with the imagery of capture and surrender, yet it may also evoke our sense of the coercion of Criseyde by Pandarus's manipulations on Troilus's behalf.

The narrating voice now interjects once more in a two-stanza exclamation. He exclaims that it is indeed truly said that in order to be healed of a fever or other serious illness, one must first take medicine which tastes very bitter. Similarly, one must endure pain in order to achieve happiness, as demonstrated by that which is here described. Troilus has found a cure for his **lovesickness** by enduring suffering. The narrating voice makes the proverbial observation that sweetness seems more sweet when one has previously tasted bitterness. Troilus and Criseyde likewise have floated out of a state of sorrow and into a state of never-before-experienced joy. The narrating voice approves, commenting that it is better to be united in joy than both to perish through suffering. He advises every woman to make sure that she acts in the same manner as Criseyde if the same circumstances arise (we are here invited to decide for ourselves whether this is good advice).

Now her fear has abated and now that she knows of what is called Troilus's sincerity and the purity of his **intention** (here perhaps referring to the pledges of devotion which he made in lines 1142–5), Criseyde treats him so affectionately that we are told it was a joy to see (again reminding us that we are complicit observers). The lovers entwine themselves in each other's arms just as the fragrant honeysuckle wraps itself tightly around a tree for support. Criseyde opens her heart to Troilus, just as the nightingale, who stops singing when she hears shepherds talking in the fields or any creature moving in the hedgerows, then makes her song ring out loudly when she feels safe again. Troilus delights in this moment of happiness just like a man suddenly rescued from certain death. The narrative lists and describes different parts of Criseyde's body as Troilus touches and kisses them. Criseyde's beauty is objectified and enjoyed by the narrating subject (and by us his readers) just as it is by her lover Troilus.

(vi) Lines 1254 to 1274: Troilus praises love

Having kissed Criseyde a thousand times (according to the narrating voice's hyperbole), Troilus now praises **the God of Love**, Cupid's mother Venus, goddess of love (here named *Cythera*, the place where according to legend she arose from the sea), and Hymen (here *Imeneus*), the god of marriage. Given that marriage does not appear as a possibility in this poem, Troilus perhaps celebrates Hymen not so much as god of wedlock but as Venus's husband. He appears as such in the *De planctu Naturae* ('the complaint of Nature'), a satire on human vices by the French poet and theologian Alain of Lille (*c.* 1116–1202), in which Venus, Hymen and their son Cupid are said to work under the guidance of Nature to ensure the sexual reproduction of humans from generation to generation.[1] Troilus says that there was never anyone as indebted to these deities as he is because of the great happiness which has been granted to him. Cupid is named both as Love and as 'Charite' (1254). By *charity*, Troilus might simply mean that Cupid embodies the love and affection shown by one person to another, yet the word itself cannot but evoke the Christian virtue of charity, that is, the love, mercy and benevolence shown by God to mankind and by one Christian to another. Troilus also addresses 'Benigne Love' (1261), that is, love which is gracious, kind, gentle and merciful. He names such love as **the holy bond of things**, the sacred force which unites and orders everything.

In order to express his belief that he could not have been granted this happiness without **the God of Love**'s merciful intervention, Troilus next

[1] Alain of Lille, *Plaint of Nature*, trans. J. J. Sheridan, Mediaeval Sources in Translation 26 (Toronto: Pontifical Institute of Mediaeval Studies, 1980), p. 146.

says that if someone wishes for Love's help or mercy yet does not wish to worship Love, it is as if this wish wants to fly without wings (that is, to do something without having what is most necessary for success). Even the actions of those who serve Love best and strive the most would be entirely futile if Love were not minded to assist them. Troilus is certain that unless Love's grace does not match but far surpasses 'oure desertes' (1267, that is, our worthiness to receive Love's grace), everything will be in vain. We cannot earn or expect Love's grace in some automatic way but must rely on his generosity. Troilus argues that because Love has helped him when he was likely to die of **lovesickness** and brought him to so high a place that no happiness could surpass the limits of his present joy, he cannot adequately express his thanks. He will instead simply offer praise and worship to Love's goodness and greatness. Line 1271, in which Troilus describes himself as being at the highest possible point of happiness, comes at the very centre of Chaucer's poem, the 4120th of its 8239 lines.

Chaucer adds this speech of praise to his source and through it raises questions at the heart of his text about the nature of earthly romantic love. He adapts lines 1262–7 from the prayer made to the Virgin Mary by the French mystic and theologian St Bernard of Clairvaux in the last canto of the *Paradiso* ('Paradise'), the third and final part of the *Divina commedia* ('the divine comedy') by the Italian poet Dante Alighieri (*c.* 1265–1321).[2] Chaucer thus has Troilus, his pagan hero, describe the lover's need for **the God of Love**'s grace using the same simile employed by one of Dante's characters to praise the vital role played by the Virgin as mediator between God and mankind. Do we agree with Troilus (given what we have seen of its bringing about and what we know to be its future) that his love for Criseyde should be celebrated in these highest terms of sacred intervention in the human world which demonstrates divine benevolence and generosity? Are these allusions to divine grace and charity in fact ironies which reveal how mistaken he is, how much romantic love falls short of these ideals? Yet if Troilus is mistaken or unaware, or even potentially sacrilegious in making such correlations, how else might the sheer joy of reciprocated love be accounted for and conveyed? How can it inspire such a sense of universal harmony and such enlightened praise?

[2] 'Lady, you are so great, and have such power, that whoever seeks grace without recourse to you is like someone wanting to fly without wings. You are so benign that you not only help whoever asks you but, very often, spontaneously give help before the prayer is made.' Dante Alighieri, *The Divine Comedy*, trans. C. H. Sisson, Oxford World's Classics (Oxford University Press, 1998), p. 495 (*Paradiso*, XXXIII.13–18).

The holy bond of things

The belief that God's divine love acts as a sacred bond which orders and controls everything in the universe is celebrated in four of the short poems uttered by Boethius and Lady Philosophy in ***De consolatione philosophiae*** (see Book I, *metrum* 5; Book II, *metrum* 8; Book III, *metrum* 9; Book IV, *metrum* 6). As evidence of this divine bond, Boethius and Lady Philosophy cite the observable patterns of the moon, sun and stars in the heavens, the yearly cycles of the lengthening and shortening of day and night, the way the changing seasons permit the annual growing and harvesting of crops, the harmonious interaction of the four elements of water, air, earth and fire (the four primary properties of the physical universe in medieval science), and the tides which rise and fall daily without flooding the land. Each poem differs on the question of whether humanity can recognize this divine bond sufficiently and whether human affairs themselves are likewise controlled by divine love.

In *Troilus and Criseyde*, Troilus, in celebrating his love for Criseyde and praising love itself, equates **the God of Love** with this divine ordering. For Troilus, the attraction of men and women and the joy of sexual love and reciprocated affection prompt praise of the divine ordering of the universe by love. Yet, given that we know that Criseyde's love for Troilus will prove mutable and short-lived, we may have a more sceptical view of the relationship of this particular example of human love to Love's divine bond. Can we conceive of the lovers' union as an example of the divine ordination of Love when we have witnessed Pandarus's role in its creation and when we know it will not prove long-lasting? How might this secret, sexual love be part of God's ordering of the universe (and hence be dignified, exalted and celebrated by association with the holy bond of things)? Or is it something fundamentally different or inferior, mislabelled and misunderstood by Troilus? Yet, if this is so, how else might the intensity of Troilus's happiness be explained? Why should human love not form a part of the holy bond of things?

(vii) Lines 1275 to 1309: Troilus renews his vows

Having praised Love, Troilus now renews the vows of service that he made at the earlier meeting in Deiphebus's palace. Troilus fervently desires to know how to please Criseyde and wonders whether there has ever been a man who felt as content as he feels now. He is so unworthy of her favour that her acceptance of his love proves that mercy surpasses justice (by allowing someone who feels himself unworthy to gain more than he strictly deserves). Despite his unworthiness but as a result of her mercy and the beneficial experience of being in her service, he will inevitably become a better person. Troilus next says that God created him in order to serve her. God thus wishes Criseyde to act as his 'steere' (1291), the person who navigates the course of a ship, thus choosing whether he lives or dies. Troilus begs her to teach him how to deserve her thanks so that he does nothing wrong out of ignorance. He pledges that she will always find loyalty and attentiveness in his actions and that he will do nothing which disobeys any of her commands. If he does indeed disobey her, he prays that he will be killed in the same instant that he commits the erroneous deed. Criseyde thanks him for these vows and, taking the initiative, she ends the conversation, saying that what has been already said is sufficient. Criseyde welcomes Troilus to her bed, her arms and her body, naming him as her knight, her source of peace and her 'suffisaunce' (1309), a source of perfect contentment.

(viii) Lines 1310 to 1337: the narrating voice's incapacity

Chaucer avoids describing the lovers' union too explicitly. Instead, the narrating voice acknowledges his own inability to describe their happiness fully. He says that it would be impossible to convey even the smallest part of their delight and joys. At this delicate moment, he remains discreet and pre-emptively defends himself from any criticism by attributing responsibility for his poem's content and form to his source and to his readers (because of his inexperience as a lover). He therefore commands those who have themselves experienced and celebrated such happiness to determine whether it was the lovers' wish to 'pleye' (1313, a verb which can mean both 'to enjoy oneself' and 'to make love'). (Lovers are thus urged to draw on their own experiences of sexual fulfilment to supply the physical details which he circumspectly omits.) He himself can say no more than that these two lovers themselves discovered the great value and splendour which can be found in love. The narrating voice implicitly demands that we too celebrate love in this way, leaving aside criticism or irony and valuing this moment of unalloyed happiness in its own terms.

The narrating voice next addresses the happy night itself, exclaiming at how joyous it was to the lovers. Unlike Boccaccio's narrator, who is experienced in love but feels he lacks the poetic ability to describe such a night, here the narrating first-person laments his own inexperience in love, asking enviously why he himself had not achieved such a night even if he had to pay for it with his soul (a reckless question which perhaps brings his judgement into question). He banishes *daunger* (see p. 43) and fear, those things which might inhibit happiness in love, so that the lovers can dwell in what he calls the bliss of heaven (as sexual ecstasy might be described within **the religion of love**), so superior he cannot fully convey it.

Though he is not able, he claims, to describe the lovers' union in as much detail as his superior source, he nevertheless promises that he has conveyed all of his source's meaning. If he has added any words in order to praise love in the best way, he invites lovers to do with such words just as they please (that is, either to accept or censure them as they see fit). He claims that his words here and throughout the poem are spoken subject to checking by such experienced readers. He leaves his poem under their control, asking them to add or delete words as they see fit. The narrating voice justifies and defends his text by reference to the praise of love and its regulation by lovers. Such an intervention inevitably puts forward matters for speculation. What might an audience of lovers add or subtract, or is this depiction of love beyond improvement or correction? What might Chaucer have added to make this scene a greater celebration of love? Is a text written for and supervised by lovers thereby exempt from other types of response?

(ix) Lines 1338 to 1414: the remainder of the night

The narrating first-person now returns his attention to the two lovers whom he left in a passionate embrace. They are so reluctant to leave each other that they each think the other would have to be snatched away violently by some other person for them to become separate once more. They are so happy that they fear they might be dreaming. Troilus kisses each of Criseyde's eyes and addresses them directly, saying that it was they who caused his suffering because they acted as nets with which Criseyde ensnared his heart, enslaving him without physical restraints. He tells her eyes that though mercy is written in their looks, those words of mercy are hard to find (presumably because her gaze is so overpowering). He embraces her once more and sighs a thousand sighs, happy sighs rather than expressions of distress or illness. In a stanza which Chaucer adds to his source, the lovers then exchange rings 'pleyinge' (1368), that is, in a playful manner. The fact that the exchange is playful suggests it is not a type of clandestine marriage (though the detail might nevertheless remind us that the lovers do not envisage marriage at any point). Criseyde also gives Troilus a brooch made from gold and lapis lazuli set with a heart-shaped ruby.

The narrating voice here interjects in order to contrast the love of money with the greater and more authentic pleasure of romantic love. Such a contrast forestalls the opinion of any reader who might be sceptical about the true value of this moment of happiness, aligning those who do not recognize the value of love with those who are greedy or miserly, though it also reveals his own bias (and perhaps his own blindness about the true nature of worldly **felicity**). He asks his audience whether they think that a covetous person or a miser, who finds fault with and despises love, gains more delight from the coins that he hoards than there is in a single moment of love. He is certain that such a miser could not enjoy such perfect joy as that experienced by lovers. Such anxious misers might say that they do but they would be lying. They dismiss love as insanity or stupidity, but he predicts that they will soon lose their money (though has he here lost sight of the fact that human love too is not a perfect joy in the sense of being permanent and without flaw, as Criseyde's monologue on false **felicity** makes clear?). In an addition to the *Filostrato*, the narrating voice prays that those who disparage love might be taught that they were in the wrong just as Midas (here *Mida*) and Crassus were. King Midas, who was granted his wish that everything he touch turn to gold, was eventually punished by growing ass's ears, whilst Crassus, famous for greediness, was killed by having molten gold poured into his mouth.

Returning to the lovers, we are now told of the conversation that passes between them. They recall how and when and where they first knew each other and all of their previous suffering and anxiety. The narrating voice says that it would be unreasonable to talk about sleep at this point because the lovers do not care about sleep and thus it does not fit with his subject matter. Instead, he claims that, in order that no part of that very precious night slip away without being put to use, their time together is spent in joy and in diligent pursuit of everything that is in accordance with noble behaviour (a euphemistic assurance which nonetheless might lead us to speculate once again whether such secret sexual love is indeed honourable).

(x) Lines 1415 to 1471: aubades at dawn

The narrative now signals the coming of dawn. The cockerel begins to crow and 'Lucyfer' (1417, another name for Venus, the morning star, which, as the proem of Book III makes clear, has a favourable influence on human affairs, particularly those of lovers) rises, as does 'Fortuna Major' (1420, meaning 'the greater fortune', referring perhaps to the planet Jupiter or to a group of stars which reproduced the shape of a particular geomantic figure), though the latter was invisible, remaining beyond the horizon and therefore known only to those with some skill in astrology. Yet despite the presence of these propitious celestial objects, each lover now makes a three-stanza lament, Criseyde criticizing the night and Troilus criticizing the day and the sun. These addresses, much expanded from the equivalent passage in the *Filostrato*, are part of a literary tradition of dawn-songs or aubades. Such aubades address the night, sun or dawn as personifications, chastising them for ending the lovers' night together. They illustrate how lovers become entirely self-absorbed in their own happiness, resisting the inevitable passing of time and unrealistically demanding that dawn be postponed for their own pleasure.

In her lament, Criseyde tells Troilus how sorry she is that the coming daylight will force them to part. He must leave before the household awakes or else her reputation will be lost forever. She addresses the night directly, asking why it will not hover over them for as long as it did on the night that Jove slept with a Greek noblewoman called Alcmena, when Jupiter extended one night into three nights for his own pleasure. She prays that God will bind the night so tightly to the part of the heavens visible from Troy that it will never again pass by as the Earth turns. Troilus is so distressed by Criseyde's lament that it seems to him that tears of sorrow and compassion flow from his heart. He calls day an 'accusour' (1450), someone who reveals confidential matters, in this case potentially making public the happiness which night and love have together gained and hidden away. He curses the day's arrival in Troy, saying that every opening has one of its bright eyes (that is, its rays of light peep into the dark houses through every chink). He questions day's motives and its supposed prejudice against lovers. When it peers into houses in the morning it does not give lovers anywhere to hide. He asks why day is trying, as it were, to sell its light here. It should sell it to those who engrave small seals (and hence need bright light for their detailed work). He also criticizes the sun (named here as Titan and conflated with Tithonus, the lover of the dawn goddess Aurora), saying that he has lain in bed next to his mistress, the dawn, all night long yet now it lets her rise up so early in order to harass lovers.

(xi) Lines 1472 to 1533: Criseyde pledges constancy

Troilus now asks himself whether he really must leave Criseyde's bed. He feels that his heart will break in two if he does indeed leave. How can he preserve his own life even for an hour once he has left her when he feels that he only has a life when he is with her? He despairs because he does not know when they can once more spend the night together. Troilus tells Criseyde that he could endure this pain more easily if he knew without any doubt that he was fixed as firmly in her heart as she is in his. He says that he would rather have such a reassurance than possess 'thise worldes tweyne' (1490), meaning perhaps the two kingdoms of Greece and Troy or perhaps two worlds such as this one, the one in which they live.

In response to his request for reassurance, Criseyde makes him an elaborate promise of constancy and devotion, beginning with a series of *impossibilia* which Chaucer adds to his source. (The rhetorical figure of *impossibilia*, in Greek *adynata*, is a form of extreme hyperbole which suggests the utter impossibility of some event by saying that it will occur only after various miraculous and hence extremely unlikely phenomena have been seen.) She tells him that matters between them have progressed so far that the sun god Phoebus Apollo will fall from his heavenly sphere, every fierce eagle will become the mate of a dove, and every rock will move of its own accord before Troilus leaves her heart. He is so deeply imprinted in her heart that she could not expel the thought of him from her mind even if she were threatened with torture. Criseyde makes her promise with sincerity, yet we know that she will break this promise in due course. We are thus shown the futility of hyperbolic promises such as these which can be overturned by future events.

Criseyde next commands Troilus not to let any other delusion creep into his mind, in case his doubt of her loyalty causes her to die from sorrow. In turn, she requests that he keep her as firmly in his mind as he is in hers. If she were sure of this, she feels that God could not increase her happiness by the smallest amount. Their conversation at this moment is filled with reciprocal promises and requests. Thus reassured, Troilus arises and dresses, embraces her a hundred times (according to narratorial hyperbole) and makes his farewell.

(xii) Lines 1534 to 1582: their afterthoughts and Pandarus's reappearance

We are now told of the distress which parting causes the lovers. Criseyde is too upset to respond to Troilus's farewell and he returns to his palace equally distressed. He creeps into bed, intending to sleep late into the morning. Yet he is kept awake by thoughts of how Criseyde has proved to be worth a thousand times more than he had imagined. In his mind he revolves all of her words and expressions and fixes in his memory the smallest detail which gave him pleasure. At each memory, he burns anew with desire and his love grows even greater. Criseyde likewise stores Troilus's good qualities and the details of their affair in her heart. She thanks **the God of Love** for providing for her so well and often longs to meet with Troilus again in secret.

Once his household has arisen, Pandarus visits his niece in her chamber (a visit which does not occur in the *Filostrato* where Troilo and Criseida meet without Pandaro's assistance in her own palace). Greeting her, Pandarus comments that the noisy rain may have kept her awake all night, as it did him. (His joke is of course that she has not been kept awake by the rain but by the presence of her lover.) Speaking to her more discreetly, he asks how she is doing on this happy morning. From her reply, it is clear that Criseyde has now realized how Pandarus has manipulated the lovers. Embarrassed and angry, she says that his interference has not made things at all better. She says he has acted as a fox (a crafty and deceiving person who shares that animal's supposed traits) and has brought these events about with his 'wordes white' (1567), his fair-seeming but deceptive words. Whoever merely looks at him, she says, knows him very little (because he conceals his true **intention** from everyone). Blushing in shame, she hides her face under the sheet.

Pandarus peers under the covers to see her face and says that if he should be punished with death for his actions, Criseyde can take his sword and cut his head off herself. Then he very suddenly thrusts his arm under her neck as she lies in bed and gives her a kiss. As elsewhere, Pandarus manhandles the lovers' bodies without seeking permission. The narrating voice now says he will skip over everything which is not important. Though some readers of the poem have found the phallic connotations of Pandarus's words and deeds suspicious in combination with this stated omission, the literal meaning is that the narrative will omit the details of how Pandarus defused Criseyde's anger. Quoting the proverbial example of Christ's forgiveness of those who crucified him (in a way which might seem profane or ill-judged, or at least a little casual), the narrating voice says that Criseyde likewise forgave her uncle and began once more to talk playfully with him because there was no reason to remain angry (this stanza hinting perhaps that her anger was merely a temporary and face-saving pose of embarrassment which was easily dealt with rather than a genuine and deep-seated emotion). He ends this section of the narrative by commenting that Pandarus has fully accomplished his **intention**, his mission to unite the lovers in secret.

LINES 1583 TO 1820: HAPPINESS BEYOND FELICITY

(i) Lines 1583 to 1666: Troilus thanks Pandarus

Troilus now sends a messenger in secret to fetch Pandarus. Pandarus visits his friend in his bedchamber, thus providing the privacy necessary to discuss his secret love affair. Troilus addresses Pandarus as the very best friend of all friends. He tells Pandarus that by arranging his tryst with Criseyde it is as if he has brought his soul from Phlegethon (here *Flegitoun*), which Troilus himself glosses as the fiery river which runs through the underworld, to a state of tranquillity in heaven (as such happiness might be imagined to be within **the religion of love**). (Chaucer adds this classical geography to his source, which refers simply to a move from hell to Paradise.) Even if Troilus sold his own life a thousand times a day for Pandarus's benefit, it would not at all be sufficient to repay him. He would bet that the sun, which can see all of the world, has never seen a woman so very beautiful and gracious as Criseyde. He describes their reciprocal devotion, giving thanks both to **the God of Love** and for Pandarus's kind efforts. Employing litotes, he says that Pandarus has given him no little thing, for which his life will forever be pledged to Pandarus's service.

Pandarus graciously accepts his thanks. After cautioning him not to take his advice amiss, he warns that Troilus should take care that he himself does not end his current happiness. Of all of the hardships sent by **Fortune**, the worst kind of misfortune is the pain of remembering former and now lost prosperity. (Here Chaucer gives Pandarus a version of the observation made by Boethius about the loss of his good fortune to Lady Philosophy in ***De consolatione philosophiae***, Book II, *prosa* 4.) In order to prevent such a loss, Pandarus instructs Troilus not to make mistakes or act rashly. Pandarus advises Troilus to keep his speech and desire in check, because worldly happiness is, in figurative terms, only kept in place by a thin wire. Its fragility is often demonstrated by its frequent breaking, showing that one must handle it gently. Pandarus's comments on fortune and worldly happiness are added by Chaucer to his source, the *Filostrato*, where Pandaro simply advises Troilo to act with prudence and restraint. Pandarus sees good fortune as precarious and fragile (a view comparable with Criseyde's earlier monologue on the brittle nature of worldly happiness, III.813–36, the false **felicity** as described by Lady Philosophy in response to the observation made by Boethius which Pandarus has just repeated). Nevertheless he believes that an individual's behaviour can have some influence on the future course of events. Proceeding with care will allow Troilus's good fortune to be sustained for as long as possible. Yet we readers, who foreknow the future events of this story, realize that these comments on the fragility of good fortune are more accurate than Pandarus can himself know. The lovers' happiness will soon be ended by unexpected events and Troilus will not prevent their separation.

Troilus tells Pandarus that his advice is unnecessary. If Pandarus knew what was in his heart, he would not worry about his future conduct. Next Troilus tells his friend about his joyous night with Criseyde, confessing that he never before felt half so hot with desire as he does now. He cannot say exactly what he feels, but he feels a new degree of love and emotion, one that he has never felt before. Pandarus agrees, saying that he who has first-hand experience of heaven's bliss feels very differently than he did when he first heard tell of such delights. Troilus repeats these topics until nightfall, describing his love, praising Criseyde and thanking his friend repeatedly, always beginning again as if the topic were brand-new.

(ii) Lines 1667 to 1708: more meetings

The time soon comes when Troilus is told that he should make his way to where he was before (presumably entering Pandarus's house in secret and hiding in the *stewe* once more). We are told that this blissful moment occurred as **Fortune** would have it (though the practical arrangements must be Pandarus's). In happiness and with discretion, Pandarus brings the lovers together in bed where they spend the night in peace and tranquillity. The *Filostrato*'s narrator describes this meeting in brief, relating Criseida's descriptions of the intensity of her desire for Troilo. Chaucer's narrating voice avoids direct descriptions and instead suggests that the lovers' union is inexpressibly superlative. He tells his audience that it is unnecessary for them to ask him whether the lovers were happy. With hyperbole, he says that if they were happy during the first night they spent together, then this time it was a thousand times better. Every sorrow and fear has departed and the lovers each experience as much happiness as an individual heart can comprehend. Employing litotes, he tells his audience that this happiness is 'no litel thyng' (1688) to speak about. Their happiness, he says, cannot be put down on paper with ink and it surpasses anything that one's heart could imagine. It is not even sufficient to call it **felicity**, the type of perfect happiness praised by wise scholars. Yet despite his hyperbole, we cannot forget that this joy supposedly beyond **felicity** will prove to be short-lived and precarious as the lovers are first separated and then Troilus is betrayed by Criseyde. We might both doubt his judgement here but also acknowledge how hard it is to dismiss such keenly felt joy as merely temporary, imperfect or illusory.

The lovers' second night together is once more brought to an end by the arrival of dawn. First the narrating first-person, and then the lovers themselves, again address dawn in the form of an aubade (see p. 102), criticizing daylight for its cruelty and betrayal. In a speech added by Chaucer, Troilus complains that Pyrois and the other three horses who were said to draw the sun's chariot across the sky each day have taken some short cut to spite him by making dawn come sooner. He says that he will never again make sacrifices to the sun god and his horses because of this act of spite. Having made their farewells, the lovers agree another time to meet and then we are told that they spent many nights together in this way. For a time the lovers have **Fortune** on their side and are thus happy (though if we remember Pandarus's lesson at I.848–9 that **Fortune**'s very nature is to change, we will be conscious that such happiness is indeed only likely to be sustained for a short time).

(iii) Lines 1709 to 1743: Troilus ennobled

The narrative now describe Troilus's behaviour during this blissful period. Troilus spends all of his days in contentment, singing joyful songs to express his happiness. He spends money liberally, jousts at tournaments, holds feasts and gives generously (either to his retinue or in charitable alms-giving). He changes his clothes often (presumably to show off various fashionable garments) and keeps a 'world of folk' (1721) about him, a hyperbolic expression implying that he has a great number of people in his retinue and as guests. His sociability leads to such public comment on his courtesy and generosity that it is as if his reputation rang up to heaven's gate (that is, reports of his fame reached the far edges of the mortal world). His devotion to Criseyde is such, we are told, that the beauty given by nature to any other lady could not untie even a single knot of the net which Criseyde has fixed about his heart (that is, another lady's charms could not loosen the hold which Criseyde has on his affections). He is so tightly enmeshed and bound fast in Criseyde's net that it cannot be unfastened. He often takes Pandarus by the hand and leads him into a private garden in order to praise Criseyde. He celebrates her womanliness and beauty to such a degree that the narrating voice says it was 'an hevene' (1742), an utter delight to hear his words.

(iv) Lines 1744 to 1771: Troilus's song

Chaucer now gives the text of one of Troilus's songs of joy in full. Having used part of Troilo's corresponding song as the basis of the proem to Book III, Chaucer now substitutes a song based directly on the eighth *metrum* in Book II of **Boethius's *De consolatione philosophiae*** (which itself provided Boccaccio with inspiration for parts of Troilo's song). Troilus entreats **the God of Love** to 'Bynd this acord' (1750) about which he is singing, that is, to make perfect and everlasting **the holy bond of things**. Troilus invokes Love repeatedly by name, each time describing one aspect of his powers. It is Love who rules on land, at sea and in heaven and Love who keeps different nations joined together by means of an advantageous alliance (for example through marriage and diplomatic treaties). It is Love who has established the law of friendship (that is, the customs and principles which govern reciprocal relationships) and Love who causes couples to live in virtue. (In this last detail, Chaucer alters Boethius's reference to Love establishing the sacrament of marriages based on true love to something which better fits the situation of his narrative, where Troilus and Criseyde's affair is clandestine and the possibility of their marriage is never discussed.)

The next two stanzas record all of the things which occur as a result of Love's divine control and ordering. Lines 1751 and 1758 both begin with two conjunctions 'That, that ...'. In each case the first *that* refers to 'all of *this*' which Love does and the second *that* (which is paralleled by the *thats* of lines 1753, 1755 and 1756) introduces what it is that Love does (i.e., 'namely that the world ... that the sun ... that the moon ... that the sea'). Love ensures that the world constantly and dependably changes from one state of balanced harmony to another (for example from autumn to winter or day to night). This constant flux means that 'elementz' (1753, that is, the four primary properties of the physical universe, hot, moist, cold and dry) which are in their natures so prone to incompatibility nevertheless maintain an everlasting bond with each other (because each dominates in turn). Love ensures that the sun and moon alternate day and night as they should and that the sea which is eager to overflow keeps his high tides within a fixed limit so that they do not surge so violently that they might drown the world and everything in it. If Love were ever to let his bridle go (that is, to slacken his control of the universe), everything which is now joined together by Love would fly apart and everything which is now united by Love would be destroyed.

The song ends by praying that Love encircle all human hearts with his bond and bind them so tightly that no one could escape, just as he binds together the physical universe. Troilus also wishes that Love would torment those people with unfeeling hearts in order to make them love and have pity on those with grief-stricken hearts, and also that he would support those who are faithful in love. Anaphora (see p. 42) binds the song intricately together just as Love tightly binds the physical universe together. In his praise, Troilus implicitly correlates his own union with Criseyde with **the holy bond of things** which keeps the fluctuating universe bound together in harmony. Yet despite the supreme power of Love, through our readerly foresight we know, though Troilus cannot, that Criseyde's heart will not remain bound to him for very long. Is such a correlation, like the associations made in the proem to Book III and in Troilus's praise of love at III.1254–74, mistaken, ironically deluded and incomplete in its insights? Or is it evidence of love's capacity to enlighten and inspire, entirely authentic and expressive of great joy when considered in its own moment in time? If the universe is itself ordered by love, if love is thus natural and necessary, why should the happiness of romantic love and sexual union not be celebrated in these terms?

(v) Lines 1772 to 1806: Troilus ennobled (continued)

We now once again see how Troilus's happiness affects his day-to-day activities. He is always the first to make himself ready to fight when needed in the town's defence and he is the most feared soldier of all the Trojan warriors except Hector. This increase in his bravery and prowess derives from his love for Criseyde which has so transformed his nature. During the times when a truce has been agreed by both sides in the war, he rides out from the city and goes hunting. When he returns to town, Criseyde often greets him from her window, looking as bright and beautiful as a falcon emerging from its moulting cage. All of Troilus's talk is of love and virtue and he despises immoral or ignoble behaviour. We are told that there was no need to implore him to praise those people who deserved praise and to comfort those who were in distress (because evidently he did those things without being asked). Troilus (in contrast with his previous mockery of love) is pleased if he witnesses or hears about any lover having success in love and he consideres all those who were not in the service of **the God of Love** to be lost. The narrating voice here clarifies that he means people who ought by their nature to be in Love's service (implying that Troilus is not damning those who are not meant to be lovers). Although he is of royal blood (and thus has the power to treat people in whatever way he wishes), he does not harass or harangue anyone by acting haughtily. Instead he treats everyone graciously, for which he is thanked everywhere. As **the God of Love** desires him to do, Troilus shuns pride, envy, anger, avarice and every other vice.

(vi) Lines 1807 to 1820: Book III ends

As Book III comes to an end, the narrating first-person addresses Venus, goddess of love (here called the daughter of Dione), her son Cupid and the nine Muses, the goddesses who in classical mythology are said to inspire the creation of all forms of art. The Muses are said here to dwell by Helicon on Mount Parnassus, their sacred home (here *hil Pernaso*). (Mount Helicon was another location sacred to the Muses, but Chaucer here takes Helicon to be the fountain sacred to the Muses as a source of creative inspiration.) These mythological figures have guided the narrating voice this far in the narrative (showing that the presiding spirits of Book III are love and creativity), but now since they wish to depart he can do or say nothing but offer them everlasting praise. Their imminent and unpreventable departure signals the impending change in the lovers' fortunes. With their help, the narrating first-person says, he has fully expressed in his verse, just as his source describes, both Troilus's service to his lady Criseyde and his consequent happiness, though he concedes that Troilus did experience some distress along the way. As the third book of the poem ends, Troilus and Criseyde are together, united in peace and happiness.

Book IV

LINES 1 TO 28: THE PROEM

Book IV begins with a proem marking this moment as the turning point in Troilus's fortunes. Chaucer follows the final stanza of Book III of Boccaccio's *Filostrato* in blaming **Fortune** for the short-lived nature of worldly happiness such as that experienced by the lovers. **Fortune** will now, like a haughty noble lady, turn her attractive face away from Troilus and pay him no attention, removing him completely from Criseyde's good favour. In Troilus's place on the ascending part of her wheel, **Fortune** will place Diomede, the Greek nobleman who will in Book V replace Troilus in Criseyde's affections. Thinking ahead to Troilus's imminent suffering, the narrating first-person tells us that his heart begins to bleed with compassion. His pen shakes with fear at the thought of what he is about to write. Yet although he acknowledges that his subject matter must now be the manner in which Criseyde deserts Troilus because that is what is written in his sources, he immediately interjects that at least it must be how Criseyde was 'unkynde' (16) to Troilus, how she was indifferent to his suffering or acted ungraciously towards him. His qualification concedes that Criseyde's behaviour is incontrovertibly heartless and discourteous but nevertheless insinuates that in some way it might be understood as less than an outright betrayal. He goes on to lament the fact that those who have written prior versions of her story should find reasons to criticize his heroine. If they lie about her in any way (presumably if they exaggerate her culpability), he says that they themselves should be blamed. This intervention begs the question of what it is that makes the narrating voice sympathize with Criseyde, regret the fact that she is criticized and see her as a potential victim of unwarranted censure. Can we agree with him in being reluctant to condemn her?

Venus, Cupid and the Muses having left him at the end of Book III, the narrating voice appeals to new sources of poetic assistance which are appropriate to the distressing material he must now relate. He calls on the three Furies (given their alternative name of Erinyes, here *Herynes*, meaning literally 'the angry ones') and on Mars, god of war and destruction, asking for their help to complete the fourth book of this poem so that he can describe in full the loss of Troilus's love and his subsequent loss of life. Given that Criseyde's departure from Troy and Troilus's death are in fact narrated in Book v, this suggests perhaps that Chaucer originally intended the story to be completed in four books. This reference reminds readers once more of the ultimate outcome of the story and encourages them to evaluate Book iv in the light of Troilus's eventual betrayal and death.

Fortune

Both the characters and the narrating voice of *Troilus and Criseyde* make reference to the goddess Fortune and her wheel, a symbol embodying the mutability and unpredictability which is Fortune's nature. The violent turns of Fortune's wheel change the positions of those placed upon it, from good fortune and happiness at the top of her wheel to misfortune and sorrow at the bottom and vice versa. From humanity's point of view, such change appears haphazard and deceptive. Humanity has great difficulty in understanding or predicting the workings of Fortune, and thus she is said to deceive mankind. As the proem to Book iv sets out, to humankind Fortune seems most dependable when she actually intends to beguile (that is, good fortune seems most long-lasting and secure when it is in fact precarious and changeable). Fortune sings to the foolish in such a way that they are captured and deceived (that is, she beguiles those who do not remember her true nature by lulling them into a false sense of security). When an individual is thrown down from the top of her wheel, it is as if Fortune laughs and makes faces at them to indicate her malicious and capricious nature. She is thus called a 'traitour comune' (iv.5), someone who notoriously betrays everyone in due course.

Yet elsewhere we are reminded that the operations of Fortune, however haphazard and malevolent they appear, are in fact part of the divine ordering of the universe. In Book iii, the narrating first-person names Fortune as the 'executrice' (617) of each of our individual fates (an executrix being the female equivalent of an executor, the person appointed to put the provisions of a will into being). She exercises her power under God as a deputy, acting as our 'hierdes' (619), our shepherds. Human beings are guided by her just as beasts are controlled by their herders, and like dumb beasts we cannot understand the complex causes by which God's Providence (the plan of all human events as understood by God in eternity) is put into action by Fortune (see also v.1541–7).

These different understandings of Fortune are discussed by Boethius and Lady Philosophy in ***De consolatione philosophiae***. Lady Philosophy consoles Boethius on his sudden fall from power by reminding him that change is Fortune's normal behaviour. If you commit yourself to Fortune's governance, you must accept that she cannot be controlled and that your own fortunes will change, with any good fortune being inevitably short-lived (Book II, *prosa* 1). Lady Philosophy then impersonates Fortune as she questions humanity as to whether the accusations it makes (that Fortune, in choosing to take back her gifts of good fortune, thus acting in accordance with her intrinsic nature, is unfair) are in any way justifiable (Book II, *prosa* 2). Later in their discussion, Lady Philosophy explains how humankind cannot fully comprehend either Providence or Fate (that is, God's divine plan as it is played out in each individual happening) and so events seem chaotic and unfair, the work of an unjust and capricious Fortune (Book IV, *prosa* 6).

These exchanges provide Chaucer with his source for the contrary views of Fortune put forward by Troilus and Pandarus (see I.837–54, IV.260–87, 384–92). Troilus believes that Fortune acts antagonistically towards him (see also IV.1189 and 1192) despite the fact that he has worshipped her above all other gods. The complaints Troilus makes against Fortune are those which Lady Philosophy (when imitating Fortune) mocks as entirely unreasonable. Pandarus reminds Troilus of Fortune's inevitable mutability, not to caution him about the foolishness of basing his happiness on inevitably transient good fortune, but in order to cheer him up with the thought that future joys may soon replace his present sorrow (just as Fortune herself beguilingly does at the end of Lady Philosophy's impersonation). If evaluated in this way, Chaucer's characters fall short of the insights offered by Lady Philosophy in ***De consolatione philosophiae***, yet given that they are characters in a pagan love story rather than a philosophical dialogue, should we thus criticize or sympathize? Lady Philosophy herself acknowledges the considerable difficulty humanity has in trying to comprehend the workings of Fortune.

LINES 29 TO 60: HECTOR'S SALLY

We are now told how Hector made plans for a sally, a sudden counterattack in which the Trojan troops rush out from their besieged city and attack the Greek forces. Chaucer adds to his source several lines of description of the encounter between the Trojan and Greek warriors. Some of these added lines (39–42) contain two or three alliterating words, imitating the form of alliterative Middle English verse romances which often described battle scenes. After a fierce and lengthy battle, the Trojan army make so many mistakes that they are repelled and have to flee back to the city at nightfall. During this ill-fated sally, Antenor, a Trojan nobleman, is captured by the Greeks despite the efforts of various Trojan soldiers listed. The Greeks then request a period of truce from Priam. The truce having been granted, the two sides arrange to meet to negotiate prisoner exchanges and ransoms.

LINES 61 TO 140: CALCHAS'S REQUEST

News of the truce quickly reaches both the besieging Greek army and the citizens of Troy. Once Calchas, Criseyde's father, hears that a diplomatic negotiation concerning the exchange of prisoners will soon be held between the Greeks and Trojans, he rushes into the Greek council chamber along with other senior Greek lords. He reminds the council that he was formerly a loyal Trojan before defecting to the Greek side in order to tell them how they would soon destroy the city of Troy. He emphasizes that he came to the Greeks in person to reveal these prophecies and that he left behind all his wealth and sources of income. As he intends to ask for a favour, he stresses his love for the Greek nobles and his desire to please and assist them. He says that he was happy and willing to leave everything behind in Troy except for his daughter Criseyde. He laments his abandonment of her, wishing that he had not left her sleeping but instead brought her with him.

Emphasizing his sorrow and regret, he begs the Greek lords to help him. The capture of Antenor now offers him an opportunity to be reunited with his daughter. Calchas asks the lords to exchange one of the Trojan prisoners for Criseyde. He argues that there is no reason to deny his request (perhaps, for example, because it would be unwise to return a Trojan soldier during a time of war) by stressing the credibility of his prophecy of imminent victory. In comparison with his source, Chaucer makes this restatement of Calchas's prophecy more specific and more convincing. Calchas swears that the god Apollo told him that Troy will soon be destroyed by fire, a prophecy which he has confirmed by other forms of divination. To Calchas, the destruction of Troy is inevitable and almost self-evident. Here referring to one of the myths of Troy's origins, Calchas reminds the councillors that the gods Apollo (here given his alternative title of Phoebus) and Neptune, who had built the walls of Troy for Priam's father, King Laomedon, are angry with the Trojan citizens because they had not been rewarded for their work as promised. They intend to bring the city to eventual destruction and, Calchas implies, it is the Greek army who will fulfil this mythological curse.

We are next told of Calchas's demeanour during his address to the council, his elderly appearance, humble speech and copious tears. He asks the Greek lords for help at such length that, in order to assuage his obvious distress, they quickly grant him Antenor to exchange for Criseyde. Calchas now repeatedly asks those ambassadors chosen to travel to Troy to negotiate to bring home King Thoas and Criseyde in exchange for Antenor.

LINES 141 TO 217: THE TROJAN PARLIAMENT

Once Priam learns of the arrival of the Greek ambassadors, he summons his parliament. Whereas in his sources this consultation is presented as a council of noblemen, Chaucer presents it as a parliament in which the king and his lords discuss matters with representatives of the common people. The narrative now concentrates on Troilus's reaction. At the moment when the ambassadors request that Criseyde be exchanged for Antenor, Troilus's expression suddenly changes, as if he nearly died of sorrow upon hearing those words. Yet he conceals his grief in case anyone should detect it. Thinking ahead about what he should do if the Trojan parliament agrees to the exchange, Troilus considers two matters. Firstly, he wishes to protect Criseyde's honour (a priority which Chaucer adds to his source). Secondly, he considers how he could best oppose the proposed exchange. Troilus's inner debate about what he should do is presented as the conflicting advice of two personifications, just as it is in the *Filostrato*. Love makes him eager to have Criseyde stay in Troy by any means, to die rather than to let her leave the city. Yet Reason tells him that he should not act without Criseyde's approval, in case he were to displease her so much that she become his enemy rather than his lady. If he intervenes publicly, she might later criticize him for making their secret love public. He resolves that he will first tell Criseyde what the lords propose.

Once she has told him her opinion on the matter, he will quickly act in accordance with her wishes. Troilus's desire to preserve his lady's honour and to act faithfully as her servant leads him to remain silent and to defer to Criseyde.

In the *Filostrato*, Troilo faints with sorrow when the news that the exchange has been granted is conveyed to the Greek ambassadors. Chaucer omits this faint and instead describes a difference of opinion between Hector and the Trojan commons present in parliament. Hector (in keeping his earlier promises to protect and assist Criseyde) opposes the exchange, reminding the ambassadors that Criseyde is not a prisoner but a free woman. The ambassadors should tell whoever has given them their orders that the Trojans are not accustomed to sell women in exchange for captured soldiers. Such an objection nevertheless articulates our sense that, without their consent being sought, women are indeed offered to men and exchanged by men in this story. In response to Hector's views, an outcry arises, its vehemence compared to the ferocity of flames which spread through burning straw. To the commons, Hector is making the wrong choice because protecting Criseyde will result in the permanent loss of Antenor, whom they consider to be one of Troy's greatest noblemen, a wise and courageous lord who is greatly needed during the siege. They tell Priam that their united opinion is that Criseyde should be surrendered in order to release Antenor.

Though their wish to release Antenor makes sense in the short term, it nevertheless reveals how blind the Trojan citizens are to their ultimate fate. The narrating first-person draws our attention to their blindness and to the irony of their choice by pausing to make an apostrophe to the Roman satirist Juvenal. The decision of the Trojan commons here proves as true Juvenal's maxim that men know so little about what is desirable that they can't see the potential harm in their desire because a cloud of error prevents them from seeing the best course of action.[1] The Trojan commons demand the return of Antenor, the very person in medieval tradition who will eventually betray Troy by assisting the Greeks to bring about the fall of the city. The narrating voice laments the parliament's hasty decision, sarcastically congratulating the foolish world on its ability to make sound decisions. Criseyde, who never did them any harm, will

[1] The maxim referred to forms the beginning of Juvenal's tenth satire, lines 1–5: 'In all the lands extending from Cadiz as far as Ganges and the Dawn, there are few people who can remove the fog of confusion and distinguish real benefits from their opposites. After all, what is rational about our fears and desires?' *Juvenal and Persius*, ed. and trans. S. Morton Braund, Loeb Classical Library 91 (Cambridge, MA: Harvard University Press, 2004), p. 367.

no longer enjoy her happiness with Troilus and will be made to leave the city, whilst Antenor, Troy's future betrayer, will return. Yet even though Hector frequently objects, the majority of those present decide to agree to the exchange, a decision which is decreed by the president, the official in charge of the parliament.

LINES 218 TO 343: TROILUS'S GRIEF

Troilus now returns to his bedchamber, dismissing his servants by telling them that he intends to sleep. Chaucer compares the loss of each of the sources of Troilus's happiness to the loss of every leaf from a tree in autumn. Just as nothing is left but bark and branches, so Troilus is said to be left confined in the black bark of sorrow. The prospect of Criseyde's exchange with Antenor drives him almost to the point of madness. Closing all of the doors and windows, Troilus then sits down on the side of his bed, so paralysed with grief that he appears to be a lifeless statue. Yet despite this momentary paralysis, his sorrow soon bursts forth. Troilus's physical response to his pain is compared to the death throes of a bull once it has been mortally wounded. He rages around his bedroom, beating his breast with his fists, hitting his head against the wall and throwing his body to the ground. Crying copiously and racked with sobs, he can hardly speak. Throughout Books IV and V, descriptions of Troilus's second sorrow echo earlier representations of the sorrows and suffering of falling in love in the first half of the poem. Here he make a brief appeal to death, asking why death will not kill him and cursing the day on which Nature created him. Eventually the anger which so squeezes his heart subsides a little and he lies down to rest. Yet soon more tears begin to flow and the narrating voice expresses his surprise that Troilus's body could endure even half of the sorrow which he is describing.

Troilus now addresses a series of questions to **Fortune**, asking what it is that has led her to treat him so cruelly. He asks why she has decided to take away his source of joy even though he has worshipped **Fortune** above all the other gods and goddesses. In a question which reveals the deranged quality of his sorrow and his preoccupation with Criseyde above anything else, Troilus asks why, if his happiness made her so jealous, **Fortune** did not rather kill his father, King Priam, or his brothers, or kill Troilus himself. He names himself as a 'combre-world' (279), someone who is a burden to himself and to the world, always sorrowfully dying yet never dead. Troilus recognizes that **Fortune** frequently robs a man of what is most precious to him in order to demonstrate her 'gerful violence'

(286), the unpredictable and forceful movements which occur as **Fortune** without warning turns her wheel. Yet if he comprehends this, we might then ask why he devoted himself so fervently to such an unreliable goddess. Troilus has been blind to the true nature of **Fortune** and he is now so devoted to Criseyde that he is unable to see her exchange as anything other than a certainty which will result in his own death.

He next addresses **the God of Love**, asking him what will happen if he has to give up the happiness which he has so painfully acquired through the sorrow of **lovesickness** and through devoted service to his lady. Given that **the God of Love** has so favoured the lovers and has 'seled' (293) both their hearts, joining them together like two parties contracted together in a sealed legal document, how can he allow such a deeply binding agreement to be revoked? Chaucer adds the comparison Troilus makes between his own projected death and that of Oedipus, king of **Thebes** (who blinded himself when he discovered that he had, without knowing, killed his father and married his mother). Like Oedipus, Troilus will end his life in darkness, not literally blinded but imprisoned by grief. This allusion might also make us speculate about other ways in which Troilus is blinded by love and sorrow in this complaint.

Troilus next addresses his own soul, asking why it will not leave his body, which he thinks has become the most grief-stricken body alive. He commands it to 'unneste' (305), to take flight from his heart like a bird leaving a nest, and to follow its mistress, Criseyde. Next he addresses his eyes, asking how, since they derived all of their happiness from gazing at Criseyde's bright eyes, they can now be anything other than useless. They should weep away their capacity for sight, since Criseyde, whom he feels gave his eyes the power of sight, is now 'queynt' (313), extinguished just as a candle is put out. Since they will soon no longer be able to see Criseyde, he says that from this moment it is as if his eyes were created in vain. The intensity of Troilus's sorrow and near-madness drives him to demand these unnatural consequences. Next he addresses Criseyde, the lady to whom he is devoted above all others. He asks who, in her absence, will now comfort him, concluding that no one will. When he dies of sorrow and his spirit is freed from his body, he begs her to welcome his soul, which will be irresistibly drawn to her. At this moment, Troilus can think of no other afterlife but a posthumous reunion with Criseyde.

Next Troilus addresses lovers in general, those who are currently placed high on **Fortune**'s wheel (that is, those who are currently enjoying good luck in love). He prays that they always experience 'love of stiel' (325), a love which endures like hardened steel. Anticipating his own death, he asks that when they pass by his tomb they remember that he, their former companion in love, lies there. Lastly he addresses Calchas, denouncing him as an old and wicked man. He tells Calchas, as the causer of his death, that he was born at an ill-omened time as far as he, Troilus, is concerned. This scene concludes with hyperbolic descriptions of the thousand sighs which emerge from Troilus's breast, each hotter than a glowing coal on a fire. These sighs are mixed with new complaints, fuelling his sorrow so that he cannot stop crying. His grief is thus amplified to such an extent that he becomes insensible to all emotion and faints.

LINES 344 TO 658: PANDARUS VISITS TROILUS

(i) Lines 344 to 392: Pandarus arrives

Pandarus, having himself witnessed the Trojan parliament's decision, rushes to Troilus's palace. The unexpected news of the exchange momentarily confounds the usually resourceful Pandarus. He is here so distressed and confused that he doesn't know what he intends to do or what to say. His deep sympathy for his friend causes him to share as far as he can the physical and emotional effects of such sorrow.

Pandarus does not blame himself in any way but instead he poses a series of rhetorical questions (echoing the friends' earlier discussion of **Fortune** at 1.834–54). Who could have believed that this could happen, that **Fortune** could overturn 'oure joie' (385, the first-person plural showing the extent of his involvement) in such a short time? Indeed, who could avoid every misfortune or predict every eventuality? To Pandarus, the answer to these question is obvious: no one could. He concludes that such unpredictability is the nature of the universe. No one should ever expect to attain private property within **Fortune** (that is, no one should believe that he will receive special treatment from **Fortune** or be allowed to retain a piece of good fortune as one would have ownership of something). Her gifts, he says, are common (meaning both that her changeability is experienced alike by everyone and also that any happiness is likely to be redistributed to someone else without warning).

(ii) Lines 393 to 433: Pandarus's nonsense

Pandarus now seeks to console his friend by any means possible. Adopting a callously dismissive tone, he reminds Troilus that there are many ladies to choose from in Troy, claiming that he could find at least twelve (or, he quickly qualifies, at least one or two) more attractive than Criseyde. He instructs Troilus to be happy because, if he is indeed deprived of Criseyde, it will be easily possible to acquire another lady. God forbid, Pandarus exclaims in a stanza added by Chaucer to his source, if we could only find happiness in one person. He hypothetically assesses the merits of different ladies, contrasting one with another (*if one has x, the other has y*). He concludes with a proverb: everything is valued for a particular individual quality, just as one values both the falcon trained for hunting herons and the falcon which hunts other waterfowl by the river. Pandarus next advises that new affection will drive out any memory of a previous love affair. Chaucer has Pandarus attribute this proverb to 'Zanzis' (414), an alternative name for the Greek painter Zeuxis to whom the Roman author, lawyer and politician Cicero refers in *De inventione* ('about the composition of arguments') when explaining why he is selecting his material from many different arts of rhetoric rather than a single source (though there is no record of such a proverb being attributed to Zeuxis).[2] Zeuxis chose five models for his picture of Helen of Troy because he felt that the epitome of beauty could not be found in a single woman (and hence Zeuxis's example might imply that Troilus can transfer his love from one lady to another by appreciating that each individual offers different attractions). Pandarus says that Troilus must find some other way to preserve his own life. This is possible because such passionate love will inevitably grow cold in time. Since it was (according to Pandarus) a 'casuel plesaunce' (419), a happiness which came about by chance, some other chance event will drive it from Troilus's mind. Moreover, just as day follows night, so something will inevitably cause former desires to pass away, whether it be a new love, the distraction of some other pain or distress, or infrequent meetings with the loved one. One of these cures will indeed alleviate Troilus's present sorrow, because Criseyde's absence from Troy will, Pandarus predicts, eventually expel her from his heart. In contrast to the *Filostrato*, where the equivalent advice is presented without narratorial comment, Pandarus's words are here labelled as 'unthrift' (431) or nonsense, advice given in order to alleviate Troilus's distress without any thought for its morality or wisdom (echoing his similar strategy at I.551–67).

[2] Cicero, *De inventione*, II.1, in *De inventione, De optimo genere oratorum, Topica*, ed. and trans. H. M. Hubbell, Loeb Classical Library 386 (London: Heinemann; Cambridge, MA: Harvard University Press, 1949), pp. 166–9.

(iii) Lines 434 to 522: Troilus's response

Troilus reacts strongly to Pandarus's *unthrift*, showing that it has done its work in provoking him out of his stupor of misery. His tone here is one of outrage and disbelief, using hyperbole to demonstrate the extent of his love and grief and dismantling Pandarus's argument with sarcasm and mockery. This medicine (namely Pandarus's suggestion that he betray Criseyde's loyalty by loving another lady) would, says Troilus, be appropriate only if he were morally a monster or a devil. He would rather die than do as Pandarus instructs. Chaucer replaces the *Filostrato*'s description of the evolution of Troilo's love for Criseida with a pledge of unshakeable devotion from Troilus. Troilus is entirely hers and will serve her and her alone until he dies. He says that Pandarus should not make any comparison between Criseyde and any other earthly lady (implying that only a goddess could equal or surpass her beauty). With exaggerated civility, he tells his friend that he cannot agree with his opinion in this matter and asks him to remain quiet because his advice is mortally distressing him.

Troilus next mocks Pandarus's seemingly inconsistent advice (previously encouraging his love for Criseyde and now dismissing it) and also the idea that love can easily be transferred from one person to another. He asks him whether Pandarus himself can change his own affections and also alter his advice just as one quickly alternates strokes in a game of tennis. He quotes part of a medicinal charm that one might repeat when applying dock leaves to a nettle sting ('the nettle makes the sting go in, the dock takes it out'). Pandarus provides instant remedies just as a dock leaf provides quick remedy from the pain of a sting. Troilus tells his friend that he is behaving like an over-eager and thoughtless advisor.

Troilus now warns that even though his sorrow will penetrate his heart to such an extent that he is likely to die, 'Criseydes darte' (472), the arrow of **the God of Love** which has fixed Criseyde in his heart, will never leave his soul. When he is dead, he will dwell with Proserpina, queen of the underworld, tormented and eternally lamenting his grief and separation from Criseyde. He next turns to Pandarus's suggestion that it will be less painful to lose Criseyde because he has already possessed her and enjoyed a period of happiness. He asks why Pandarus is now talking nonsense, reminding him in the form of proverb that he had earlier argued that it is the worst kind of misfortune to have happiness and then to remember it when it is lost (see III.1625–8 where Pandarus's observation echoes the one made by Boethius to Lady Philosophy). If he thinks it is so easy to transfer one's affections, he asks why Pandarus himself has not done everything he can to exchange the lady who causes his pain (that is, Pandarus's unnamed lady who will not reciprocate his affections) for another woman. If Pandarus cannot supplant love which has always been unsuccessful, how can he, who has had so much pleasure, quickly forget the source of this prior happiness?

Troilus thus dismisses the entirety of Pandarus's *unthrift*, ending his reply with another apostrophe to personified Death. He invites his own death, saying that happy is that death which, having been often requested, finally arrives and puts an end to suffering. Since Death kills so many people who do not wish to die, Troilus argues that Death should certainly kill him because he invites death willingly. He begs Death to free the world of him because, if he is separated from Criseyde, he can serve no useful purpose here. Having thus pleaded with Death, Troilus expresses his sorrow in copious tears. His tears are compared to the distillate which pours out of an alembic (a round glass vessel with a long neck used to distil liquids in science or medicine).

(iv) Lines 523 to 658: Pandarus suggests abduction

In the face of Troilus's desire for death and refusal of his advice, Pandarus is momentarily silenced and subdued. Yet whilst his friend fatalistically sees no solution to his sorrow, Pandarus cannot help but give advice rather than let Troilus die as he wishes. With a vigorous imperative, Pandarus urges him to 'Go ravysshe' (530) Criseyde, meaning here to seize and abduct her by force and then resist any attempt to exchange her for Antenor. Troilus should either accept that she will leave Troy or keep her there by some means (whether legal or not). In mock surprise, Pandarus questions how Troilus can be a resident of Troy (alluding to Troy as Troilus's power base, as a city of bold warriors, and as a city already besieged because of the abduction of Helen) and not be daring enough to abduct a woman who loves him and who is likely to agree with this plan of action.

In contrast to his earlier bitter mockery, Troilus answers this latest suggestion quietly and with measured reason and forethought. He claims to have thought about this possibility but already rejected it. For him, the abduction of Helen does not give him sanction to abduct Criseyde but rather precludes such action. Because Troy is already at war for this reason, Troilus could not be allowed to make the same mistake or commit a similarly significant impropriety. He would be blamed by everyone if he challenged his father's decree in this way. He has considered the possibility, if Criseyde were willing, of asking his father for her. But, because Priam has ratified the exchange in parliament, the king cannot rescind this parliamentary decree on his son's behalf. Chaucer omits from his source Troilo's comment that Priam would also think that Criseida is not a suitable choice for his son because of her lower social status. Troilus concludes that because Priam will not overturn the decision, to ask him would simply make their love known and thus endanger Criseyde's reputation. Chaucer here alters the order of Troilo's arguments in the *Filostrato*, making Troilus's fears about frightening Criseyde and slandering her good reputation his last and most important reason for rejecting the proposed abduction. As her knight and lover, he would rather die than defame her honour. The discretion required of a lover according to **the art of love** means that he cannot act in a way which might expose her to shame and he is thus torn between the impulses of desire and reason. Desire advises him to prevent her from going whilst reason will not allow him to do so (because of the consequences and restrictions he has outlined above). He ends his reply in tears, setting out his predicament in a counterbalanced image of expansion and diminution. Both his love and the causes of his sorrow are increasing at the very same time that his hope is decreasing.

Having had his suggestion of abduction rejected, Pandarus responds by offering arguments which, as Troilus later identifies, are intended to 'priken' him (633), to incite him to action. Such suggestions also incite our readerly sense that Troilus could act more impetuously, that he should set aside the constraints which limit his actions and thus that this predetermined story should, however impossibly, unfold in an entirely different way. Rather than reflecting too deeply or thinking too meticulously about the argument one might make against abduction, Pandarus argues Troilus should act to help himself. Pandarus does not consider it to be a 'rape' (596, here primarily meaning an abduction by force) or a vice to protect and to refuse to return the woman whom Troilus loves. Moreover, Criseyde may think that Troilus is foolish to allow her to go to the Greek army encampment. Pandarus reminds Troilus of the proverbial advice that **Fortune** favours the brave but spurns the wretched if they are cowardly. Even if Criseyde is a little displeased at an unexpected abduction, the lovers will soon be reconciled, though Pandarus does not believe Criseyde would react in this way. Chaucer here omits Pandaro's ignoble comment that if Criseida's reputation were lost in this way matters would be less troublesome (because their affair could then be conducted openly, if dishonourably). Pandaro says that Criseida can do without her reputation, just as Helen of Troy now does, if Troilo's desires are satisfied.

Chaucer instead has Pandarus ask why Troilus should be afraid to act when Paris, his brother, has gained his lover by a similar abduction. Such discussions highlight the treatment of women by Trojan men. Criseyde has been exchanged for Antenor by her father without her consent and might now be seized and controlled by her lover, just as Helen has been abducted by Paris. In such circumstances, women may have no choice but to assent to such abductions after the fact.

In a stanza added by Chaucer to his source, Pandarus now refers to Criseyde's love for Troilus, saying that if Criseyde loves him she will not disapprove of such a plan. He says that if Criseyde wishes to leave Troilus and go to the Greek camp, then she is 'fals' (616, a prediction which of course proves to be true) and he should love her less intensely. Pandarus next exhorts his friend to act courageously, playing upon Troilus's sense of knightly honour. If Troilus were to die whilst attempting to abduct Criseyde he would become a martyr (within **the religion of love**) and thus go to heaven. Yet despite Pandarus's efforts to goad him into action, Troilus remains steadfast in his views. Even if he might indeed die from sorrow, he does not intend to abduct Criseyde unless she herself instructs him to do so. Seeing the strength of his friend's conviction, Pandarus quickly changes his tune and claims that consulting Criseyde is what he has been suggesting all along. He establishes that Troilus has not yet discussed matters with her, and therefore cannot know what her reaction would be unless Jove were to tell him (by means of divine omniscience). He commands him to get up, wash the tears from his face and visit his father, King Priam, before his absence is noted. Troilus must continue to deceive his own father and others, whilst Pandarus will arrange another private meeting at which Troilus can discover Criseyde's **intention**.

LINES 659 TO 805: CRISEYDE'S REACTION

(i) Lines 659 to 730: the news reaches Criseyde

We are now told how Fame, who spreads both truth and lies alike, flies with swift wings throughout Troy, spreading the news of the exchange. Criseyde does not have any feelings for her father and hence is not pleased to hear the news that she will be reunited with him. Chaucer here adds to his source a stanza which emphasizes the depth of Criseyde's love for Troilus. She is so devoted to Troilus in heart and mind that nothing in the world could unravel this love or remove Troilus from her heart. Her heart is thus inflamed with both love for Troilus and fear about their future. Seeming to speak Criseyde's thoughts for a moment, the narrating voice says that she will be Troilus's lady for as long as she lives. Yet for us readers, this sincere profession of love must coexist with our foreknowledge that Criseyde's love will not be as long-lasting as she and the narrative avow at this moment.

We now see a scene in which a group of Criseyde's female friends visit her upon hearing about the exchange. Their visit is motivated by a compassionate wish to share or cultivate happiness. Both the narrating first-person and Criseyde are dismissive of these well-meaning attempts to portray the news as a positive development. The narrating voice sees the visit very much from Criseyde's perspective, calling the women fools and their conversation foolish chatter. Criseyde hears their comments as if she is present in body but absent in spirit. Her thoughts are elsewhere, her spirit constantly seeking her soul-mate Troilus. Trying to cheer her up, the women make light conversation, but Criseyde burns with such different emotions to the ones which they assume she is feeling that she finds their company utterly distressing. She cannot conceal her emotions for long and thus she wells up with tears and sighs as she contemplates the loss of Troilus. She feels as if she has fallen from a heaven of happiness into a hell of sorrow. Again, the women mistakenly believe that she is distressed because she will soon no longer have their companionship. They themselves weep for her distress and try once more to comfort and distract her from her sorrow. The narrating voice comments that such comfort is as ineffective as the relief one might get if someone scratched your feet when you were in fact suffering from a headache.

(ii) Lines 731 to 805: Criseyde's complaint

Once her visitors have departed, Criseyde retires to her bedchamber in private in order to lament. She falls on her bed as if she were dead with sorrow. She tears at her wavy hair, here described as the colour of bright sunlight. She wrings her long slender fingers and her complexion grows pale. She begs God to take pity on her and end her suffering by ending her life. She makes a solitary complaint, calling herself a sorrowful wretch and an unfortunate creature who must have been born at a moment of unfavourable planetary influences. She also curses the day on which she first saw Troilus. Her tears fall quickly like a swift April shower and she beats her breast and cries out for death a thousand times.

Her complaint continues with a series of despairing questions and apostrophes. She asks what on earth she and Troilus will do if they are separated and who will comfort Troilus. She blames Calchas briefly and invokes her dead mother Argia (here *Argyve*), cursing the day that she gave birth to her. She asks why on earth she should carry on living when she is in so much sorrow. Just as she asks how a fish can live without water or a plant or animal without nourishment, so she asks what Criseyde is worth without Troilus. In support of this she cites a 'by-word' (769), a proverb: rootless greenery will soon die (implying that to be separated from Troilus is to be separated from the source of life itself). Given that she is too afraid to take hold of a sword or spear to kill herself, she resolves that if sorrow does not kill her she will starve herself until her soul leaves her breast just as a knife or sword is unsheathed from its scabbard.

Addressing the absent Troilus, Criseyde next says that, once they are separated, she will always wear black clothes to signify that she has withdrawn from daily life (just as nuns do when entering a convent). Until she dies, her 'observance' (783, that is, the rules, rituals and regulations of this imagined religious order) will be a life of sorrow, lamentation and fasting. In keeping with these thoughts of death (either by starvation or by a death-like retreat from the world), Criseyde now bequeaths (as if writing her will) her heart and soul to be eternally united in lament with Troilus's soul. Even if their bodies are separated, their two souls will be together in Elysium (here *Elisos*), a place of compassion beyond pain (Elysium being that part of the classical underworld occupied by the souls of heroes and of the virtuous). They will be just like Orpheus and Eurydice, mythological lovers who were ultimately reunited in death.

Finally, having already accepted that she will soon be exchanged for Antenor, she asks the absent Troilus how he will bear such a loss. Chaucer omits from his source the final two stanzas of Criseida's lament in which she curses her father more extensively and blames her own sufferings on his sinful betrayal. The narrating first-person concludes this scene by acknowledging his supposed inability to do justice to Criseyde's complaint (as Boccaccio's narrator likewise does in the *Filostrato*). He asks how her lamentation could ever be authentically read or sung (a formulaic phrase meaning 'conveyed in any way'). If his 'litel tonge' (801), that is, his limited literary ability, were to attempt to describe her grief, it would diminish her sorrow and clumsily misrepresent her noble complaint. He will therefore move on in his narrative. Such comments highlight the difficulty of conveying such sorrow authentically, yet also assert the intense and exceptional nature of Criseyde's despair.

LINES 806 TO 945: PANDARUS VISITS CRISEYDE

Pandarus now visits Criseyde discreetly in order to obtain her consent to another meeting with Troilus. He finds her still prostrate with grief in her bedchamber. Her chest and face are wet with tears and her luxuriant sun-bright hair is not neatly braided but hangs loosely down around her ears. These physical signs of her distress give Pandarus an unmistakable indication that Criseyde's heart desires to die, that she wishes to undergo the suffering of death just as a martyr does. When Criseyde sees her uncle, she buries her tearful face in her arms. His arrival prompts Criseyde to bemoan her sorrow a thousand times more powerfully than she had previously done when alone in her chamber. Chaucer here adds Criseyde's three stanzas of complaint to his source, making his heroine much more eloquent in her distress. She addresses Pandarus obliquely in the named third person, telling him that he was the 'cause causyng' (829), that is, the primary or initiating cause, of all her happiness. Chaucer here gives Criseyde a term from scholastic logic, the vernacular equivalent of the Latin *causa causans* (as opposed to a *causa causata*, literally a 'caused cause', a secondary or subsequent cause). Criseyde identifies Pandarus as the ultimate author of the affair, an attribution which is in keeping with our readerly sense of his indispensable involvement in the bringing together of the lovers.

Because Pandarus was the person who first brought her into the service of **the God of Love**, she does not now know whether to welcome him or not. She asks herself and him whether love does indeed end in misery and immediately answers her own question. Love ends in sorrow as do all types of worldly happiness (as she herself predicted in her earlier monologue on false **felicity**, III.813–36). Whoever does not believe this proverbial wisdom should look to her for proof. She describes herself as demonstrating every aspect of sorrow simultaneously, compiling a lengthy list of near-synonyms for the physical and emotional effects of grief (841–5). Pandarus does not indulge Criseyde's sorrow but instead demands that she regain her composure. He commands her to put aside such grief and to listen to his message from Troilus. The mention of her lover prompts new sorrow from Criseyde. She asks despairingly what Troilus has said. The narrative now describes Criseyde's appearance as if we are looking at her ourselves. If you looked at her features, you would see that she resembled a corpse tied to a funeral bier. Her face, which was once a kind of mirror image of Paradise itself, has been entirely changed and now reflects other things (doubtless, life-threatening pain and grief).

All of her happiness, the merrymaking and laughter which were usually witnessed in her demeanour, are entirely gone. Switching to the present tense, the narrating voice says that Criseyde now lies alone, the purple ring which encircles each eye giving an authentic indication of the pain she feels.

Pandarus, though moved to tears by her pitiful appearance, now does his best to convey Troilus's message. Troilus is, Pandarus says, like someone who is preparing himself for certain death. Although he and Troilus have despaired so much that it has nearly killed them both, Pandarus tells Criseyde that he has managed to advise Troilus in such a way that his sorrow has lessened a little. Whilst in the *Filostrato* Pandaro tells Criseida simply that Troilo now wishes to be with her, in Chaucer's version Pandarus tells Criseyde that Troilus wishes to spend the night with her in order to plan some sort of remedy for their predicament. Chaucer ends Pandarus's speech with an additional stanza in which he comments on his own brevity in conveying this message. He tells the message as briefly and plainly as he can because he knows that she is too upset to pay attention to any lengthy preamble (echoing his earlier preamble at II.255–63). He demands an answer and urges her to cease her sorrow before Troilus arrives.

Criseyde's reply demonstrate how the lovers' grief is as reciprocal as their love. Her sorrow is considerable but her own sorrow is doubled by news of Troilus's grief because she loves him even more than he loves himself. She laments that he has such sorrow because of her and wonders that he laments so piteously for her. She says that leaving Troy and Troilus pains her terribly, but it will be even harder to witness Troilus's sorrow. She tells Pandarus to ask Troilus to visit before she dies from sorrow. Pandarus, who suspects and fears that witnessing such extreme sorrow will drive Troilus mad or lead him to kill himself, is certain that he will not allow him to observe the full extent of her sorrow. He thus commands Criseyde to get up from her bed so that Troilus will not find her in tears.

In the *Filostrato*, Pandaro's sole instruction to Criseida is this command to conceal her sorrow from Troilo. Chaucer adds further advice, having Pandarus tell Criseyde that she must prepare herself to comfort Troilus and not increase his sorrow. She must be more a 'cause of flat than egge' (927), that is, she must not wound him further as the edge of a sword-blade might do but heal him just as the flat of the sword was thought to be able to cure a wound created by the edge. He instructs Criseyde that the lovers should spend the night planning how her departure from Troy can be prevented or how she can quickly return to the city if she does indeed leave. She should take the lead because women, he says, are good at thinking quickly. He anticipates that they will find a solution and says that he will help in any way he can. Pandarus's instructions deepen our immersion in the temporal world of the narrative. Although we know the ultimate conclusion of the story, we may nevertheless feel that the lovers have the opportunity to change the course of events. More particularly, his instructions place the initiative in Criseyde's hands. This may seem unfair (in that Criseyde rather than Troilus is encouraged to take control) or it may later lead us to blame her to some degree (because she does not subsequently bring about the solutions she proposes). It may be wise (because Pandarus knows that Troilus will defer to his lady and thus any action must be initiated by Criseyde) or it may be unwise (because Pandarus places responsibility for action with his niece, who, as we will see in the portrait of her in Book v, is noted for her changeability). Thus decided, Criseyde dismisses Pandarus and agrees to do her best to comfort Troilus if she can.

LINES 946 TO 1123: TROILUS IN THE TEMPLE

(i) Lines 946 to 1085: Troilus's monologue

Pandarus now goes in search of Troilus and finds him alone in a temple (a location not specified in Chaucer's source). We are told that Troilus no longer cares about life itself and that he begs the gods to allow him to die very soon because he cannot see any other help that might be had. We, like Pandarus, now eavesdrop on the reasoning that lies behind and stems from Troilus's despair. Troilus's long soliloquy, added by Chaucer to his source, is based closely on the third *prosa* of Book v of ***De consolatione philosophiae*** in which Boethius describes to Lady Philosophy how God's foreknowledge of all of human history appears to preclude humanity's freedom to decide their own fate. Troilus believes that everything which happens occurs 'by necessitee' (958), by some inescapable predetermining of the future course of events. It must therefore always have been his destiny to be doomed to destruction in this way (and hence he despairs because he can do nothing to prevent this course of events). He is certain that the divine insight which results from God's foreknowledge and governance of events must have seen that he would lose Criseyde (something which he here takes to be an unavoidable certainty). This is, he tells himself, because God undoubtedly foresees all things and by divine decree arranges how all things will come to pass in an immutable predetermined order.

Though he thus begins by firmly expressing a belief in the predestination of all human history, Troilus then asks despairingly in whom he should trust when it comes to these matters. There have been many great scholars who have proved predestination to be true by philosophical reasoning, yet others say that logic demands that there is no predestination but rather that each of us retains free choice in all our actions. He now outlines some of the possible arguments in more detail. Some men say that if God foresees everything and it is certain that God cannot be mistaken, then that which Providence (that is, God's foresight and foreknowledge) has foreseen must occur, even if men had sworn to do the contrary. Therefore Troilus concludes that if God has foreknown our future thoughts and actions from eternity (before time itself began) then we cannot have any free choice. There can be no other thoughts or actions except those which Providence has exactly foreseen. If there could be a 'variaunce' (985), some alternative by which Providence could be evaded, then God would not truly possess foreknowledge of future events but rather His foreknowledge would be merely an unreliable opinion and not reliable prescience. It would be a heresy (and hence an unthinkable conclusion) to deduce that God's knowledge is the same as humanity's own uncertain and unreliable understanding of the future.

Troilus now outlines the opposite point of view. Other scholars argue that it is not because Providence has foreseen a future event that it must therefore occur, but rather that because a future event will occur Providence must therefore foreknow it accurately. As Troilus explains, in this second argument *necessite* (that is, what must logically and necessarily be the case) has changed places (the necessity now being that Providence must foreknow accurately and not that future events must inevitably occur). In this alternative argument, it is not the case that those events which are foreseen by God must inevitably occur (and hence humanity retains freedom of will), but it must be the case that all events which occur are indeed foreseen by Him (because God's foreknowledge cannot be incomplete or unreliable).

Troilus next says that in this he speaks as if he were taking the trouble to investigate which is the cause and which is the consequence. He puts forward the two possibilities: either God's prescience is the invariable cause of the inevitability of everything that will occur, or the inevitability of everything that will occur is the invariable cause of God's Providence. Yet he reiterates that at this moment he is not attempting to demonstrate the order of causation. Nevertheless he is certain that it must be the case that events which are foreknown must certainly occur (because God's foreknowledge cannot be incomplete or unreliable), even though it does not seem as a result that God's prescience makes the occurrence of future events inevitable. (Troilus's conclusion is that it is not that God's foreknowledge causes events, but that this foreknowledge *presupposes* certain future events.)

As Boethius does, Troilus now gives a simpler example of the same situation. If a man is sitting over there on a seat, then it must be the case that your opinion that he is sitting is true (because it is not possible, without lying, to say that he is not sitting). The converse is also true: if your opinion about the man is true because he is sitting, then it must be the case that he is sitting (because if he were not sitting the opinion would not be true). There is thus a type of interrelated necessity (that is, what must logically and necessarily be the case) in both statements. In the second statement it must be the case that the man is sitting and in the first statement it must be the case that your opinion is true. The next step is to consider which is the cause and which is the consequence. One could point out that the man does not sit there in order that your opinion that he is sitting be true, but rather, because the man was already sitting there, your opinion is therefore true. Troilus thus concludes that although there is a type of interrelated necessity in both statements, it is the fact of the man sitting there that is the cause of the truth of your opinion.

Having worked through this example, Troilus is confident that he can reason in the same way as regards God's Providence and all the events which will occur in the universe. One can, Troilus reasons, clearly see that all events happen 'by necessite' (1050), by some inescapable predetermining. For though it is true that because an event is going to occur it is therefore inevitably foreseen and not that it occurs *because* it is foreseen (just as it is the man sitting which causes the viewer's opinion to be true and not the opinion which causes the fact of sitting), yet nevertheless it must also be the case either that future occurrences are inevitably foreseen by God or else that events which are foreseen then occur.

This, Troilus is certain, is enough to obliterate any possibility of free will. Yet it is of course heresy to say that the occurrence of temporal events is the cause of God's eternal foreknowledge. Having set aside such obvious errors, Troilus argues that just as when he *knows* that something is, it must be the case that it *is* (because it must exist in order to be known), so when he knows that something is going to occur, it must be the case that it will occur (because it must be going to occur in order to be foreknown). Likewise it must be the case that God's foreknowledge of future events presupposes that they must occur (even if it does not *cause* them and they cannot possibly cause it). Thus Troilus concludes that the occurrence of every event that is foreknown cannot be avoided in any way (and hence that the exchange of Criseyde for Antenor cannot be prevented).

Chaucer here omits the last part of Boethius's argument that God's knowledge cannot be uncertain and therefore all human thoughts and actions must occur in a single, predetermined manner. From this, Boethius extrapolates despairingly that vice and virtue must cease to exist because men's actions are not their own but those of predestination. Moreover, hope and prayer must have no meaning because everything is already determined and so humanity is isolated from God without means of communication with Him. Troilus, by contrast, concludes that if humanity cannot change the course of events then the only solution is to plead for divine intervention. He thus ends his soliloquy by begging Jove to have pity on him, or alternatively to end his life quickly, or to save him and Criseyde from this suffering. In ***De consolatione philosophiae***, Boethius's argument for determinism is immediately countered by Lady Philosophy's proofs that God's foresight does not in fact obliterate human free will because God sees all events simultaneously in an eternal present without causing or presupposing events (see Book v, *prosae* 4, 5 and 6). Troilus's argument receives no such rejoinder, and instead the narrative next describes how Pandarus enters the temple in search of his friend. Troilus thus has not Lady Philosophy (who personifies Boethius's own philosophical learning and insight) but Pandarus to offer advice.

Chaucer's addition of this monologue on predestination challenges us to think about causality, both fictional and actual. How do individual action and choice interact with the workings of Fate, **Fortune** and chance, the means by which God's eternal view of all things simultaneously is put into operation as a series of events in time? Why do the story's key events – the love of Troilus and Criseyde, the exchange of Criseyde for Antenor, Criseyde's betrayal of Troilus – occur? In comparison with their Boethian origin, Troilus's conclusions about causality are limited and incomplete because he does not have access to the insight offered by Lady Philosophy. Does this reveal inadequacies in Troilus's own character, learning and understanding or does the inadequacy lie within the pagan world-view of this story's Trojan setting? Yet, given that what we are reading is a historical fiction in which characters refer both to classical deities and to a monotheistic God, and are given some but not all of the dialogue between Boethius and Lady Philosophy, on what grounds should we judge their insights (or lack of them)?

Moreover, do characters in this narrative have free will to act or are events predetermined as Troilus argues? According to Lady Philosophy, God's foresight does not negate human free will and therefore we might conclude that Troilus could have acted to avert the proposed exchange (and hence his future betrayal, though this part of his future remains as yet unknown to Troilus). Yet, given that Chaucer is composing a poem whose plot is already fixed by prior versions, events are in some senses predetermined and cannot be escaped (even if within the temporal world of the narrative there are many moments at which free will is exercised and choices are made).

Boethius's *De consolatione philosophiae*

De consolatione philosophiae ('the consolation of philosophy') was written by the late Roman scholar, author, translator and royal and public servant Anicius Manlius Severinus Boethius (*c.* 480–524). Boethius translated and wrote commentaries upon works by Aristotle and Cicero, as well as writing his own treatises on logic, on theology and on the liberal arts. In the service of King Theodoric the Ostrogoth, Boethius was arrested and imprisoned on charges of treason. It was during this period of imprisonment, as he awaited his eventual execution, that Boethius wrote *De consolatione philosophiae*. The work takes the form of a dialogue between the prisoner Boethius and the allegorical personification Lady Philosophy who visits him in prison. Divided into five books, each book alternates passages of prose (each labelled as a *prosa*) and sections of verse (each labelled as a *metrum*). The fictional Boethius represents a version of his self blinded by self-pity and despair, having forgotten the consolations which philosophy's wisdom can offer during his great misfortune. Lady Philosophy represents the insights learned during his education and studies which are now temporarily obscured by his own preoccupations. With Philosophy's help, Boethius is shown and hence relearns both the true nature of **Fortune** and that true happiness cannot be found in worldly success or pleasure. By dialogue, question and exposition, Philosophy helps Boethius relearn that evildoers (such as those whom he feels have wrongly brought about his downfall) are not, as he temporarily believes, powerful and unpunished, but are in fact ultimately powerless in a universe which God guides and controls benevolently. Four verse sections describe the way in which **the holy bond of things**, the sacred bond of God's love, orders the universe and keeps it in harmony. Finally, following Boethius's complaint that what he has experienced and witnessed leads him to believe that human affairs are chaotic and haphazard, Lady Philosophy explains how God's Providence, His benevolent plan for all of human history, is unfolded in time as Fate. God's Providence, despite Boethius's argument to the contrary, does not obliterate human free will (and hence render meaningless good and evil, hope and prayer). Boethius is thus urged to remain hopeful and prayerful, to strive to be virtuous and to trust that God will ultimately reward his piety.

Chaucer had translated the Latin text of the *De consolatione* into English prose in his *Boece* ('Boethius') shortly before beginning *Troilus and Criseyde*. Boethius's *Consolatione* is thus a major influence on *Troilus and Criseyde*, not only in the form of direct borrowing and allusion but also in supplying imagery, mythological allusion, and the roles of complainant and consoler, amongst other things. There is a full list of potential points of connection between the two works in B. A. Windeatt's *'Troilus and Criseyde': Oxford Guides to Chaucer*, pp. 99–100. Such borrowings invite us to compare the fictional Boethius's complaints and questions and Lady Philosophy's explanations and assurances as they appear in the *De consolatione* with the uses to which they are put *in situ* in *Troilus and Criseyde*. The Boethian borrowings placed by Chaucer in his characters' mouths are often tellingly partial or applied to a different context or purpose, reminding readers who know *De consolatione* of what is missing or redirected and prompting judgements about each character's wisdom and insight. Yet as well as evaluating Chaucer's characters in terms of the quality and completeness of their Boethian insights, we should also remain aware of differences of genre and circumstance. Both Criseyde and Pandarus quote Lady Philosophy's explanation of the fragile and imperfect nature of worldly **felicity** accurately enough, yet once the lovers are united in happiness such cautions are forgotten. The true nature of **Fortune** is remembered and forgotten within the poem. Characters fall short of Philosophy's full insights, but Chaucer's text is not an internal dialogue in which reason and learning lead a mind from despair to enlightenment. It is a set of events unfolding in time, in which characters both reason and feel. As their circumstances change, Chaucer's characters grapple with theory *and* actuality, idealizing, extemporizing and despairing rather than questioning, explaining and understanding.

(ii) Lines 1086 to 1123: Pandarus's counsel

Pandarus seems to have overheard at least some part of Troilus's monologue, as his own response begins with a derisive appeal to God enthroned which echoes Troilus's appeal to Jove. With a series of exasperated questions, Pandarus expresses his amazement at (yet offers no answers to) Troilus's philosophical speculations. He asks whether a wise man ever behaved in this way (prompting us perhaps to consider the ways in which Troilus's arguments are not wise). Pandarus reminds Troilus that Criseyde has not yet left the city. He asks why Troilus so destroys himself with anxiety that his eyes seem dead in his skull. Trying to reason with him, Pandarus now asks Troilus whether it isn't the case that he lived comfortably for many years without Criseyde. Was he only born in order to serve her? Has Nature created him simply for the purpose of pleasing Criseyde? Pandarus advises him to console himself with the thought that when in love happinesses come and go as randomly as the throws of a dice.

Pandarus is most amazed that Troilus laments his fate in this way when it is not yet certain how or when Criseyde will leave. Given that he has not yet found out what she thinks about the proposed exchange, he cannot know whether she will be able to prevent her departure. Pandarus tells Troilus that he has discussed matters with Criseyde and that he senses that she, in her most secret thoughts, has a plan to delay her departure. We readers know that this is not entirely accurate, as it is Pandarus himself who has instructed Criseyde to take the initiative. In the equivalent passage in the *Filostrato*, Pandaro presents the forthcoming meeting as an opportunity for *both* of the lovers to find a solution.

Pandarus concludes by advising Troilus to visit Criseyde that night. In an addition to the *Filostrato*, Pandarus prays that the goddess Juno will through her great power send them grace. Pandarus is optimistic that the lovers can change their fates, saying that he feels in his heart that Criseyde will not leave the city. In contrast to Troilus's assumption that he cannot change what he assumes has been foreseen by God, to Pandarus other possibilities remain open.

LINES 1124 TO 1701: THE LOVERS' MEETING

(i) Lines 1124 to 1246: Criseyde's swoon

In secret, Troilus now visits Criseyde. Their mutual sorrow is so immense that at first they cannot exchange greetings but simply embrace and kiss. We are told that even the less sorrowful of the two was insensible and could not speak for misery and weeping (implying of course that the more sorrowful was in a yet worse state, and making us wonder whose emotion was greater). Their tears, which because they are caused by such pain are said to be entirely unlike normal tears, are as bitter as gall or as the purgative drug produced from the aloe plant. The narrating voice comments that even Myrrha did not weep such bitter tears through the bark of the tree into which she was transmuted. (Myrrha, in order to escape her father's rage on discovering that his daughter had tricked him into incest, was metamorphosed by the gods into a myrrh tree. Myrrh trees exude an aromatic resin, imagined in this myth to be Myrrha's tears.)

For both Boccaccio and Chaucer, extreme grief is imagined to drive out the lovers' spirits (both their immortal souls and the physiological spirits which were thought to link the soul to the body) temporarily from their hearts. Criseyde is only able to speak once their spirits have returned to their bodies and once, through the length of time they have already spent lamenting their sorrow, the flowing of their tears begins to decrease and their hearts are less swollen with emotion. Yet she is only able to announce that she is at that very moment dying from sorrow, appealing to Jove for mercy and to Troilus for assistance. This appeal is much more dramatic than the equivalent speech in the *Filostrato*, where Criseida asks Troilo despairingly about the forthcoming exchange. Criseyde's voice trembles with emotion and is hoarse from shrieking in grief. Laying her face upon his chest, she loses the ability to speak. As she says those words, we are told that her soul is again at the point of being driven out of its usual home.

Criseyde now faints, her complexion pale and sallow. Troilus tries to revive her, calling out her name. She is insensible, not breathing and cold to the touch, looking and feeling as if she has died. All of these events create a convincing collection of signs that Criseyde is dead. Troilus exclaims in grief and distress, and makes a long lament. Finally, we are told that he says what should be said on such an occasion. (This unspecific formulation allows Chaucer to evade presenting what exactly Troilus did say, giving neither a re-creation of a pagan rite nor a contemporary Christian prayer for the dead.) Nevertheless, Troilus prays for Criseyde's soul and asks God for pity on his own soul because he intends to follow her in death. He wipes away his salty tears which have rained down on her breast and arranges her limbs as if she is a corpse lying on a funeral bier.

Convinced that Criseyde has died, Troilus now unsheathes his sword. He intends to take his own life so that his soul can follow Criseyde's to wherever the judgement of Minos, judge of the dead in the classical underworld, decides that his soul should reside (thus evading yet also raising the question of whether Troilus would be posthumously punished for his suicide). He will kill himself because it seems to him as if **the God of Love** and **Fortune** do not wish him to remain in this world (presumably because they allow such events to occur which would drive a lover to death). Troilus denounces both hostile **Fortune** and cruel Jove, whom he now sees as his antagonists. He asserts that they have wrongfully killed Criseyde but says that he will not allow them to defeat him in this cowardly way by separating him from his lady. (Ironically of course it is his own suicide which would in fact separate him from Criseyde in death.) Since (as he thinks) his lady is already dead, nothing can prevent him from leaving this world and following her soul (though Chaucer does not translate Troilo's speculative reference to loving Criseida in the underworld, *Fil.* IV.123). He promises that no future lover will be able to say that Troilus was too scared to join his lady in death. Since **Fortune** and Jove will not allow them to be together in life, he asks that their souls be allowed to be together posthumously.

Troilus now makes his farewells to the city of Troy and to his family (showing how his love for Criseyde has superseded these loyalties). He begs that Atropos, the third of the three Fates (see p. 85) who cuts the thread of life, make his own funeral bier ready. He tells Criseyde to prepare her soul to welcome his own spirit and places the point of his sword against his heart, ready to die. At that very moment, Criseyde comes to her senses, sighing and calling out Troilus's name. Chaucer adds to his source both the narrating voice's idiomatic reference to Criseyde's timely awakening occurring 'as God wolde' (1212), as God would have it, and Criseyde's later reference to it occurring 'as grace was' (1233). Troilus's suicide is thus prevented by God's Providence, the divine foreknowledge which allows benevolent and protective intervention in human affairs. Troilus lowers his sword and asks Criseyde in wonderment if she is indeed still alive. Her soul, which has been hovering above her between death and life, between departure and return, now returns to her heart. After a time, she notices Troilus's unsheathed sword on the floor. In distress, she asks why he has drawn his sword and Troilus thus explains his narrowly averted plan to commit suicide. Criseyde responds with shock, gazing at him and embracing him tightly. She says that if she had come to her senses after Troilus had killed himself, she would not have remained alive for the amount of time it would take to walk a furlong, one-eighth of a mile. She would have killed herself with Troilus's sword even if she had had the chance to be crowned queen of all the land on which the sun shines brightly (that is, to be queen of the whole world). Criseyde now quickly changes the subject to avoid too much contemplation of the potential tragedy of their double suicide. She urges that they should now go to her bedchamber to discuss their shared sorrow further. Looking at how far the wick of the lamp has burned down, she urges haste, telling Troilus that it is not far from dawn.

(ii) Lines 1247 to 1421: Criseyde's heap of ways

With Troilus and Criseyde now abed, the narrative first contrasts their sorrowful embraces with previous joyful nights spent together. As she has been encouraged to do by Pandarus, Criseyde then takes the initiative. Since they have met in order to find a solution, it is high time they begin to do so. Criseyde describes her proposals as the type of womanly quick thinking which Pandarus had earlier advised. Criseyde tells Troilus that their grief is unreasonable because, between the two of them, they have enough ingenuity to put right what is currently wrong and to end their distress. Their sorrow stems from nothing more than the fact that they must be apart from each other for a period of time. It therefore seems straightforward to Criseyde that they must therefore merely find a way to meet again after their separation. She is entirely confident that she can soon find a means to return to the city within a week or two. She promises to show Troilus a whole heap of different routes by which her return can undoubtedly be brought about. Criseyde sounds confident, but her vagueness and hyperbole make us suspicious. Sounding rather like Pandarus, she promises not to make a long speech but to omit her reasoning and instead present her final conclusion about what is best. Although she has clearly taken charge, she begs forgiveness from Troilus if she says anything which might disturb his peace of mind. Again rather like Pandarus, Criseyde takes the initiative whilst deferentially submitting to Troilus's authority. Here, as elsewhere, Chaucer exposes the complexities of identities, relationships and authority in this story: man and woman, knight and lady, prince and subject, agent and patient, advisor and recipient of advice.

Criseyde now reminds Troilus that her departure from Troy has been ratified by the Trojan parliament so conclusively that the agreement cannot be overturned for any reason. Since thinking about her departure will not prevent it, they should stop speculating about ways to prevent her leaving and instead try to find a better way to proceed. She acknowledges that a separation will be painful for them, but consoles Troilus with the thought that a servant of **the God of Love** must necessarily suffer periodically if he or she wishes to achieve happiness. Moreover, she will not travel a great distance from him but will only ride a little way out of the city to the Greek camp. Because there is now a truce between the Greek and Trojan armies (and hence all sorts of commercial and diplomatic interactions between the citizens and their besiegers), Criseyde tells Troilus that she will not be so hidden from him that he will not hear news about her welfare. And when the truce has ended, she says confidently, she will be here, having returned to Troy. Then Troilus will have regained both Antenor, his fellow soldier for whom she has been exchanged, and his lady. Criseyde thus encourages Troilus to be happy. When the time comes, he should accept that she has departed but be undaunted by this because she will soon return. Criseyde asks and answers her own question about the length of her absence. In a sequence of too confident-sounding exclamations (1319–20), she says she will undoubtedly return before ten days have elapsed. Once she has returned, they will be for the first time truly happy because they will remain together forever. They will be so happy that the combined expressive power of the whole world could not convey their happiness. She points out that even whilst she remains in Troy, they often go a fortnight without speaking to each other or without her seeing him ride by her window because they conceal their private matters, their love affair, from public knowledge. Shouldn't he therefore be able to do without her for ten days?

Criseyde now begins to list some of the heap of reasons which supposedly makes her return inevitable. She reminds him that, except for her father Calchas, her entire family and all her possessions are in Troy. Most importantly, Troilus himself, he whom she could never stop seeing for anything, will remain in Troy. Next she asks Troilus to consider why Calchas so desires to be reunited with his daughter. It must be, she says, because he fears that the Trojan citizens despise her for his betrayal. If he knew how she prospered in Troy, the lovers would have little reason to worry about her departure (presumably because once told about her good fortune, Calchas would allow her to return to the city). Furthermore, Criseyde reminds Troilus that peace between the Greeks and Trojans is thought to be increasingly likely. It is believed that Queen Helen will be returned (to Menelaus, her Greek husband) and the Greeks will offer the Trojans some kind of compensation (another potential example of the quasi-commercial exchange of women by men). Even if there were no other means to assuage Troilus's fears than this, the fact that peace is being proposed by everyone should, she thinks, make him wait for her return less anxiously.

Criseyde now argues that her return is inevitable whether or not a final peace is negotiated between the Greeks and Trojans. If peace is agreed, then there will be many dealings between the citizens and the besiegers, and people will go back and forth between the Greek camp and the city as frequently as bees fly to and from a beehive. Everyone will have permission to remain wherever he prefers, so presumably either Criseyde can return to the city or Troilus can visit her in the Greek camp. If peace is not agreed, then Criseyde nevertheless feels she will still return because it is inconceivable to her that she should go elsewhere with her father or live in constant fear in an army camp for any length of time. Criseyde's discussion of the likelihood of a peace treaty shows that she is as oblivious to the eventual fall of Troy as she is to her own future betrayal of Troilus. Our readerly foreknowledge of these outcomes makes her reasoning seem hollow and unconvincing even if it is meant entirely sincerely.

Finally, Criseyde offers Troilus yet another reason if he has not been persuaded by the ones she has already put forward. In the *Filostrato*, Criseida simply says that she will remind Calchas that he has property in the city which requires his management. She will persuade her father, who is elderly and avaricious, to allow her to return to Troy to act as his agent in order to guarantee the safety of his properties in any event. In contrast, Chaucer has Criseyde plan not to exploit current reality as Criseida does but instead, like Pandarus, fabricate an alternative reality with an elaborate lie. As Criseida does, Criseyde reminds Troilus that her father is old and that old age is traditionally a time of covetousness. In light of this, she claims to have devised a way in which she can catch him without using a net (meaning that she can entrap him through his own weakness and without being observed). Criseyde plans to take her personal possessions to her father and to tell him that these items have been sent to him by one or two of his friends. These friends will (according to the story Criseyde will tell him) beg Calchas quickly to send for more of their possessions, supposedly in order to guarantee the safety of their belongings while the city is under attack. Criseyde will tell her father that there is a large amount of property which might be sent to him, but that only she can arrange its delivery. (The implication here is that, tempted by the thought of acquiring such a quantity of valuable goods, Calchas will allow Criseyde to travel back to Troy.)

Criseyde next says that she will also explain to her father how many influential friends she has in every faction of Priam's court. She will offer to use her influence to persuade Priam to forgive Calchas for his defection and to restore him to favour. Summing up her reasoning, Criseyde now tells Troilus that she will so beguile her father that he will dream his soul is in heaven (presumably because he is so cheered and enticed by thoughts of wealth and renewed favour). Chaucer now adds to his source Criseyde's confident explanation of how she will beguile her father despite his scholarship and prophetic abilities. She predicts triumphantly that Apollo (the god who spoke to Calchas through the oracle at Delphi), Calchas's clerical learning and his ability to divine the future will all be worthless in the face of her persuasions. His avaricious desire for gold will so blind his soul (here meaning his intellect and his capacity for foresight) that she will be able to create the result the lovers want. If Calchas decides to try to test whether she is lying by casting lots, Criseyde says that she will impede him, making him believe that he hasn't understood his divine sources correctly. She will remind him that the gods often speak in ambiguities (that is, their oracles are often open to more than one interpretation) and that they tell twenty lies for each truth they offer. She will remind him of the proverb that 'fear first invented the gods' (which implies that men only believe in gods at times of great need when they are fearfully in search of assistance and hence less likely to be sceptical). She will suggest that his own cowardice made him interpret Apollo's prophecy incorrectly when he hurried away from Delphi in fear (because of his prediction that Troy would fall). Criseyde ends by saying that unless she makes her father change his mind and follow her advice within a day or two, she promises Troilus that she will die instead. Throughout this speech, Criseyde sounds increasingly like her uncle Pandarus, employing a welter of words to manipulate, persuade, guarantee and deceive, confident that she can shape the future yet arousing our suspicions about her methods and motives.

The narrating first-person here interjects to reassure his readers that he finds in his source that everything Criseyde said here was said with a good **intention** and that her heart was faithful and kind towards Troilus. He says that she said exactly what she meant to say, that she nearly died of grief when she left Troy and that she intended to remain faithful forever. This, he claims, is what those previous authors who fully understood Criseyde's actions have written (though this stanza has no equivalent in Chaucer's unacknowledged source). Though it notionally reassures us about the authenticity of her words, **intention** and emotions, such reassurances in fact crystallize our unease about Criseyde's sincerity. Her Pandarus-like persuasion of Troilus, her lack of foresight and her overconfident dismissal of her father's predictive abilities make these plans ring hollow. Moreover, her willingness to lie to her father, in combination with our knowledge of her eventual betrayal, makes her promises harder to believe. All of this might make us wonder whether Criseyde, like the gods, is here speaking in ambiguities and telling twenty lies (or at least twenty well-meant but questionable hopes) for each piece of truth.

(iii) Lines 1422 to 1526: Troilus's doubts and counter-suggestions

It seems to Troilus that he agrees with Criseyde's way of thinking. Yet his heart (the seat of his true feelings) causes him to have misgivings (just as we readers might already have). Despite these doubts, however, he forces himself to put his faith in Criseyde and to accept her plan willingly. The hope of her swift return abates his immense torment and Troilus and Criseyde now make love. Just as birds delight in singing in spring sunshine, so we are told that the lovers' words now delight them and make their hearts serene. Yet despite this brief moment of happiness, Troilus cannot stop thinking about Criseyde's impending departure. He frequently pleads with her to reassure him that he will find her true to her promise to return after ten days. He warns her that if she is 'unkynde' (1440, that is, if she proves untrue to him or indifferent to his devotion) and unless she returns to Troy on the day she has specified, he will never again prosper. Troilus assures her that just as the sun inevitably rises in the morning and just as surely as he hopes God will eventually end his suffering, so he will without doubt kill himself if she delays her return. Although he self-effacingly says that his death would be insignificant, he begs her to decide to remain in Troy.

Troilus now explains his doubts about Criseyde's plans because he thinks all of them are very likely to fail in some way. He reminds Criseyde that it is said that the bear thinks one thing but its keeper thinks quite another. (By this he implies that whatever she might wish, her father will, like a bear's trainer, ultimately control her actions.) Calchas, Troilus argues, is shrewd and ingenious. Although Calchas has been separated from his property, he has not lost his former cunning and so Troilus predicts that Criseyde will not be able deceive him with any of her womanly wiles. Chaucer here adds to his source Troilus's assessment of Criseyde's plans and Calchas's own guile, an assessment which further undermines Criseyde's earlier confidence in her ability to deceive her father.

Troilus now observes that he does not know whether peace will be made between the Greeks and Trojans. Yet he is certain that whatever occurs, Calchas will be too ashamed to return to Troy because he has ruined his reputation in such a shameful and treacherous manner. To imagine that

Calchas might want to return to Troy is nothing but a fantasy. Given his desire to remain in the Greek camp, Calchas will therefore cajole her into marrying one of the Greek nobles whom he will praise and commend, either overwhelming her with his persuasive words or compelling her to marry by physical force. Referring to himself in the third person, Troilus says mournfully that he himself, to whom she will thus have shown no pity (by marrying another), will therefore die unjustly, faithful in his love for her but unjustly betrayed. Troilus also fears that Calchas will disparage all of the Trojans and say that the city is about to be lost. Because of the Greeks' unity and resolve, the siege will never be lifted until the city walls are destroyed and all of the Trojans are killed. Calchas will thus frighten Criseyde into remaining permanently in the Greek camp. In an addition to Chaucer's source, Troilus also jealously fears that Criseyde will encounter so many fine knights in the Greek camp, each of whom will do his best to please her, that she will become tired of what he calls the vulgarity of us simple Trojans. All of these doubts are so painful for Troilus to think about that he feels it will tear his soul from his breast. He cannot remain hopeful of her return if she does indeed depart because he is certain that Calchas's cunning will destroy the lovers' relationship. If she leaves, she should consider him as good as dead (because he feels that either his fears or her failure to return will kill him). From our position of readerly foreknowledge, we are painfully aware that Calchas's predictions and Troilus's intuitive misgivings will both prove correct and, just as Troy will indeed be destroyed, so Criseyde will indeed switch her affections to one of the Greek knights.

Although Troilus earlier rejected Pandarus's proposal that he should abduct Criseyde forcibly, he now fears her departure so greatly that he begs her to leave Troy secretly with him. They should think that it is madness, when one has a choice, to lose what is essential for what is more trivial or unimportant. (By this he implies that they should not jeopardize what to him is an essential reality, their being together, for less fundamental concerns.) Criseyde has thus become everything to Troilus, more important than his loyalty to his family and fellow citizens, Criseyde's honour or his own reputation. Troilus here (1505) uses two terms from elementary metaphysics (*substaunce* being an object's essential, permanent nature and *accident* being a non-essential attribute or quality), but then goes on to pun on other senses of these words, namely 'wealth' (as in the phrase 'a man of substance') and 'a random or unpredictable occurrence'. Since they can easily leave Troy in secret before dawn and therefore remain together, he asks why they should opt for a more uncertain choice, to put to the test whether or not Criseyde will be able to return to Troy once she joins Calchas in the Greek camp. Troilus thinks that it would be madness to put in jeopardy the certainty of a life together if they elope by going along with the exchange whose outcome cannot be known. Explaining his own pun, he says that if he now talks about *substaunce* in its usual, everyday meaning, they have enough wealth to live in pleasure and honour for the rest of their days. Troilus says that in his heart he cannot consent to any other plan which Criseyde might devise. Troilus reassures Criseyde that if they do elope in secret, she should not fear a life of poverty. He urges Criseyde to leave with him as soon as possible because, if this plan meets with her approval, in his opinion this course of action is best. Despite his earlier fatalism, Troilus is here prompted by the doubtfulness of Criseyde's plans to propose a means by which they can elude the forthcoming exchange.

(iv) Lines 1527 to 1596: Criseyde's certainty and her objections

Criseyde is not persuaded by Troilus's counter-suggestion. They could indeed, she says with a sigh, leave in secret and follow such unprofitable courses as the one he suggests which they would later regret very deeply (a choice of words which makes clear her reluctance though not her reasoning). She tells Troilus that he is worrying about the future unnecessarily. To Criseyde at this moment, it is inconceivable that she will not return to Troy as she has promised. In order to prove her sincerity, she invokes terrible curses upon herself if she breaks her pledge. She invites Saturn's daughter, the goddess Juno, to condemn her to live forever in madness like King Athamas (here *Athamante*) in Styx (a place that Criseyde calls the pit of hell though Styx is in fact one of the rivers in the classical underworld) if she were to betray Troilus in order to marry another. (King Athamas was driven mad by the Fury Tisiphone on behalf of Juno who was angered by Athamas and his wife Ino.) Criseyde next swears on a host of mythological figures both major and minor, a much more extravagant promise than the equivalent passage in the *Filostrato*, where Criseida simply swears on **the God of Love**'s arrows. Criseyde entreats Atropos, the third of the three Fates (see p. 85), who cuts the thread of life, to kill her if this promise proves false. She also invites the River Simoeis, which she says runs like a bright arrow through the city of Troy to the sea, to bear witness to her pledge. If she were to betray Troilus, the river should flow backwards to its source and she herself should sink alive into the underworld. Given that we know that she will indeed betray Troilus, these hyperbolic promises and *impossibilia* (see p. 103) cannot but seem hollowly overconfident and foolish in their extremity.

Having once again promised faithfulness, Criseyde now explains her objections to Troilus's plan to leave in secret. God forbid, she says, that anyone should abandon their friends for a woman in this manner, especially when the city is in such a perilous position. She points out that if their elopement were discovered, her life and his honour would be in danger. If peace between the Greeks and Trojans were established, she exclaims at the sorrow she predicts Troilus would feel because he would dare not return to his home (because of the shame of having abandoned it during a time of need). She warns him not to act hastily and not to put his good name at risk. She asks him what he thinks the citizens of Troy would say about an elopement. To Criseyde the answer to this question is obvious: they would be certain that it was not love which caused him to leave Troy but sensual desire and cowardice. Troilus would thus lose his honour and Criseyde would likewise lose her honest reputation once their elopement caused their relationship to become public knowledge (this echoing her concern for honour and reputation in Books II and III). She says that if she lived forever she would never again regain her good reputation (an ironic conclusion given that the course of action she follows will lead to her notoriety as a betrayer). Chaucer here omits the more worldly-wise argument made by Criseida in the *Filostrato* that familiarity breeds contempt. It is, Criseida says, the illicitness of their relationship which so pleases Troilo and so, if they left Troy and lived together openly, their passion would soon be extinguished.

Criseyde concludes by instructing Troilus to erase with rational thought this impetuous plan to leave Troy. She tells him to make 'vertu of necessite' (1586), to submit to an unalterable situation with good grace. She tells him that the man who does not care about **Fortune** is always **Fortune**'s superior and hence **Fortune** can frighten only those who are too wretched to be indifferent. There are of course ironies in Criseyde's stoical response. By considering this situation to be unalterable and by refusing any alternative plan, Criseyde, though she does not yet know it, in fact begins to create the circumstances of her future betrayal.

Once again, Criseyde promises that she will see Troilus again after ten days in the Greek camp, before Lucina, the moon, has passed out of the zodiacal sign of Aries, through Taurus, Gemini and Cancer, and beyond out of the sign of Leo. The moon completes its circuit through the twelve signs of the zodiac every twenty-eight days, so it will pass through four signs in approximately ten days.

(v) Lines 1597 to 1701: Criseyde's pledges

In the face of Criseyde's promises Troilus initially agrees to wait patiently for ten days since she has persuaded him that her plan to leave and return is the path they must follow. But he still cannot suppress his own misgivings about this plan and once again begs her to leave Troy secretly with him. No matter how vehement her promise to return, his heart tells him that eloping in order to live together in peace is the best course of action. Criseyde, however, reacts to his renewed request with distress and indignation. She demands for the love of Cynthia (another name for the goddess of the moon) that he does not doubt her without good reason since she has already given him her word that she will remain faithful. Swearing on this goddess, emblematic of change because of the moon's changing phases, here reminds us ominously of Criseyde's forthcoming change of heart. He should drive out such deluded notions from his mind, forget his sorrow and trust her. If he does not do this she promises that she will not survive another day. If he really understood how painful his doubts are to her, she tells him, he would stop mistrusting her. If it were not for the fact that she is confident she knows a solution which will allow her to return, she claims, she would die here and now. She tells him that she is not so foolish that she can't imagine a way to return to him as she has promised. Quoting another proverb, she asks who can keep hold of something that wishes to get away (a question which ironically anticipates Troilus's loss of his lady). Answering herself in terms of her own situation, she says that her father will not be able to keep her away from Troilus for all his ingenious tricks. Before she leaves, she begs him to show her that he is comforted and cheered by her promises. This will set her heart, which is currently at breaking point, at peace.

Moreover, Criseyde begs Troilus that, since she has pledged herself entirely to him, he likewise will not allow the pleasure of anyone else's company to cause him to forget her while she is absent from Troy. She is continually fearful, inasmuch as it is said that love is a state in which anxious fear is constantly present. If she thought otherwise (i.e., that Troilus was not the epitome of loyalty) she would do nothing other than die on the spot. She begs him for the sake of God's love not to be unfaithful or treat her indifferently unless he finds a reason to act in this way. In the light of our readerly foreknowledge, this comment inevitably and ironically reminds us that Criseyde will indeed eventually give Troilus plentiful cause to reject her.

In the *Filostrato*, Troilo here goes on to explain why he could not possibly betray Criseida, describing how he did not fall in love with her because of more superficial qualities such as her beauty, good breeding, grace or wealth but because of her innate nobility. In Chaucer's version, Troilus instead replies by asking God, who understands the cause of every human action, to grant him happiness because he is certain that he has never betrayed and will never betray Criseyde. He tells her that she should have faith in this brief promise because he cannot say any more. His loyalty to her will be proved by his actions. Criseyde thanks him for his promise and prays to Venus, goddess of love, not to let her die before she is in the fortunate position of being able to reward Troilus for his loyalty. She promises that, for as long as God keeps her in her right senses, she will, because she has indeed found him as loyal as he has claimed to be, continue to act in such a way that honour will always attach itself to her. Chaucer now reworks Troilo's speech (in which he explains why he fell in love with Criseida) for Criseyde who reiterates the source of her love for Troilus. It was not his royal status, nor idle sensuality, nor simply his exploits in war or at tournament, nor the trappings of his nobility which made her take pity on his **lovesickness** and accept him as her knight. It was instead his virtuous thought and conduct, those virtues which derive from his nobility and integrity, as well as his gentility, his manliness and his disdain for anything that was liable to lead to wickedness, for example discourtesy or vulgar urges, and because his reason remained in control of his pleasure-seeking. These are the reasons why she became his lady and intends to remain so for the rest of her life. Speaking the words which Troilo speaks in the *Filostrato*, Criseyde says that her devotion to him cannot be destroyed by the passing of time or be sullied by the effects of fickle **Fortune** (a prediction which will of course be proved false). Whereas Troilo's praise of Criseida seems brutally ironic in the face of her forthcoming betrayal, Criseyde's recognition of Troilus's innate virtue and her promises of constancy are both ironic but also sincerely heartfelt, raising the question of why she forgoes Troilus and what it is that undoes her love for him. Why are promises not kept and why is a good **intention** not always put into effect? How can love and devotion survive the vicissitudes of **Fortune** or of time itself?

Finally, Criseyde begs Jupiter to grant them the favour of meeting again in this same place before ten nights have elapsed, so that both of their hearts are content. She ends by bidding Troilus farewell because she sees (presumably by the approaching light of dawn) that he must soon leave her bedchamber (in order to leave without being detected). Troilus gets dressed and looks sorrowfully at Criseyde like someone who feels the cold pains of death. He bids her farewell formally by recommending himself to her favour. The narrating voice thinks there is no question as to whether Troilus was grief-stricken at this moment. No human mind can imagine, nor any intellect evaluate, nor any tongue narrate the bitter pains of such a sorrowful man, sorrows which surpass every infernal torment. When he accepts that Criseyde cannot remain in Troy, a realization which we are told tore Troilus's soul out of his heart, Troilus leaves the bedchamber without saying or doing anything else.

Book V

LINES 1 TO 87: THE EXCHANGE

As Book v begins, the narrating voice speaks again to the Fates (see p. 85; here named as the angry Parcae), telling them that the lovers' predetermined destiny, governed by Jove and entrusted to the Fates to perform, draws near at hand. Criseyde must soon leave Troy and Troilus must therefore suffer her loss until the Fate Lachesis no longer spins out the thread of his life (Chaucer here gives the task of spinning, usually allocated to Clotho, to Lachesis who usually measures the thread of life). Next, in an addition to Chaucer's source, we are told that the sun had melted the snows of winter and Zephyrus (a name for the warm westerly wind) had heralded the tender spring leaves three times since Troilus fell in love with Criseyde, for whose imminent departure he now grieves. Three springs have therefore passed since Troilus observed Criseyde in the temple in Book I. We see little evidence in the narrative of such a lengthy romance apart from the summaries of time passing given in III.435–511 and 1713–15. Chaucer's addition makes both Troilus's intense sorrow more plausible and Criseyde's betrayal more heartless because of the duration of their love.

We are now told how Diomede (the Greek nobleman to whom Criseyde will transfer her affections) was ready early in the morning to escort her to the Greek camp. Criseyde is so distressed that she feels as if her heart is bleeding. Troilus is equally grief-stricken, waiting in attendance on her like someone who has lost all of his sources of pleasure. Accompanied by some of his servants, Troilus waits for her at the gate where she will leave the city. He conceals his sorrow manfully yet we are told he could hardly remain seated on his horse because of his grief. This torment is conveyed in a sequence of self-reproachful questions. He once more contemplates abducting Criseyde by force, asking why he does not give everyone, rich and poor, enough to do before she leaves (meaning why not occupy them in trying to prevent such an abduction). Why does he not kill Diomede and abduct Criseyde, why does he not remedy his grief himself? The narrating first-person answers these questions for him, telling us that he will not do any of these things in case Criseyde were to be killed in the chaos that might result if he abducted her by force. Troilus's fear of the worst possible outcome prevents him from taking the initiative. Despite this explanation, however, such questions tempt us to conclude, despite the predetermined outcome of this story (of which we are reminded in lines 27–8), that the exchange is not inevitable and that some other future might have been possible.

Once she is ready to ride out from the city, Criseyde accepts the inevitability of her departure, sighing and briefly exclaiming in sorrow. In the *Filostrato*, Criseida gives voice to her feelings, questioning Jove and **Fortune** once more and speaking disdainfully and haughtily to her escort Diomede. It is clear that Criseida is scornful of the Trojans who have bartered her for Antenor and is leaving against her will. In Chaucer's version, Criseyde is more sorrowful but also more passive. Troilus accompanies Criseyde as she rides out of the city. As they approach the Greek army camp, Antenor rides out and is warmly welcomed by the party of Trojans. Despite his private distress, Troilus greets Antenor just as he should. Finally, he bids farewell to Criseyde, and, speaking quietly and privately, he urges her to keep her promise to return by the tenth day and not to kill him by failing to return. Pale with grief, he turns his warhorse around quickly and returns to Troy without speaking to Diomede, Criseyde's escort, or to any of his own retinue.

LINES 88 TO 196: DIOMEDE ESCORTS CRISEYDE

Troilus's abrupt departure is noticed by Diomede, who is described as being as perceptive as someone who knew more than the creed (that is, who knew far more than the basics) of **the art of love**. As he leads her horse away from Troy by the bridle, Diomede plans how he will speak to Criseyde. We are not shown a moment in which Diomede falls in lust or in love with Criseyde. Instead his wish to pursue her appears unwarranted, simply an instance of masculine competitiveness, a wish to win something currently possessed by another man. Diomede tells himself that he will not labour in vain if he engages Criseyde in conversation. At the very least, he thinks, it will pass the time on their journey to the Greek camp. He tells himself that he will achieve nothing if he talks to her straightaway about matters of love or if he is too persistent. If Criseyde is, as Diomede suspects, devoted to Troilus then he will not be able to drive him from her mind very quickly. Nevertheless, he plans to find a way to speak to her so that she will not yet realize his full **intention**. In his premeditated and proverbial inner discourse, Diomede resembles Pandarus and so Criseyde is now in the hands of a second calculating persuader.

Diomede begins with small talk, then asks Criseyde why she is in such distress, offering his service if he can console her in any way. Although the *Filostrato* does not have such a conversation at this point, Chaucer here adapts the account given in Benoît's *Roman de Troie* of Diomedes' immediate declaration of love for Briseida.[1] Diomede swears on his honour as knight that there is nothing he would not do to please her and ease her heart. He begs her to be less distressed, tactfully seeming to interpret her sorrow as anxiety about her prospective welcome in the Greek camp. He acknowledges that it must be a strange experience for her to exchange the familiarity and companionship of Trojans for that of the Greek nation which is new and unknown to her. God forbid, he swears, that amongst them she should not find a Greek who is as true and honourable as any Trojan. Without giving Criseyde a chance to reply, Diomede now argues that because he has already pledged to serve her as a friend and because he, as her escort, knows her better than other strangers in the Greek camp, she should command him as a lady would her knight and treat him with as much familiarity as she would her brother. He claims not to know the cause of her sorrow (though we have already seen him perceive the cause) but says that he wishes to help her as soon as possible.

Diomede here moves quickly from courtesy to friendship, brotherly love and more (a faster-moving echo of the various stages of Pandarus's wooing of Criseyde on Troilus's behalf in Books II and III). He tells Criseyde that although the Greeks and Trojans are at war, they both serve the same **God of Love**. He asks in the name of that god that she should not be angry with him because there is no one else who could serve her who would be half as reluctant to do anything which might deserve her anger. Again without allowing her to respond, he assumes the role of her knight and servant. He commands her to give him her hand and formally pledges to be hers for the rest of his life. He claims never to have made such a pledge to another woman and to be inexperienced in matters of love (a claim already contradicted in lines 88–90). Already calling her his lady, he tells her not to be surprised that he reveals his love to her so quickly because he has heard of many cases in which a person falls

[1] *Chaucer's Boccaccio*, trans. Havely, pp. 172–3.

instantly in love with something he has never seen before. He claims that he cannot struggle against **the God of Love** (though we have not witnessed him being struck by Love's arrows, and so his story seems a paltry echo of Troilus's earlier swift conversion to love). More pragmatically, he points out that there are so many noble knights in the Greek camp and Criseyde is so beautiful that many of them will try to gain her favour. If she would favour him by calling him her servant, no other knight could serve her so faithfully and humbly.

In Benoît's version of this scene in the *Roman de Troie*, Briseida makes a polite but somewhat equivocal reply in which she neither accepts nor fully declines Diomedes' advances and does not admit her love for Troilus.[2] Criseyde by contrast is distracted by grief, hearing only a few words of Diomede's speech and making little answer. Yet the narrative nevertheless describes in summary how she thanks Diomede for his efforts and hospitality, accepts his friendship, agrees to do whatever might please him and agrees to trust him. In Boccaccio's version of this same scene, Criseida is then too overcome with sorrow and thoughts of Troilo to greet her father appropriately. In Chaucer's poem, Calchas greets his daughter warmly and Criseyde manages to respond a little before retreating into herself, silent, obedient and meek. Chaucer's characterization of his heroine is again ambiguous. Criseyde is both distracted by grief and capable of social niceties. We are left to speculate on whether or not she fully understands Diomede's **intention**.

LINES 197 TO 273: TROILUS'S TERRIBLE DREAMS

Troilus returns to his palace feeling unprecedented sorrow, going to his bedchamber with such an angry expression that no one dares speak to him. Once alone, he gives vent to all of the grief which he had earlier suppressed. This solitary expression of sorrow recalls similar scenes in Book 1. Here he curses his gods, his own birth and destiny, Nature and every created thing except Criseyde. Taking to his bed, he tosses and turns in agony. In an addition to Chaucer's source, Troilus is compared to Ixion, a Greek king punished in hell for his crimes by being bound to a perpetually turning fiery wheel. His intense emotion is expressed in a sequence of questions and apostrophes to Criseyde. The source of these last two stanzas of Troilus's speech and the subsequent description of his nightmares is

[2] *Ibid.*, p. 173. Guido's account of Diomedes' love for Briseida describes such equivocation as part of Briseida's womanly wiles, intended to increase his love for her (*Historia destructionis Troiae*, trans. Meek, p. 164).

the conversation between Pandaro and Troilo which follows this scene in the *Filostrato* (v.23–8). Calling her his 'lode-sterre' (232), his guiding star, Troilus asks who sees her at this moment, who is with her and who can now soothe her inner conflicts. Who does she listen to now and who will speak on his behalf when they are apart? Troilus answers this last question by saying that no one will speak for him and that he is certain that Criseyde fares as badly as he now does. With readerly omniscience, we might answer his questions in a different way, suspecting that Diomede is the person who will offer her comfort. Troilus ends his complaint by asking how he can endure ten days of such torment and how Criseyde will bear such suffering.

Whenever Troilus falls asleep, he soon begins to moan and experience terrible nightmares. Such nightmares cause him to wake up suddenly and he then experiences an intense palpitation which makes his entire body tremble with fear. At other times, Troilus tries to reassure himself, telling himself that it is madness to suffer such fear without any real cause. Yet his painful sorrows soon begin once more. The narrating voice concludes by saying that everyone would have pity on Troilus. He asks who might be able to fully express the extent of Troilus's suffering and grief. Answering himself with hyperbole, he declares that not even everyone alive now and in the past could do so collectively. Addressing an individual reader directly (the only occasion in the poem in which a single reader is so identified), the narrating first-person tells him or her they can undoubtedly guess that his mental powers are not able to describe Troilus's sorrow in sufficient detail. He says that he would labour in vain to describe it given that his mind is emotionally drained from trying to imagine it. The narrating voice here uses two versions of the topos of inexpressibility to convey the full intensity of Troilus's sorrow, claiming both that Troilus's suffering is beyond description and that he himself is incapable of adequately describing it.

LINES 274 TO 434: PANDARUS VISITS TROILUS

(i) Lines 274 to 322: Troilus plans his funeral

We are now told of the changes in the night sky as darkness gives way to dawn. Once the sun has arisen, Troilus sends for Pandarus. Pandarus goes straight to his friend when he can because he knows intuitively that Troilus has been awake all night and will wish to tell him about his suffering. Having converted Troilo's half of the dialogue in this scene into Troilus's preceding monologue and the narrative description of his nightmares, Chaucer here adds to his source Troilus's instructions for his own funeral and the disposal of his possessions.

Troilus tells Pandarus that he cannot endure his present sorrow for much longer. He believes he will not survive the night and therefore he wishes to describe the rituals he would want at his burial. As if he is making an oral testament, he instructs Pandarus to dispose of his personal possessions as he thinks best. He begs him to make sure that various aspects of his funeral are done properly. He instructs that his horse, sword and helmet be presented to the war god Mars as a religious offering and that his shield be offered to the goddess Pallas Athena. He instructs Pandarus to collect the ashes of his heart once he has been cremated, and to store them in a golden vessel called an urn. The fact that Chaucer has Troilus gloss this unfamiliar word with a physical description shows how alien these details of a pagan cremation may have been to a fourteenth-century audience. Troilus asks Pandarus to give this urn to Criseyde and ask her to keep it as a memento of his devotion. He is convinced that he will die because of his **lovesickness** and his nightmares, and also because he has heard an owl screech at him for the last two nights (owls were thought to be harbingers of death or misfortune). Troilus concludes by appealing to the god Mercury (in his role as the guide who escorts the souls of the newly dead to the underworld) to guide his soul and to fetch it from his body when he chooses. Although it indicates the strength of his grief and despair, Troilus's meticulous concern for his own funeral may seem premature and melodramatic, indicative of his tendency to accept that future events are inevitable and not open to change. Criseyde has only recently departed and Troilus does not know for certain that she will not return. Yet Troilus's preparations are indeed accurately prescient because, as we readers already know, this story will end in his death.

(ii) Lines 323 to 385: Pandarus's advice

Pandarus tells his friend that it is foolish and to no purpose to grieve as he does. Because Troilus is in such despair, Pandarus says that he is unable to do or say anything to help. If someone will not accept the advice he is given, Pandarus says that he can see no means of relief for him and so he should be left alone with his own delusions. Yet of course Pandarus cannot help but offer his friend advice and try to talk him out of his extreme and perhaps untimely sorrow. He asks him mockingly if he thinks that anyone else has in the past loved as passionately as he loves Criseyde. Of course, says Pandarus, other men have loved in the same way and indeed many worthy knights have been separated from their ladies for any entire fortnight (a comically short period of separation) without making half such a fuss as Troilus here does. He reminds Troilus that friends (and by implication lovers) cannot always be together. Trying to get him to put his own situation in some perspective, Pandarus asks Troilus how those who witness their beloveds marry someone else cope with their grief. Pandarus says that such people endure this with forbearance, wisdom and self-control. Troilus should likewise endure his suffering, remain cheerful and let time pass. Ten days, says Pandarus, is not long to wait. He reassures Troilus that Criseyde will not break her promise and swears on his life that she will find a way to return.

Turning to Troilus's morbid fears, Pandarus urges him to dismiss all his dreams and imaginings. In Pandarus's opinion, Troilus's nightmares are simply the result of his 'malencolie' (360), a depression brought on by his love and grief. Pandarus dismisses the significance of such dreams, saying that they are not worth a straw or a bean, two idiomatic measures of insignificance. Chaucer here adds three more stanzas of dream lore to his source. No one, argues Pandarus, can accurately interpret dreams because there is such disagreement about their origins. Priests in the temple say that dreams are both divine revelations *and* delusions sent by wicked spirits. Doctors say they are caused either by fasting or overindulgence or by physiological and psychological predispositions caused by a predominance of one particular humour in an individual. Other people say that dreams are caused by mental images of whatever the dreamer has been concentrating on when awake. Others say that we dream different things at different times of the year depending on the phases of the moon. Because we cannot be sure, no one can know what they truly signify and hence Troilus should not believe his own dreams. Believing in dreams, says Pandarus, is all right for superstitious old women, as is giving credence to divination based on the cries of particular birds. Fear of supposedly ominous birds leads men to think they will soon die (as Troilus has interpreted the owl's screeching), but Pandarus says that to believe in dreams or augury is erroneous and shameful. He laments that such a superior creature as man might believe 'swich ordure' (385), such crap.

(iii) Lines 386 to 434: Troilus and Pandarus decide to visit Sarpedon

Pandarus now begs Troilus to rise up from his bed and join him in thinking how they can most profitably spend this period of time while they wait for Criseyde. In order to cheer his friend, he encourages him both to reminisce about earlier happy times and to anticipate how happy they will be when she returns, which he is certain will be soon. Pandarus urges that they should remember the enjoyable and happy existence which they have previously enjoyed in Troy and make plans to enjoy themselves with some merry company. As Pandarus points out, the truce arranged by King Priam is still in force and so they are free to visit King Sarpedon, one of the many noblemen currently in residence in the city. He instructs Troilus to get out of bed, warning him that it is shameful to weep and to hide himself away like a bird roosting at night. If he remains in bed for several days, people will say that he is pretending to be sick because of cowardice (intending thus to avoid fighting the Greeks when the truce is lifted).

Troilus replies by justifying his despair. No one who has not felt such pain can understand his grief. Nevertheless he accedes to Pandarus's requests. Troilus prays that God make the tenth day since Criseyde's departure arrive quickly because, he says, there was never a bird so happy to see the arrival of May as he will be when he sees Criseyde return (in medieval folklore birds were thought to choose their mates on the first of May). Seeming not to have heard Pandarus's earlier suggestion, Troilus now asks where he suggests that they can enjoy themselves most in Troy. Pandarus suggests once more that they visit Sarpedon, one of Troy's allies and king of Lycia, one of the Anatolian kingdoms.

LINES 435 TO 511: THE VISIT TO SARPEDON

We are now told of King Sarpedon's unrivalled household and hospitality. The narrating voice reports the opinion of everyone, great and small, that such splendour had never before been seen at any feast. There is not in the known world any wood or string instrument which was not heard harmonizing with the other instruments at the feast. Likewise, no one had ever before seen such a beautiful company of ladies dancing. The superlative nature of these festivities, however, does not cheer and console Troilus but instead exacerbates his distress. He cannot enjoy the hospitality because his heart always longs for Criseyde. Because she is absent, looking at the other noble ladies present at this feast is not a delight but a sorrow. Similarly, Troilus's self-centred delusion is that no one should play music because his lady is not in attendance. We are told that there is no hour in the day or night that, when in private, Troilus does not rehearse the moment when Criseyde would return. He practises the terms of courtly address, welcoming her and asking how she has fared since they last spoke. The narrating voice laments that such rehearsal is nothing but a fantasy. Troilus's rehearsals are deluded and futile because **Fortune** intends to better glaze his cap. (*To make* or *to give a glass houve* is an idiomatic expression meaning to mock or to delude someone, because to give someone head-gear made from glass would be to provide ineffective protection.) **Fortune**, in thwarting their plans so that Criseyde will not return, thus deludes Troilus as to the actual outcome of events. Troilus also rereads Criseyde's letters a hundred times between noon and the following morning, inwardly imagining her appearance and her femininity and remembering every word and deed in their affair.

At the end of the fourth day, Troilus tells Pandarus that he wishes to return home. He argues that it would be more seemly to make their own farewells (presumably rather than outstaying their welcome). Pandarus disagrees, asking him in proverbial terms whether they have come here simply to fetch fire and run home again (because someone who borrows a light must return to their own hearth quickly before the flame goes out). To leave precipitously would be an act of rudeness because they have agreed that they will stay for a week. Sarpedon would be surprised and puzzled if they left after four days. By reminding him of his social obligations, Pandarus makes Troilus stay for an entire week. In Boccaccio's *Filostrato*, Troilo and Pandaro leave on the fifth day even though in doing so they offend their host. In Chaucer's version, Pandarus has more influence over his friend and Troilus is more constrained by the demands of courtesy.

On their return journey, Troilus prays that God will send him such grace that he will find Criseyde has returned when he arrives at his palace. Optimistic about this prospect, he beings to sing as they ride. Pandarus (though he earlier claimed to be certain that she would return) now responds to Troilus's optimism with private cynicism. He thinks 'Ye, haselwode' (505) to himself, a proverbial expression meaning 'nonsense' or 'foolishness'. Pandarus now thinks that Criseyde's return is so unlikely that Troilus's love for her will eventually fade. Yet he conceals his true feelings from his friend and returns to his former role as entertainer. He swears to Troilus that his heart tells him Criseyde will return as soon as she can. Is Pandarus here being a good friend, supporting Troilus in his hopes whilst planning to let him down gently in due course (as he does at 682–6)? Or should we be troubled by his capacity to think one thing whilst saying another? What is it that Pandarus knows about Criseyde or about her circumstances that makes him doubt her return?

LINES 512 TO 686: TROILUS'S NEW SORROW AND OLD JOYS

The narrative now describes how Troilus spends the eighth and ninth days of Criseyde's projected ten-day absence from the city. Troilus wakes at dawn and begs Pandarus to go with him to visit Criseyde's empty palace. He argues that since they cannot at present have any other form of merriment (because his lady is absent), they can at least look upon her dwelling-place. Troilus invents a reason for going about the town in order to conceal his true purpose from his retinue. The narrating voice exclaims at how unhappy Troilus is when he sees the locked gates of Criseyde's house. When he sees how every window is closed (signifying that the house is unoccupied), he feels that his heart grows as cold as frost. With a changed and lifeless expression, he rides past in silence so quickly that no bystander detects his grief-stricken expression.

Troilus now addresses the house directly. This address (which Chaucer expands from one stanza in the *Filostrato* to two) is a form of *paraclausithyron*, a classical literary motif in which an excluded lover speaks to the door of his lady's house. In a sequence of vocative addresses, Troilus contrasts the house's former glory with its present emptiness and desolation. He extends his adoration of Criseyde to a remembrance of her house's virtues. When Criseyde was in residence, the palace was called the best of houses, lit up like a lantern or like daylight by her whom Troilus calls the sun of all bliss. Now she is absent, the house has had its light extinguished and is in darkness. These contrasts work both figuratively and literally, as a house whose owner is absent is left empty and unilluminated. The palace is also compared to a ring whose ruby has fallen out, figuring it as the setting and Criseyde as its jewel. Troilus says that the palace now ought to fall down, just as he ought to die, for lack of Criseyde's presence. Since Troilus cannot get any closer to his lady, he says that he would gladly kiss the cold doors of her palace. As he rides away, he bids farewell, calling the house a shrine whose saintly relics are now missing.

As he rides away, Troilus is so distressed and his face is so altered and made deathly pale that the narrating voice asserts that anyone who saw him would feel great pity. He rides through the city, seeing places in which he formerly enjoyed great happiness and remembering all of the details of their love affair. Through direct speech, we eavesdrop on the comments Troilus makes to himself as he notes each location. In contrast with the *Filostrato*, where Troilo remembers Criseida's varying moods both cheerful and aloof, Chaucer has Troilus celebrate Criseyde's accomplishments and remember only happy memories. Such reminiscence prompts Troilus to look back over the entire course of his love affair. As he thinks, he makes an address to Cupid, **the God of Love**. When he thinks back over the story, how Cupid has attacked him in every way, Troilus observes that someone could write a book about it, a book in the form of a 'storie' (585). *Storie* here means not a fiction but a narrative account of all the events which have occurred (just as Chaucer is himself doing). Troilus next asks Cupid why he needs to seek victory over him since he has already submitted to his will. He assures him that he has fully taken revenge for his anger (Troilus angered him by formerly mocking love), acknowledging him as a powerful god whom it is dangerous to offend. Troilus begs for mercy and pledges his loyalty. Troilus asks only one thing in reward for his devotion, namely that Cupid soon return Criseyde to him. He asks him to compel her heart to want to return as much as Cupid makes his heart long to see her. If Cupid does this, Troilus says, he will feel confident that she will not tarry in the Greek camp. Troilus ends his appeal by asking Cupid not to be as cruel to the Trojans as the goddess Juno was to the people of **Thebes** in bringing about the destruction of their city (an ironic request given what we know of Troy's future destruction).

Troilus now visits the gates through which Criseyde rode out of the city. He paces back and forth, begging God that he might see her return to Troy once more. Now his thoughts turn to the effect of his distress on his appearance and health. He imagines himself to be disfigured by grief, paler and thinner than he used to be. His melancholic depression leads him to imagine in paranoid fashion that those around him are gossiping about his ill health. Similarly, he imagines that all who pass him in the street pity him and say to themselves how sorry they are that Troilus looks as if he will die. We are told that Troilus spent a day or two like this, like a man who was poised between hope and fear. Because of these conflicting emotions, it pleases Troilus to explain the cause of his sorrow in songs because such song-making alleviates his distress a little. Chaucer replaces Troilo's five-stanza prayer to **the God of Love** for death to end his suffering with a single stanza of direct address to Criseyde whom Troilus names as his lode-star once again. In her absence, he is like a sailor who has lost his guiding light. He tells her that he should indeed lament that night after night, in distress and darkness, he feels he is sailing towards his death, driven on by a prevailing wind. If he is without her guidance on the tenth night (that is, if she does not return to Troy), he imagines that Charybdis (a legendary sea monster who created dangerous whirlpools) will swallow up him and his ship. In his song, Troilus recapitulates the nautical imagery used in Book II, offering us parallels between the sorrow of unrequited love and the sorrow of parted lovers.

Having expressed his grief, Troilus now once again sighs in distress. At night he cannot sleep but stands and looks at the moon. He tells the moon that he saw her 'hornes olde' (652) on the morning on which Criseyde left the city and that he will be happy when the moon is 'horned newe' (650) because that is when he expects Criseyde to return. These horns are the two tips of the crescent moon. Troilus saw the waning crescent when Criseyde departed and, ten days later, after the new moon will come the waxing crescent. He urges the moon therefore to hurry in its orbit around the Earth. Time seems to drag for Troilus as he waits for Criseyde to return. He feels that the days and nights are longer and that the sun must be travelling some longer route in the sky. He fears that Phaeton (the sun god's son who was killed by Jupiter because he lost control of his father's chariot which carries the sun around the heavens) has returned to life and is once again driving the sun-chariot on an erratic and hence lengthier route.

Troilus often walks on the ramparts on top of the city's walls and looks out at the Greek army. The narrative once again reports his mutterings to us as direct speech. Troilus imagines he can see Criseyde in the distance. Feeling the fragrant breeze on his face, he imagines that the air which every hour blows stronger and which seems to restore his soul must be Criseyde's deep and grief-stricken sighs. He thinks this must be true because he does not feel such a breeze in any other place in the town (though cynical readers might conclude this is because of the height of the city walls). Yet Troilus feels that the noise of the wind blowing sounds so much like the sound of distress that this proves his fancy to be true. The wind seems to speak Criseyde's words and ask 'Why are we two parted?' Scenes such as this demonstrate how Chaucer's narrative can be read sincerely or sceptically or both at once: Troilus's fancies are irrational and perhaps absurd, yet pitifully evocative of his noble sensibility and the strength of his love.

LINES 687 TO 770: CRISEYDE'S INTENTION

The narrative now turns its focus back to Criseyde, highlighting the difficulty of her situation. She is accompanied by a small number of women servants and surrounded by warlike Greeks. Chaucer here adds Criseyde's lament to his source. She bemoans her own existence and says that her heart is right to wish for death because her sorrow makes her feel that she has been alive for too long. She now realizes that her father will not allow her to return for any reason, however she might try to sweet-talk him. She fears that, if she does not return on the appointed day, Troilus will think she is untrue to him and she will be blamed by everyone. If she risks trying to escape from the Greek camp at night and is caught, she will be considered a spy (and presumably imprisoned or executed) or she will fall into the hands of some other man and be entirely ruined even though her **intention** was honourable. She begs God to have pity on her for the sorrow this perilous situation causes her. Chaucer's addition makes us see how constrained and difficult Criseyde's situation seems and how fearful she is as a woman in the midst of a besieging army.

Throughout the description of Criseyde's sorrow, many of the details given mirror the representation of Troilus's despair, creating a sense of reciprocal sorrow which parallels their earlier reciprocal happiness. We are told how Criseyde's face has grown pale with grief and her limbs thinner because she has spent all of her time standing and looking back at Troy. She inwardly pictures Troilus's very many good qualities and remembers his words of love. The narrating voice says that there is in the world no one so cruel-hearted that they would not weep for pity if they were to hear her weeping in such distress. To emphasize the extent of her crying, the narrating voice exclaims that Criseyde certainly did not need to borrow any tears from anyone else (implying that she had plenty of her own). The worst aspect of her sorrow is that she has no one to confide in. In piteous fashion she looks back at Troy, seeing its tall towers and grand buildings. She laments the fact that the pleasure and happiness which she formerly enjoyed within the city walls has now turned to sorrow (here figuratively called *gall*, the epitome of bitterness). She addresses her absent lover, asking Troilus what he is doing now and whether he is still thinking about her.

Criseyde next laments the fact that she did not trust in Troilus's advice and elope with him as he earlier suggested. She questions her reasons for refusing to elope, asking who could have criticized her for absconding with someone such as Troilus. Criseyde tells herself that it is now too late to wish with the benefit of hindsight that she had acted differently. Chaucer adds to his source Criseyde's lament that she always lacked one of the three eyes of Prudence before she left Troy. Prudence was thought to have three eyes in order to be able to see past, present and future, contemplation of all three giving one the greatest chance of acting wisely. Criseyde says that she was able to remember time past and could fully see time present, that is, she understood both past and present. Yet before she was in this present perilous situation, she could not see the future and it was this lack of foresight which brought about her present sorrow. The lament applies not only to Criseyde herself but to the Trojans as a whole (and also, beyond the text, to Chaucer's readers, then and now). The Trojans look back at the fall of **Thebes** and at the examples of the mythological and historical figures they name but are their perceptions ones of insight or blindness? And to what degree can the Trojans correctly perceive their current situation? How do they respond to those who see the future? What, in the face of the vicissitudes of time and **Fortune,** might constitute prudent action, both in love and in war?

Criseyde now decides that whatever the consequences she will secretly escape from the Greek camp and elope with Troilus wherever he wishes. She will pay no attention to the tittle-tattle of any malicious gossips (who might comment on such an elopement) because such wretched people are always jealous of those in love. Criseyde strengthens her resolve with proverbial wisdom. If you try to take account of everyone's advice and views you will never succeed, because that which some people criticize is conversely praised by others. In the face of such diversity of opinion, Criseyde decides that she will say that **felicity** is sufficient for her (implying that the private joy of a reunion with Troilus will allow her to cope with the loss of her reputation or status). She therefore resolves conclusively to return to Troy. Yet the narrating voice immediately undermines Criseyde's own certainty of purpose through his atemporal ability to look into the future of the story. He exclaims that within two months (a time period not specified in Chaucer's source) such an **intention** will become a distant memory because thoughts of Troilus and the city of Troy will slip out of Criseyde's heart 'knotteles' (769), just as a thread without a knot slides through a piece of material. Rather than returning to Troy, Criseyde will change her mind and decide to stay in the Greek camp.

Intention

In *Troilus and Criseyde*, there are many references to characters' intent or intention and what it is that they mean or intend. Such assertions about a character's inner purpose prompt the reader to speculate about matters of volition, ethics, morality and culpability as the narrative progresses. In the process of courtship, Pandarus and Troilus claim initially that they are asking for only limited concessions from Criseyde, but we are frequently suspicious (and rightly so) that Pandarus and Troilus intend far more than their initial requests.

And can Criseyde really be unaware of what they intend? Characters also make claims about the morality of their intentions. Troilus claims to Pandarus, and Pandarus claims to Criseyde, that each does not intend anything which might be sinful or shameful but only that which is virtuous. Elsewhere, the lovers' intentions towards each other are described as 'cle(e)ne' (II.580, III.1166, 1229), as pure, decent and faithful. Yet can a love which is secret and brought about by dubious means also be noble and virtuous? As Troilus and Pandarus discuss the affair, what Pandarus is doing is very like the actions of someone who procures women for men for sex. Is intention (and especially intention which appears disingenuous or suspect) enough to distinguish a virtuous action from a shameful one?

At times we are given access to a character's inner intention in speaking or acting in a certain way, whilst at other times we can only guess at their true purpose. At key points, Chaucer shows us that the intentions of different characters (Pandarus and Criseyde, Diomede and Criseyde) are in direct conflict. We can also speculate on how far one character understands another's intentions. When are Troilus and Criseyde fully aware of Pandarus's intention to arrange an opportunity for the lovers to consummate their relationship? At what point does Criseyde become aware of Diomede's intention towards her? At times, it seems as if Criseyde in particular may not even fully understand her own intentions. When does she become conscious of her own decision to remain in the Greek camp? What is her intention in sending Troilus such a misleading letter after her failure to return?

Our readerly foreknowledge of the inescapable conclusion of the story also allows us to compare a character's intention with the eventual outcome of events. Criseyde's intentions (such as her promises to remain faithful to Troilus, her plans to find a way to return and her decision to escape secretly from the Greek camp) are, presumably, sincere and well-meant at the moment at which they are stated, but they are inevitably compromised by our knowledge that they will not be kept. Chaucer's narrative thus challenges us to think about the nature of intention, and particularly good intentions, and why some intentions are not able to be implemented. By extension and via the narrating first-person's comments on his own intentions, we are also challenged to think not only about the nature of an author's intention, but also about the relationship between what an author intends and what his text might be thought to mean.

LINES 771 TO 1015: DIOMEDE VISITS CRISEYDE

(i) Lines 771 to 798: Diomede's deliberations

The narrative now turns to Diomede's deliberations about the best way to win Criseyde's love. This is in contrast to Chaucer's source in which Diomede first doubts his ability to supplant Troilo in Criseida's affections. Employing all his cunning (and with echoes of earlier descriptions of Pandarus's guile), Chaucer's Diomede debates with himself how he can quickly and successfully bring Criseyde's heart into his net. He cannot stop himself, spending all of his time casting out hook and line to fish for her (that is, thinking of ways to capture her affections). Despite his eagerness, Diomede knows intuitively that Criseyde must have a lover in Troy because, in the time since he escorted her from the city gates, he has never seen her laugh or rejoice. Yet he encourages himself that it can do no harm to try to woo her by citing the proverb that he who does not try anything does not gain anything. He also, however, asks himself whether he isn't acting foolishly to address her about matters of love when her present sorrow is caused by the love of another man. Changing his mind once again, Diomede argues that whoever might win such a flower (here meaning a prize) from someone for whom the lady mourns day and night could call himself a conqueror (a formulation which again figures his wooing as a competition between men). Diomede resolves that whatever the consequences, even if he should die, he will pursue her love because he can lose nothing but words.

(ii) Lines 799 to 840: character portraits

The narrating voice now digresses in order to paint portraits of Diomede, Criseyde and Troilus. Such portraits are not present in Chaucer's immediate source, though the *Filostrato* does include a description of Diomede at the end of his visit to Criseida (*Fil.* VI.33). The portraits here are based in large part on the versions given in Joseph of Exeter's *Daretis Phrygii Ylias.*[3] Joseph's fourth book begins with a sequence of brief character portraits of the leading figures, both men and women, who play a part in the story of the fall of Troy. Such a list of character portraits was a notable feature of retellings of the Troy story, appearing in Dares, in Benoît's *Roman de Troie* and in Guido's *Historia destructionis Troiae.*[4] By

[3] Joseph of Exeter, *Iliad of Dares Phrygius*, trans. Roberts, pp. 40–1, 43.

[4] *The Trojan War*, trans. Frazer, pp. 142–5; *Chaucer's Boccaccio*, trans. Havely, pp. 167–8; Guido, *Historia destructionis Troiae*, trans. Meek, pp. 82–6.

including his own sequence of character portraits, Chaucer supplements the *Filostrato* with other historical sources and associates his poem with the wider literary traditions of Trojan storytelling. The reader is implicitly invited to compare their own perceptions of the central characters in Chaucer's version of the story with these traditional descriptions of each character's notable qualities.

Diomede is portrayed as quick to act and brave whenever needed, with a loud voice and sturdy, powerful limbs, valiant and impulsive. Some people thought him to be intemperate or presumptuous in his speech. The portrait compares him to his father Tydeus (one of the seven warriors who led the Argive army in its attack on the city of **Thebes**). Criseyde is said to be of average height and more beautiful than any other woman in her physique, her face and her bearing. There was no flaw in her appearance apart from the fact that her eyebrows were joined together as one. Though such a mono-brow was a mark of particular beauty in the ancient world, in the Middle Ages it was thought to be an undesirable blemish (and hence might be seen as a token of a flawed nature). The narrating voice counters this minor imperfection by reporting that those who saw Criseyde said that it was as if Paradise itself had been created and located in her eyes. Moreover, it is as if love and her splendid beauty were always in competition to see which predominated in her. As well as listing her many virtues, Chaucer, following comments made in Benoît's *Roman* and Guido's *Historia*, adds the detail that Criseyde was 'slydynge of corage' (825), unsteady and perhaps unreliable in her attitudes and **intention**.[5] This detail invites us to consider whether her betrayal of Troilus is somewhat inevitable, given that it is in her nature to be changeable, and thus whether we might therefore blame her for it a little less. Criseyde's changeable nature might also align her with the goddess **Fortune**, whose nature was earlier defined by Pandarus as one of inevitable and unavoidable mutability (see 1.848–9).

Troilus's portrait presents him as a superlative example of a young knight. He is said to be tall and his body so perfectly created in proportion that Nature itself could hardly improve on it. The narrating voice

[5] Benoît's portrait of Briseida says that 'She was greatly loved, and she herself loved greatly, but her heart was not constant' (*Chaucer's Boccaccio*, trans. Havely, p. 167). Guido's portrait of Briseida says that 'She attracted many lovers by her charm, and loved many, although she did not preserve constancy of heart toward her lovers' (*Historia destructionis Troiae*, trans. Meek, pp. 83–4). In keeping with her betrayal of Troilus, Benoît, and following him Guido and Chaucer, in contrast to earlier portraits by Dares and Joseph of Exeter, make such changes of heart a notable part of her personality.

says that in the historical accounts of the Trojan war, Troilus was never in any way inferior to another knight in feats of arms. Even though a giant might surpass him in pure strength, his heart was equal to the first and best when it came to having the courage to act as he intended.

(iii) Lines 841 to 952: Diomede speaks to Criseyde

Whereas in the *Filostrato* Diomede visits Criseyde on the fourth day since her departure from Troy (*Fil.* VI.9), in Chaucer's version of the story he visits Criseyde on the tenth day, the very day on which Criseyde has promised to return. Diomede visits Calchas's tent and pretends to have matters to discuss with him. His real business, as the narrating first-person promises he will soon show, is with Criseyde rather than with her father. Criseyde greets him with courtesy and sits him beside her. Her servants fetch them wine and spiced sweetmeats as they make small talk together. They first discuss the progress of the war and Diomede asks Criseyde for her opinion about the siege. He next asks her if the manners and habits of the Greeks seem strange to her (in comparison with the Trojan mores she is used to). He asks why her father delays so long in arranging a marriage for her to some worthy man. Diomede perhaps seeks to make her anxious about this possibility and make his own advances seem a more preferable option.

Criseyde, still deeply distressed because of her love for Troilus, answers him as best she can. The narrating voice tells us that it did not seem as if she knew what Diomede's **intention** was. This statement must be taken at face value, Criseyde being so distracted by grief that it seems she does not recognize Diomede's tactics. Yet it may also make us wonder how naïve and unsuspecting Criseyde is and how much she might be playing along with his courtship. Because Criseyde does not dismiss his advances outright, Diomede grows more confident. He tells her that he has never been able to witness in her any emotion other than sorrow since the morning on which he first escorted her from Troy. He claims not to know what the cause of this sorrow is and purports to speculate that if her grief was caused by the love of a Trojan, he would be greatly distressed that she would expend even a quarter of a tear on any of the city's residents. This is because he is certain that the destruction of Troy and its inhabitants is inevitable. Diomede fiercely emphasizes to Criseyde the merciless nature of the Greeks' revenge, asserting that she herself must realize this from her first-hand knowledge of the situation. The Greeks will take such vengeance for the abduction of Helen that even the Manes (here describing not the deified spirits of dead loved ones but the deities who enact punishments in the underworld) will be frightened that the Greeks will harm them. (Chaucer adds this more specific reference to classical mythology to his source, which refers only to the dead in hell.) The Greeks' vengeance will stand as a perpetual warning against the abduction of another nation's queen.

Diomede now alludes to Criseyde's own father's prophecy to prove that this threat of vengeance will be fulfilled. Unless Calchas is misleading the Greeks with 'ambages' (897), Diomede is certain that what has been predicted will quickly come true. He glosses *ambages* as meaning a word with two faces, a word which is capable of meaning two things at once. Moreover, he asks why else Calchas would have requested that she be exchanged for Antenor if he was not certain that Troy would be destroyed. Because Calchas divined that no one will escape the city's destruction, his fears for Criseyde's safety led him to make sure that she did not reside there any longer. Diomede asks what more Criseyde might want by way of proof of the inevitability of Troy's fall. He therefore urges her to no longer care about Troy and its inhabitants. He instructs her to banish that bitter hope (Criseyde's painful desire to return to Troy) and to be happy in the Greek camp. Troy, he says, is in such peril that there is no hope of salvation (and of course we know that he and Calchas will be proved right about this). Chaucer here omits the disparaging comments about Trojan barbarity and vulgarity which Diomede makes in the *Filostrato*. Yet as he does in the *Filostrato*, Diomede goes on to assure Criseyde that she will find a more perfect lover amongst the Greeks than any Trojan is, one who is more faithfully and nobly affectionate and who will serve her better. If she permits him, he offers, he himself will be the one to serve her as her knight.

Even though we know Diomede's courtship is carefully premeditated, he is nevertheless emotionally and physically affected by the demands of wooing his lady well (if such gestures are not themselves feigned). He blushes, his voice shakes a little, he averts his gaze and pauses for a moment in order to recover his composure. Diomede's brief courtship thus provides ironic echoes of Troilus's love for the same woman. In order to persuade Criseyde of his worth as a suitor, he now reminds her of his own lineage. He tells her that he is as nobly born as is any Trojan (an important claim given that Diomede has guessed that Criseyde's lover is a Trojan prince). If his father Tydeus, who was killed during the siege of **Thebes**, had remained living, Diomede himself would now be king of the Greek city-states of Calydon and Argos.

Diomede ends his speech by asking Criseyde to agree to hear more the following morning about the distress caused by his unrequited love. He asks this as her 'man' (939), her knight and servant. Diomede here appears presumptuous: Criseyde has accepted his friendship but nothing more. Criseyde agrees to meet Diomede the next day as long as he does not talk about matters of love. Yet despite refusing to recognize Diomede as a suitor, Criseyde's agreement to a meeting raises doubts about her **intention**. If, as in Chaucer's version, Diomede's request is made not on the fourth but on the *tenth* day, then by agreeing to meet him the following morning Criseyde must either be intending not to return to Troy as promised or must be lying to Diomede if she intends to escape in the night as she earlier planned.

(iv) Lines 953 to 1015: Criseyde's reply

The narrative now gives Criseyde's response to Diomede verbatim. She speaks coldly, as one would expect, the narrating voice asserts, from someone whose heart is so firmly fixed on Troilus that no one could uproot it. Criseyde tells Diomede that she loves the city in which she was born (and so she cannot forget Troy). She prays that Jove will soon rescue the city from its predicament. She acknowledges that the Greeks desire revenge, but swears that the future will not be as Diomede predicts. Criseyde acknowledges that Calchas is wise and provident and that she is the more obliged to him because he has liberated her from Troy at such a high price (namely the exchange with Antenor). Although she acknowledges that the Greeks are men of noble status, she is certain that one could find as many equally worthy people in Troy. Yet she also acknowledges that Diomede could serve a lady very ably, in such a way as to deserve her thanks. We see Criseyde caught between a number of different obligations. She must be courteous to Diomede and his fellow Greek nobles, obedient to her father but also loyal to Troy and Troilus, disbelieving and yet aware of the future that we readers know will come to pass.

Turning to matters of the heart, Criseyde tells Diomede that she had a husband whom she loved wholeheartedly. This is of course true, as earlier references to her widowhood make clear (see I.97, 169–77, II.110–19, 221–3, 750–9, 1296–8). Yet she also denies that she has had any other lover since her husband's death. Her disavowal of Troilus here may be motivated by her desire to keep the love affair secret, but (given that we know she is about to betray him) we may see it as an indication of her impending change of heart. Criseyde also acknowledges that Diomede is from an aristocratic family. She next swears that love and she are very far apart (implying that her feelings are as far removed as possible from those of romance). Rather than love again, she would rather lament and grieve until her dying day. Yet rather than being entirely certain, she hints that this may change. She says that she cannot predict what she will do in the future, but that 'as yet' (987) she does not wish to enjoy a romance.

Criseyde thus does not completely dismiss Diomede's courtship, suggesting she is already entertaining the possibility of not returning to Troy. Whilst not acknowledging such a future plainly or directly, she refers to it in conditional terms. She tells him that when he and his fellow Greeks have conquered the city (is she here accepting this future?), it will perhaps so happen that when she sees what she has never yet seen (i.e., Troy subjugated?) then she will do what she has never yet done (i.e., accept Diomede's love?). This cryptic reply, she says, should be enough for him at present. She agrees to speak with him again tomorrow, as long as he does not discuss love. She swears by the goddess Pallas Athena that if she were ever to take pity on any Greek suitor it would be Diomede. She tells him that she does not promise to love him but that she is not saying that she refuses him. She concludes by assuring him that she means well in saying this. She looks down with a sigh, praying that she will again see the city of Troy in peace and tranquillity or if not that she will die heart-broken. We may guess here that she is also thinking of Troilus whose name echoes that of his own city. We are told that Diomede is reinvigorated by her reply and eagerly begs for her favour. He takes her glove (gloves were often exchanged as tokens of affection between lovers) and, once it is evening and everything (from his perspective) is going well, he bids her farewell.

Throughout this reply, it is hard to decipher Criseyde's ultimate **intention** through these words, which seem as two-faced as the *ambages* which Diomede earlier described. Should we think the worst, that she has already decided to betray Troilus, or should we think the best, that she is trying politely to deflect Diomede's courtship? Perhaps this is a kind of self-deception in which she does not wish to acknowledge to herself what she is doing? Does she realize the significance of agreeing to meet Diomede the next morning, after the promised deadline has passed? Does she perhaps accept that Troy will indeed fall and is she therefore safeguarding her own future in perilous circumstances? Criseyde's **intention** is hidden from us and perhaps also hidden from herself at this moment.

LINES 1016 TO 1099: CRISEYDE BETRAYS TROILUS

The narrative now describes how, once it is evening, the bright planet Venus follows the setting sun and indicates where it has descended below the horizon. Cynthia, the moon goddess, is imagined as leaning forward over her chariot-horses which pull her through the night sky to urge them onwards. She does this in order to whirl her way out of the zodiac sign Leo. This reminds us of Criseyde's earlier promise to return within ten days, before the moon passed through Leo. Given that the moon is indeed nearly leaving the sign of Leo, we have now reached the evening of the tenth day after Criseyde's departure.

As Criseyde goes to bed, she turns over in her mind the events of the day. She thinks about what Diomede said to her, his noble rank, the danger Troy is in and the fact that she is alone in the Greek camp and thus lacks support and assistance. It is from this mixture of thoughts that the reason why she resolves to stay in the Greek camp begins to 'brede' (1027), to develop or grow organically like a plant or animal. This is the point at which her decision to intend 'fully' (1029) to stay begins to grow, perhaps hinting that she has already given some thought to remaining. Diomede appears to have very successfully preyed on Criseyde's fearful nature and perhaps also her desire for social respectability. Chaucer leaves it to us to decide whether these are sufficient reasons for her betrayal of Troilus. Diomede visits Criseyde the following morning and, we are told, argues his case so well that he assuages all of her painful sighs of sorrow and takes away the majority of her distress. Though Diomede is said to console her through words, Chaucer's choices of verbs (*leien adoun*, *reven*) have a hint of erotic double entendre about them.

The narrating voice asserts that he is telling the truth and that he is telling his readers this as quickly as he can in case they interrupt (prompting speculation about what sort of audience reaction he anticipates). He also avows that the extra details he tells us (which reveal Criseyde to be too quickly concerned with Diomede's suffering and not at all troubled by the thought that Troilus may see his love-tokens on the battlefield) can be found in the various historical narratives in which these events have already been described (here he is not in fact being disingenuous as Chaucer supplements Boccaccio's account with details from Benoît and Guido, as well as his own extrapolations). The narrative describes how Criseyde returns to Diomede the fine horse which he had previously won from Troilus on the battlefield and had given to her.[6] She also gives Diomede a brooch which once belonged to Troilus.[7] The narrating voice cannot contain his shock at the callousness of this gesture, exclaiming that there was little need for her to do that. Criseyde also allows Diomede to wear one of her sleeves as a pennon (a narrow triangular flag or streamer which a knight wore on his helmet or fixed to his lance as a token of his lady's affection).[8] The narrating first-person also says that he reads elsewhere in prior versions of this story that Criseyde wept copiously when she saw the gaping wounds which Troilus inflicted upon Diomede on the battlefield. She takes great pains to nurse Diomede. The narrating voice quotes others as saying (though claims that he himself does not know whether it is true, as if he does not wish to subscribe fully to this reason being the cause of her acceptance of Diomede's love) that Criseyde gave Diomede her heart in order to heal such battle wounds (do we approve of such compassion or dismiss it?).[9] The narrating voice asserts that these details are not his own invention (and hence he cannot be accused of adding to those things for which Criseyde might be blamed) but nevertheless signals that they are authorized by prior versions of the story.

The narrative now presents Criseyde's regretful lamentation (drawing on Briseida's comparable soliloquy in Benoît's *Roman de Troie*).[10] According to historical sources, the narrating voice claims, no other woman ever lamented more than Criseyde did when she betrayed Troilus. She laments that her reputation for faithfulness in love has now been completely wiped away. She laments that in future no positive word will ever be written or sung about her (a formulaic phrase meaning 'told in any way') because 'thise bokes' (1060), imagined future versions of her story, will insult and revile her. Her name and story will be talked about by many people and

[6] Benoît describes how Briseida lends to Diomedes the horse which he captured from Troilus in battle and then presented to her, because Diomedes' own horse has subsequently been captured (*Chaucer's Boccaccio*, trans. Havely, p. 177). See *Historia destructionis Troiae*, trans. Meek, pp. 162 and 164 for Guido's account of Diomedes' courtship of Briseida.

[7] Benoît and Guido do not make mention of such a brooch. Later in his version of the story Boccaccio describes how Troilo sees a brooch which he gave to Criseida on the morning of her departure on the breast of a garment captured from Diomede in battle (*Fil.* VIII.9–10; cf. *TC* V.1653–65). Prompted by Diomede's later possession of such a brooch, Chaucer thus invents an earlier moment at which the brooch is given to Diomede.

[8] Chaucer takes this detail from Benoît (*Chaucer's Boccaccio*, trans. Havely, p. 178).

[9] Benoît describes how the anxiety and pity created by the news of Diomedes' battle injuries causes Briseida to express her love for Diomedes (*Chaucer's Boccaccio*, trans. Havely, pp. 179–80). In Guido's *Historia destructionis Troiae* (trans. Meek, p. 190), it is during Briseida's frequent visits to the wounded Diomedes that she 'inclined her whole thought toward Diomedes and changed her love'.

[10] *Chaucer's Boccaccio*, trans. Havely, pp. 180–1.

her bell will be rung throughout the world (that is, news of her scandalous story will spread everywhere). She says that women in the future will hate her most of all because they will think that she has brought shame upon womankind. (So, for example, Guido's *Historia* uses Briseida's change of heart as an opportunity to lament women's supposed inconstancy and deviousness, whilst Benoît's *Roman* places a similar account of women's supposed fickleness, callousness, self-delusion and changeability at the point at which Briseida and Troilus last speak to each other.[11]) Since she cannot now see any better way to act, and since she thinks it is too late to regret her actions, she resolves always to be faithful to Diomede. Criseyde now addresses the absent Troilus. She prays that God send him good fortune because Troilus is the noblest knight she ever saw. Now weeping, she tells him that she will never hate him and that he will always have love from her platonically, as a friend. Yet despite her tributes to him, she says that everything (including presumably their love and her regret) will pass away in time and so she bids him farewell.

The narrating voice concludes this section by affirming that no authoritative author specifies how long it was before Criseyde deserted Troilus for Diomede. He challenges every member of his audience to pay close attention to their books (that is, to search carefully in the various versions of this story) but is certain that no one will be able to find mention of a particular period of time. He concedes that Diomede began to court her very quickly after her departure from Troy, but says that before he gained her love completely he had still much work to do (implying that the process was a long one). Here the narrating voice creates a matter for speculation. Those readers who could check other versions would find that Benoît and Guido each imply a long process (though Guido's *Historia* implies that the change of heart began on the very day that Briseida left Troy).[12] The narrating voice is technically right, as no particular agreed number of days or months can be easily established from his sources (though he himself has earlier said in lines 766–7 that her **intention** to return to Troy was overturned in less than two months). Yet though his intervention evades

[11] *Historia destructionis Troiae*, trans. Meek, p. 160; *Chaucer's Boccaccio*, trans. Havely, p. 171.

[12] *Historia destructionis Troiae*, trans. Meek, p. 160. Yet, having left Troy during the truce after the sixth battle between the Greeks and the Trojans, even in Guido's account Briseida does not fully accept Diomedes as her lover until after the twelfth battle, with several months of truce between each battle. In Benoît's *Roman de Troie*, the period of time is likewise lengthy, with several battles and many months of truces occurring before Troilus inflicts the wound on Diomedes which causes Briseida to make clear her love for him. In Boccaccio's *Filostrato*, Criseida's change of heart is described in narrative summary following the account of Diomede's visit to Criseida on the fourth day after her departure (*Fil.* VI.34).

having to establish an exact moment of betrayal, it leaves us uncertain. Did Criseyde change her mind quickly or did it take many months and much effort on Diomede's part to gain her love?

The narrating voice also says that he does not wish to criticize or rebuke Criseyde to a greater degree than the historical account he is purportedly following does in relating these events. As Criseyde herself predicted, her reputation is now so widely known that such pre-existing infamy ought to be sufficient punishment for her misdeed without him adding to it further. Indeed, he says that if he could excuse her in any way because she was so sorry for her betrayal, he would without doubt excuse her for pity's sake (if not for the sake of facts). The narrating voice wishes to excuse her, yet these wishes remain conditional, as if his hands are nevertheless tied by prior versions.

We readers are here challenged to decide whether we should likewise wish to excuse her in any way. For some readers, Criseyde's insight into her own literary future and her pledge of loyalty to Diomede, alongside her tears and her farewell to Troilus, may mitigate her unfaithfulness to some degree, yet for others they may seem meaninglessly self-serving in the light of her betrayal. Moreover, by his intervention the narrating voice focuses attention on wider questions both of culpability and of authorial **intention**. Does Chaucer's version of the story add to Criseyde's infamy or will it rehabilitate her to some extent? For example, does the manner in which Criseyde is persuaded to love Troilus in Books II and III of Chaucer's version excuse her betrayal to some extent? Do the extra (if potentially paradoxical) insights we are granted into her character and psychology and the circumstances of her life in Troy and in the Greek camp make it more difficult to condemn her?

LINES 1100 TO 1197: TROILUS WAITS IN HOPE

Having moved forward in time to recount how Criseyde ultimately betrays Troilus in transferring her love to Diomede, the narrative now moves back to describe how Troilus sleeplessly spends the ninth night since her departure, making his hopes for her return seem all the more deluded because we have seen her betrayal to be a foregone conclusion. Troilus and Pandarus amuse themselves by climbing the city walls to see if they can see Criseyde returning to the city. They stand there until noon, saying that every person who approaches the city gates from afar is Criseyde until the figure comes close enough for them to recognize who in fact it is. The narrating voice says that Troilus and Pandarus are 'byjaped'

(1119, meaning either that they are deluded by false hope or disappointed by having these hopes dashed), gazing out at nothing because Criseyde will not appear.

Over the entire course of the tenth day, Troilus maintains his belief that she will return and finds reasons to excuse how long they have waited. He tells Pandarus that for all he knows Criseyde will not certainly return to Troy before noon. Calchas will make her have dinner, the first main meal of the day, before she departs. Pandarus agrees that this indeed may be the case and suggests that they likewise eat before returning to the ramparts. Once again, the narrating voice comments mockingly that the friends will have to search for a long time before they find what they are seeking. He says that **Fortune** intends to mock or deceive them both by bringing about a future which neither of them expects (though Pandarus elsewhere seems to have assumed already that Criseyde's return is unlikely). After their meal, Troilus continues to excuse Criseyde's non-appearance. He suggests that she has stayed so long with her elderly father that she will not reach the gates until nearly evening. He tells Pandarus to come with him to the city gates where he will order the gatekeepers to keep the gate open a little longer.

Criseyde of course does not arrive. Troilus looks out at every feature in the landscape, stretching his head far out over the city walls. With poignant certainty, he tells Pandarus that he has just worked out what he imagines must be Criseyde's plan. Congratulating her on her supposed prudence, he says Criseyde must be intending to enter Troy in secret, under the cover of nightfall, because she does not wish to have people gawping at her as she returns. He directs Pandarus's gaze to what he is certain must be Criseyde's vehicle returning in the twilight. Their exclamations and questions convey this moment of excitement when Troilus thinks his lady is approaching. Yet Pandarus disagrees, pointing out that what Troilus has identified is nothing but a cart used for transporting goods or provisions from place to place. (Such a humble vehicle is unlikely to be a suitable form of transport for a noblewoman like Criseyde and so Troilus's deluded optimism is making him seize on the most implausible ideas.) Though he accepts his misidentification, Troilus nevertheless feels that his optimism must be a sign that Criseyde will indeed return soon. We know, yet he cannot, that his confidence is a self-created delusion which protects his own feelings. Pandarus, who loyally supports Troilus in his delusion as far as he can, voices our scepticism here. He laughs quietly to himself, inwardly muttering proverbial expressions of disbelief.

It is now night and the gatekeeper begins to call in everyone who is still outside the gates. Very late at night, Troilus rides home in tears once he has accepted that there is no point in waiting there any longer. Yet he still manages to cheer himself up by thinking that he has made a mistake in expecting her to return that day. He remembers that Criseyde said she would return before the moon had passed beyond the sign of Leo. Rather than expecting her on the day on which the moon leaves Leo, Troilus allows her an extra day to return by remembering that she said she would come when the moon has *fully* passed beyond this sign. (This is indeed true, but Criseyde also said that she would return on the tenth day which has now ended.) He tells himself that she may still keep her promise by returning the following morning. Yet when he returns to the gate the next day, his hope entirely blinds him to the reality that Criseyde will not appear. In despair, he returns to his palace at nightfall.

LINES 1198 TO 1232: TROILUS'S HOPE FADES

Troilus's optimism now fades. This loss of hope causes such intense and extraordinary anguish that Troilus feels as if his very heart is bleeding. Since Criseyde has broken her promise to return on the tenth day and has remained for so long in the Greek camp, Troilus does not know what to think. His heart remains poised between hope and fear on the third, fourth, fifth and sixth days after the day of her promised return as he still places some belief in her former promises. But when he finally acknowledges that she will not keep her agreement to return within a short time, he cannot see any other remedy for his sorrows but to prepare himself for death. As he endures this sorrow, we are told that the evil spirit which men call mad jealousy begins to creep into his thoughts. Because of his depression and his wish for death, he neither eats nor drinks and hides away from any company.

Troilus is so disfigured by sorrow that anyone who met him could hardly recognize him. He is so thin, pale and weak that he has to walk with a crutch. He thus destroys himself with his jealous fury. His family frequently ask him why his behaviour and expression are so sorrowful and what was the cause of this distress. But Troilus remains discreet, telling both his family and anyone else who asks that he is experiencing a severe sickness or pain around his heart (though the location of the hurt hints at its true cause).

LINES 1233 TO 1288: TROILUS'S DREAM AND PANDARUS'S REINTERPRETATION

The narrative now recounts a disturbing nightmare experienced by Troilus. He dreams that he is walking in a dense forest in order to weep in private for the love of Criseyde. He comes across a wild boar with large tusks lying asleep in the heat of the bright sunshine. In his dream, Criseyde is lying beside it and kissing it, tightly held in the boar's arms. This sight causes Troilus such sorrow and feelings of outrage that he immediately awakes and calls out loudly for his friend Pandarus. He tells Pandarus that he now understands everything that has happened. He interprets his own dream, telling Pandarus that Criseyde has betrayed him by satisfying the desires of her heart somewhere else. He is certain that the gods have chosen to reveal this to him in his dream. In the *Filostrato*, Troilo identifies the boar as signifying Diomede because he and his ancestors used a boar as their heraldic device. Yet Troilus does not make this connection, meaning that the identification is delayed until Cassandra's later interpretation.

Troilus now addresses the absent Criseyde. He asks in despairing wonder what it is that could have detained her. What failings of his and what awful experience have taken her thoughts and feelings away from him? He calls out to those things on which their former mutual devotion was based, namely trust, loyalty and deep-rooted confidence in each other. He asks who has stolen Criseyde from him, why he let her leave Troy, and swears that he believed every word that she said as gospel truth. Yet, turning his own experience into a proverbial question, he asks who is better able to deceive than the person in whom one thinks it is best to trust. He next asks Pandarus what he should do. Because there is no remedy for his situation, he feels such an intense new pain that he feels it would be better to kill himself now with his own two hands than to have to lament this sorrow forever. If he killed himself his sorrow would be ended, whereas if he remains alive he will torture himself every day.

Though Troilus speaks about suicide, Chaucer here omits the passage in his source where Troilo tries to stab himself and is prevented from doing so by Pandaro. In the *Filostrato*, Pandaro now chastises Troilo for attempting suicide as the result of a dream. In Chaucer's version, Pandarus is simply exasperated by the credence which Troilus gives to his nightmare. He reminds Troilus that he had earlier explained to him how dreams can deceive all kinds of people. He asks how Troilus can dare to say that Criseyde has been unfaithful on the basis of a mere dream.

He tells him to forget his interpretation because he doesn't know how to interpret dreams correctly. Perhaps, says Pandarus, the animal represents Calchas who is old and grey-haired (like the bristles of a wild boar) and who is lying in the sun about to die. Criseyde may thus be kissing him in grief because he is on his deathbed. Yet given that we have already overheard Pandarus expressing scepticism about Criseyde's return, this counter-interpretation must be offered merely in order to console his friend and keep his spirits up.

LINES 1289 TO 1435: TROILUS'S LETTER AND CRISEYDE'S REPLY

Troilus now asks Pandarus how (if he should not rely on his own interpretation) he can be certain about what his dream means. Pandarus suggests that he should quickly write Criseyde a letter (here echoing his earlier advice that Troilus should write a love letter at II.1002–43). By writing to her he will certainly be able to discover the truth. Pandarus argues that if Criseyde is indeed unfaithful to him, she will not write back. If she does write, Troilus will then learn whether there is any possibility that she will return or, if she is prevented from returning, she will offer an explanation. Pandarus points out that the lovers have not exchanged letters since Criseyde's departure (implying that Troilus therefore cannot know Criseyde's situation). Pandarus (once again pretending to be optimistic and to think the best of his niece) bets that Criseyde may have such a rationale that, once Troilus learns about it, he will surely agree that delaying her return is the best course of action for them both.

The narrative now gives the text of Troilus's letter verbatim. Chaucer shortens it in comparison with his source, omitting Troilo's fears that Criseida has a new lover, his descriptions of the way in which former pleasures are now clouded by thoughts of her absence, and his reminders of earlier moments in their love affair. Troilus's letter employs many of the conventional formulae of contemporary French and English letter-writing, for example an exaggeratedly reverent initial address and commendation, and enquiries about the recipient's health and reports of the writer's own condition. As a knight writing to his lady, Troilus takes great care not to offend her or impose on her good will. He names her with conventional epithets of beauty and devotion and identifies himself as the epitome of sorrow. Troilus reminds her that he is and will be hers and no other's, serving her with every part of his being. He recommends himself to her noble favour as constantly as matter fills a vacuum and in every humble way which can be imagined. He respectfully invites her to remember how, a long time ago, her departure left him in intense suffering. He must remain in anguish for as long as it pleases her (because the only cure is her return). It is for this reason that he writes to her in order to convey and lament his ever-increasing grief. He tells her to blame the fact that parts of the letter are blotted out on the tears that rain from his eyes. He deferentially asks that she will not consider her bright eyes to be sullied or defiled by it (presumably by its sorry physical state). If he writes anything improper, he asks forgiveness because his good judgement is overwhelmed by his current anguish.

Having made such deferential overtures, Troilus now begins to outline his grievance as tactfully as he can. He reminds her that she has stayed in the Greek camp for two months yet she previously said that she would only stay there for ten days. He says that he dare not complain any more because (as a devoted servant to his lady) he must be content with whatever pleases her. Yet he nevertheless humbly writes to her about his troubling and painful sorrows. Each day he desires always to know how she has fared in the Greek camp and when she will return. If she wishes to hear about his welfare, he says melodramatically, he can say no more than that he was barely alive when he wrote this letter, fully prepared to end his life by banishing his wretched soul from his body yet holding back from this until he sees the content of her reply. He describes how her delayed return has turned every former joy or comfort into its contrary. So, for example, his eyes which look for her in vain have become sources of sorrowful and salty tears and his (formerly joyful) song has become a lament about his misfortune. Yet if she returns to Troy, he tells her, she can put all this right and thus make him more than a thousand times happier than he was before.

Venturing a little more boldly, he instructs her to remember her promise to return. If he has done something wrong and deserves death, or if she does not wish to see him any more, he asks, as a reward for his previous devotion, that she will nevertheless reply to him so that death can end his inner conflict. If there is another reason which prevents her from returning, he begs her to comfort him by explaining it in a letter. Even though her absence is a living hell for him, he could (if he knew the reason) endure his grief with patience and console himself with new hope. He tells her to write and thus stop him lamenting in this way, to deliver him from his pain by either giving him hope or bringing about his death (by telling him definitively their love has ended). He warns her that when she next sees him she will not be able to recognize him because he has lost his former good health and complexion. Whatever her letter will contain, he ends his missive by asking God to bless her and wishing her farewell. Whereas an everyday letter might end with the writer commending himself to the recipient with news of his condition (i.e., *yours in good spirits*), Troilus says that he writes in such a non-existent state of good health that unless Criseyde gives him health (by an encouraging reply) he will have no health at all.

In the *Filostrato*, Boccaccio delays news of Criseida's reply until after the scene with Cassandra (see *Fil.* VII.105). Chaucer in contrast has Criseyde reply immediately in a way which is cruelly misleading because it gives Troilus cause to hope. We are told only the gist of her reply: she will return as soon as she can and will put right everything that is wrong. In the conclusion of the letter Criseyde tells Troilus that she will indeed come to him but she does not know when. The narrating voice says that in this letter Criseyde swears that she loves Troilus best and pays him a remarkable number of compliments, yet in the future, he says matter-of-factly, Troilus found such promises of love to be without foundation. Addressing Troilus directly, the narrating voice tells him that he can now, if he likes, go and pipe in an ivy leaf in any direction (an idiomatic description of a futile activity). The narrating voice does not take this opportunity to criticize Criseyde but rather adopts a tone of acquiescence and generalization. He comments that the world is always like this and prays that God defend us from similar misfortune and advance everyone who intends to remain faithful. Yet this pious hope seems somewhat at odds with the events of his narrative. Criseyde meant to keep her promise but has nevertheless betrayed Troilus, whilst Troilus remains faithful but will not prosper.

LINES 1436 TO 1540: CASSANDRA INTERPRETS TROILUS'S DREAM

Despite the misleading hope offered by Criseyde's reply, Troilus's suffering increases and his hope and energy correspondingly decrease. He takes to his bed, not eating, drinking or speaking, always speculating that Criseyde has betrayed him and nearly going out of his mind at this thought. In the *Filostrato*, Deiphebo (as Deiphebus is known in the Italian) now overhears Troilo calling out to the absent Criseida. Deiphebo pretends not to have heard and urges Troilo to return to the battlefield now the truce between the Greeks and Trojans has ended. Troilo agrees because he is keen to fight the Greeks (presumably Diomede in particular whom he rightly suspects from his dream is Criseida's new lover). Deiphebo tells his brothers about the cause of Troilo's suffering and they, along with his female relatives, try to console him with music and entertainment. His sister Cassandra, who has overheard the news about Criseida, mocks Troilo about Criseida's lower social status as the daughter of Calchas, the traitorous priest. Troilo, though he denies his love affair with Criseida, nevertheless defends and describes her innate (rather than inherited) nobility, rebuking Cassandra harshly for her snobbery.

Chaucer radically revises this encounter with Cassandra. In his version, Troilus sends for Cassandra in order that she interpret his dream of Criseyde in the boar's arms. Troilus cannot stop thinking about this dream and is convinced that Jove, through his omniscient knowledge of human events, has shown him a sign of her betrayal whilst he slept. The boar has been shown to him as a symbol whose meaning (i.e., the identity of Criseyde's new lover) he can, with Cassandra's help, interpret. Chaucer names Troilus's sister as both Cassandra and as 'Sibille' (1450), taking the noun *sybil* (the name for women in antiquity who possessed powers of divination or prophecy) to be another name for the same person. In classical tradition, Cassandra was given the gift of prophecy by the god Apollo because of her beauty, yet because she did not accept his advances he cursed her to be always disbelieved, as she is here. Troilus recounts his dream and Cassandra interprets it for him. She tells him that if he wishes to learn whom the boar represents and from what family he is descended, he must listen to some old legends on the theme of how **Fortune** has overthrown various ancient noblemen.

The particular legends which Cassandra recounts are those in which Diomede's grandfather and father played a part. She first tells a version of the story of the hunting of the Calydonian boar. Because the Greek people did not make sacrifices to her or burn incense on the altars in her temples, the goddess Diana became angry with them. She avenged herself in a remarkably cruel way, sending a giant boar to ravage the countryside and eat all their corn and vines. The whole country was rallied in order to hunt and slay the animal. One of the most praised maidens in the world (in fact the mythical huntress Atalanta) came to see the boar. The prince of that country, Meleager, fell in love with her and demonstrated his prowess to her by slaying the boar and sending her its head. Cassandra says that ancient books report that this action led to conflict and great enmity. She does not report the details of this ill will (caused by jealous quarrels amongst the huntsmen which led Meleager to kill two of his uncles) and says that she will not pause to tell how Meleager's mother killed him in vengeance for the deaths of her two brothers. She tells Troilus that Tydeus, Diomede's father, was directly descended from Meleager. (Tydeus is in fact a half-brother of Meleager but Chaucer here follows the *Filostrato* (see VII.27) in calling Meleager Diomede's grandfather.) Cassandra next recounts Tydeus's part in the war of the Seven against **Thebes**. She concludes that the boar in Troilus's dream represents Diomede because he is descended from the man who killed the Calydonian boar, and that Troilus's lady (whose identity he has presumably not revealed) and Diomede are lovers. Unsympathetically, she tells her brother it doesn't matter whether he weeps or not because he is out of his lady's affections and Diomede is in.

Troilus refuses to believe this interpretation of his dream. He accuses Cassandra of lying and of being an enchantress whose gift of prophecy, her ability to tell the future through dreams, is 'false' (1521), meaning untrustworthy, spurious or mendacious. He tells her that she might as well tell lies about Queen Alcestis, the kindest and best of creatures (implying that Criseyde is similarly flawless and devoted, though we know that Troilus's faith in her devotion is entirely ironic given that Criseyde's betrayal has already occurred). In classical myth, Alcestis, when the life of her husband King Admetus was hanging in the balance, chose to die and go to hell to save his life, thus becoming a celebrated example of womanly devotion. Troilus is so angered by his sister's interpretation of his dream that he leaps up from his bed as if he has been entirely cured by a doctor. With great diligence, he spends his time seeking the truth about his dream (he would of course prefer an alternative interpretation to the accurate one Cassandra has already given him).

Thebes

At several points Chaucer's characters make reference to the story of the siege of Thebes, the history of the destruction of another city which predates their own siege. As with the story of the fall of Troy, the story of the destruction of the city of Thebes, one of the city-states of ancient Greece, was told in several different classical and medieval versions. When Pandarus visits his niece at the beginning of Book II, Criseyde and her ladies are listening to part of this story.

In Book V, Cassandra, in order to identify the boar about which Troilus has dreamed, recounts the role played by Diomede's father Tydeus in the siege of Thebes. The narrative summary of Cassandra's account is based by Chaucer on a twelve-line Latin mnemonic verse (which appears at this point in all but two of the manuscripts of *Troilus*) which gives in brief the contents of each of the twelve books of the *Thebaid*, a Latin epic poem written by the Roman poet Statius in the first century AD. Through these brief hints, the entirety of the story of the siege and destruction of Thebes is signalled to the reader. Following Oedipus's death, his two sons, Polynices (here *Polymytes*) and Eteocles, were to alternate annually as ruler of Thebes. During Eteocles' year as ruler, Polynices visits the kingdom of Argos, another of the ancient Greek city-states, and marries one of the two daughters of King Adrastus of Argos. Having been exiled by his uncle, Tydeus, son of King Oeneus of the Greek city-state of Calydon, marries Adrastus's other daughter. When Eteocles refuses to relinquish his rule of Thebes, Adrastus promises firstly to help Polynices reclaim Thebes from his brother Eteocles and then to help Tydeus reclaim Calydon. The 'Seven against Thebes', that is, Adrastus, Tydeus, Polynices and four others (the warriors Capaneus, Hippomedon and Parthenopaeus, and the prophet Amphiaraus) lay siege to Thebes. The summary picks out famous episodes which occurred before, during and after the siege. Tydeus kills all but one of the fifty warriors sent by Eteocles to ambush him and only Maeon (here *Hemonydes*) escapes. A serpent sent by Jupiter kills King Lycurgus of Nemea's infant son, left behind while his nursemaid was guiding Adrastus's army towards the nearest source of fresh water (despite a prophetic warning that she should always carry him in her arms). The funeral of Lycurgus's son (here *Archymoris*) is described, as well as how Amphiaraus, as he himself had prophesied, falls into the underworld when the earth opens up on the battlefield. The deaths of Diomede's father Tydeus, Hippomedon, Parthenopaeus (here *Parthonope*) and Capaneus are each narrated. As Diomede tells Criseyde (v.932–8), it was Tydeus's untimely death in the siege of Thebes which prevented him from reclaiming Calydon and hence Diomede could not inherit this kingdom or the kingdom of Tydeus's father-in-law, King Adrastus of Argos. Eteocles and Polynices kill each other in battle, and the story ends with the grief of Polynices' wife Argia (here *Argyve*) because Jocasta's brother Creon, who takes control of the city after the death of Polynices and Eteocles, will not allow the bodies of those killed in the siege to be buried. Ultimately, the city of Thebes is destroyed by fire, just as Calchas has predicted that Troy will likewise be destroyed.

These allusions to the story of the fall of Thebes in *Troilus and Criseyde* invite us to speculate about the larger patterns of history. Why do things go wrong, both for individuals such as Troilus and Criseyde and for nations such as Thebes or Troy? Is history always destined to repeat itself or can such patterns be altered? Troilus, in asking for **the God of Love**'s assistance in Book v (599–602), asks him not to be as cruel to the nobility of Troy as Jove's wife Juno was to the people of Thebes. Juno's wrath (caused by her husband's affairs with two Theban women) led to the destruction of Thebes and its people. But in the Theban story as heard by Criseyde and her ladies, as known by Pandarus and as retold by Cassandra, death and destruction are brought about not only by angering the gods, but by human jealousy and rivalry, by the thirst for power, by pride and stubbornness, by familial betrayal and by misfortune and unlucky coincidence. Even when the future is known through prophecy (as in the cases of Oedipus, Amphiaraus and Archemorus), such disastrous events cannot be avoided. Likewise, though we readers can see that the destruction of Thebes anticipates the fall of the Trojans' own city, the Trojan characters themselves cannot see such parallels because they do not know their own future and do not believe Calchas's prophecy.

LINES 1541 TO 1582: HECTOR'S DEATH AND TROILUS'S VACILLATIONS

Following on from Cassandra's recounting of the fall of **Thebes**, the narrative now describes how Troy's fortunes likewise began to decline. Jove, through his divine foreknowledge and ordaining, has entrusted the perpetual changing of all things to the goddess **Fortune**. Such changing can be witnessed when sovereignty over territories is transferred from the possession of one nation or race to another, or when (formerly glorious) nations or races are disgraced (*smytted* meaning literally stained or sullied). **Fortune** therefore begins to pull away Troy's bright feathers one by one until it is devoid of joy. The city here is figured as a bird whose individual feathers (in this metaphor the city's nobles who provide protection and renown) are plucked away until it is entirely defenceless and defeated. Hector is one such bright feather which is plucked away. We are warned that the end of Hector's life's term was approaching extraordinarily quickly. Hector's fate, his individual destiny, decrees that his soul should now 'unbodye' (1550), literally to un-body or leave his body. Fate thus devises a method by which Hector's soul can be driven out of his body, a destiny which Hector cannot resist. As Hector drags a king along the ground by his chain-mail neckguard, the Greek warrior Achilles stabs him through his chain-mail armour and through his body. The narrating voice comments that every type of military man should lament the death of such a noble knight. He says that the lamentation made by the Trojans upon Hector's death was too great to tell. Troilus's grief for his brother's death is particularly great. Because of this news, and also his grief at Criseyde's failure to return, he commands his heart to break (and so end his torment) many times a day. Yet he cannot quite abandon hope. Although he despairs and dreads that Criseyde has betrayed him, yet his heart (and hence his feelings of love) always returns to her. Troilus continues to make excuses for her late arrival, thinking that it is Calchas who has delayed her. He often intends to disguise himself as a pilgrim (who would be able to travel more freely than a soldier in a time of war) in order to visit Criseyde in the Greek camp. Yet he does not do this, we are told, because he is unable to disguise himself well enough that those who know him would not recognize him. Nor could he think of a sufficient excuse for his presence if he were recognized whilst amongst the Greeks (he would likely be killed or imprisoned if he, a Trojan noble, were found in the enemy camp).

LINES 1583 TO 1631: CRISEYDE'S LETTER

Because his hopes remain alive, Troilus frequently writes more letters to Criseyde, pleading with her that, because he remains faithful, she should likewise keep her word and return as promised. Whereas in the *Filostrato* Criseida's messages are summarized as 'fair words and grand promises without effect' (VIII.5), in Chaucer's version we are given the text of one of Criseyde's replies and left to judge the contents for ourselves. The narrating voice says that Criseyde wrote out of pity, though he implies that others may interpret the letter differently by acknowledging that this is his subjective opinion. Criseyde's letter features many of the formulae of contemporary letter-writing. She addresses Troilus with superlative epithets, yet, rather than conventionally sending him good health, she asks how a person who is tormented and anxious, lacking health herself, could send the recipient of this letter any happiness. She describes her own state, exclaiming that she is sick, distressed and 'herteles' (1594, meaning not 'callous' as in Modern English but 'disheartened'). Since they cannot be together, she can neither send him good cheer nor wish him good health. She has seen how his letter is entirely stained by tears and how he asks her to return. Yet evasively she says such a return is impossible, but she cannot say why because she is frightened that her letter might be intercepted. She says that to hear about his torment and his impatience is painful for her. To her he does not seem to be stoically taking for the best what the gods have ordained for them (that is, a prolonged separation). She accuses him of thinking of nothing but his own pleasure. She tells him not to be angry with her because her delayed return is caused by other people's wicked gossip. She claims to have heard a great deal more public gossip about their affair than she had expected (perhaps implying here that he has been somehow indiscreet). She tells him she will put this right by making some sort of pretence (is this an evasive description of her acceptance of Diomede?). She tells Troilus she has discovered (though we might wonder how) that he is doing nothing but leading her on. Yet despite this implied criticism of his behaviour, she says that all this doesn't matter now as she cannot suspect him of anything other than perfect faithfulness and nobility. She says she will come to him, but she is in such a predicament (again unspecified) that she cannot say on what day or in which year she will return. Yet she asks him always to have a good opinion of her and asks him for his friendship because she will always be a friend to him. These requests echo her earlier soliloquy in which she pledged to be loyal to Diomede and bid farewell to Troilus (v.1072–85), hinting that this letter is, in some implicit manner, also a farewell. She ends by begging him not to be offended that her letter is short. She claims that she dare not write letters in the Greek camp and that she has never had much skill at letter-writing. Yet she reminds him that one can write things of considerable significance in a very few words. The **intention** of the writer is everything, not the length of the letter. Such a comment invites the reader to speculate about Criseyde's **intention** in writing this letter, given that from our perspective, the letter seems deluded, deceptive and cruel.

LINES 1632 TO 1743: TROILUS'S SUSPICIONS CONFIRMED

We are next told of Troilus's reaction to the letter. Troilus thinks it very aloof and unfriendly, appearing to be a calends of change (see p. 35), a harbinger of her betrayal. Yet Troilus cannot entirely bring himself to believe that Criseyde will not keep her word. The narrative explains Troilus's reluctance in the form of a proverb: he who is deeply in love is most reluctant to believe the worst, even though he is troubled by doubts. Yet carrying on in this proverbial vein, we are told that nevertheless it is said that in the end, despite everything, the truth will be seen. As we will see, just such a revelation occurs and Troilus soon realizes that Criseyde was not as 'kynde' (1643), as affectionate and constant in love, as she should have been.

The narrative now recounts the incident which confirms Troilus's suspicions. It happens that Troilus sees a kind of 'cote-armure' (1651) being carried around the city streets. (A *coat-armour* or coat of arms was a vest or tunic decorated with an individual's heraldic arms and worn on top of his armour.) It is being carried in front of Deiphebus as a sign of his victory. The narrating voice claims that his supposed source Lollius recounts that Deiphebus had ripped the tunic from Diomede that day (this detail is in fact taken from Chaucer's unacknowledged source, Boccaccio's *Filostrato*). Troilus inspects the garment in detail, looking at its size and workmanship. As he looks his heart suddenly grows cold because he finds inside the collar the brooch which he had given to Criseyde on the morning on which she was forced to leave the city. Troilus gave her the brooch in remembrance of himself and of his grief at her departure, and Criseyde promised him that she would keep it forever. Now he comprehends that he can no longer trust her (guessing of course that in all likelihood she must have given the brooch as a love-token to the owner of the coat of arms, the identity of whom he can deduce from the heraldic device painted or embroidered on the fabric).

Troilus returns to his palace and sends for Pandarus in order to tell him about the brooch. He bemoans the inconstancy of Criseyde's heart and, in contrast, his own long devotion, loyalty and suffering. He begs death to restore him to a state of tranquillity free from distress (by ending his life and suffering). He addresses the absent Criseyde directly, asking what has become of her sworn oath and promise, her love and loyalty. He says that he would have at least thought that she would not have strung him along in this way if she didn't want to remain faithful to him. He says he could not have believed (before he had sight of this physical evidence) that she could have changed so much. Only if he had acted wrongly could he have believed that her heart could be so cruel as to kill him in this way. Just as Criseyde herself predicted in her soliloquy, Troilus also laments that her reputation for loyalty is now obliterated. He asks whether she could not have given some other brooch to endow her new lover, reminding her that she has given away the very piece of jewellery that he gave her, wet with his tears, as a keepsake. He concludes that she had no reason to do so except out of spite and also because she wished to display her changed **intention** very publicly. He can now see that she has cast him clean out of her thoughts, yet he cannot bring himself to 'unloven' her (1698), literally *to un-love* her (meaning both not to love her and not to have loved her) for even a quarter of a day.

He next asks God to grant him the favour of soon encountering Diomede on the battlefield. Troilus says that if he has the strength and the opportunity, he hopes to injure him grievously. He pleads to know why God, who should be careful to reward loyalty and punish wrongs, does not take vengeance on Criseyde's moral error. Now he addresses his friend Pandarus. Pandarus can see for himself how loyal his niece Criseyde is now. Troilus also points out that he, not Pandarus, was right about dreams. The gods reveal both happiness and pain in various ways in sleep, as his own dream proves. He concludes firstly by promising that he now intends to pursue his own death on the battlefield, even if that comes very quickly. Finally, he addresses Criseyde once more. He tells her that he has not deserved what she has done to him.

Strikingly, for someone who has previously done so much talking and advising, Pandarus cannot answer Troilus immediately even though he inwardly acknowledges the truth of what his friend is saying. He stands as still as a stone, unable to say a word because he is paralysed by two things. He is simultaneously sorry for Troilus's sorrow and ashamed at his niece's actions. After a pause, he admits his helplessness to Troilus. All he can say is that he hates Criseyde and that he will hate her forever more. He also prays that God quickly deliver her from this world by death. In comparison with the *Filostrato* (where Pandaro says he will avoid his cousin and begs God to punish her so that she will not sin in this way again), Pandarus's denunciation of his own niece is much more severe. Pandarus also defends his own actions in the love affair. He says that he did all that Troilus earlier asked him to do exactly as his friend wished, with no regard to his good repute or his own leisure (Pandarus here makes it sound as if he did not take the initiative in bringing about the love affair but merely acceded to Troilus's requests). He swears that Criseyde's betrayal is a sorrow to him and that he would gladly remedy it if he knew how. But ultimately Pandarus cannot provide any more explanations or plans for action in the face of the proof of Criseyde's change of heart. In his last words in the poem, he admits that he cannot say any more.

LINES 1744 TO 1869: THE ENDING

(i) Lines 1744 to 1764: Troilus fights Diomede

The narrative now sums up the situation by antithesis, the juxtaposition of contrasting ideas in balanced clauses or phrases. Troilus's sorrow and lamentation are immense (and hence moving) but **Fortune** always keeps to her course (and hence is unmoved by his distress). Criseyde loves Diomede yet Troilus must weep in distress. In an addition to Chaucer's source, the narrating voice again says that the world always appears like this to whosoever knows how to look at it. He concludes that there is little peace for the soul in each stage of life and in each position in society. All we can do, as the narrating first-person himself does, is ask for God's help to take it for the best. Again, he avoids criticism of Criseyde, taking her change of heart as a matter of fact and offering only generalized acquiescence.

As he had earlier vowed, Troilus now pursues his own death on the battlefield, seeking out Diomede in particular. We are told that Troilus and Diomede often encounter each other in battle, exchanging both bloody strokes of their swords and angry words. Yet even though Troilus intends to kill Criseyde's new love, **Fortune** did not wish that either should die at the other's hand. Once again **intention** is not enough – wanting something to occur does not make it happen if events are destined to be otherwise.

(ii) Lines 1765 to 1785: the narrating voice's self-justification

In an addition to the *Filostrato*, the narrating voice now excuses himself from giving more details of the fights between Troilus and Diomede. He says that if he had undertaken to write about Troilus's heroic deeds he would now compose verse about such clashes (and hence his poem would have more subject matter yet to cover). He interrupts himself to tell his readers that whoever wants to read about Troilus's noble feats of arms should consult Dares. Yet, because he commenced his poem intending only to write about Troilus's love, he has now said as much as he can (and hence his poem is drawing to its end).

Chaucer here adds material to his source in which the narrating first-person anticipates the response his text will receive. The narrating voice is keen to clarify that he did not set out to be a historian of military matters, so cannot be criticized for concentrating on matters of the heart. He also anticipates that women readers will be angered by his rehearsal of

Criseyde's betrayal. The narrating voice appeals directly to every lady and every gracious or noble woman, asking them that, although Criseyde has indeed been unfaithful to Troilus, the irrefutable fact of her guilt should not lead them to become angry with the storyteller, who merely recounts the circumstances of the matter. He tells them that they can read about her misdeed in other books too (for example the preceding versions of the story told by Benoît, Guido and Boccaccio). He thus implies that he is not the originator of this story of womanly betrayal but that he is bound to follow the pattern of his sources and of history. He tells his women readers that, if they were to ask him, he would more willingly write about the faithfulness of Penelope and about good Alcestis (see p. 181). Penelope, the wife of the Greek hero Odysseus, loyally waited for her husband to return home for twenty years, resisting the advances of other suitors. The narrating voice also claims that what he is saying in his poem is not said just for the sake of men such as Troilus (who are betrayed by women) but most particularly for the sake of women who are betrayed by deceitful people. Such people, through their considerable cunning and guile, betray the women to whom he is now speaking directly. It is the betrayal of women by men which impels him to speak out and so he tells women to beware of men. This motivation seems at odds with the particularities of the story he has chosen to tell, which more obviously demonstrates that men should beware of women. Indeed Boccaccio's epilogue warns young men to put no trust in women, especially young ones. Is it possible, as the narrating voice proposes, to interpret this story as warning about masculine betrayal? Is Criseyde betrayed in some way by the men of Troy, by Troilus and Diomede, and perhaps most particularly by Pandarus, her uncle? Why does the narrating voice avoid explicitly censuring Criseyde for her actions, as seems a more obvious response?

The narrating voice's attempts to forestall his women readers' displeasure prompt a number of other questions and inferences. If one can indeed read about Criseyde's guilt in *other* books, is his own book offering us some different verdict about its central female character, one which puts her guilt in a different context? Would the virtue of Penelope or Alcestis be more appropriate or fruitful subjects for a literary work or is a story of misfortune and human failing more absorbing and enlightening? Does the story of Troilus's love affair, however narrated, always propound one message (i.e., that women are likely to betray men) or can it be turned on its head to mean the opposite? Does the narrating voice's purported **intention** (whatever Chaucer's **intention** may be) determine the meaning of his story or is it out of his control to some degree?

(iii) Lines 1786 to 1798: the envoy to the book

The narrating voice now addresses his own poem directly, fondly calling it his little book and his little tragedy. These stanzas (added by Chaucer to his source) form an envoy, an author's parting words to his composition as he sends it forth to be read or recited by others. Though ostensibly speaking only to an author's own work, such envoys are of course intended to be overheard by their readers. Whilst an envoy might be expected to be located at the very end of a literary work, Chaucer here has the narrating voice address the work before he has even described the death of his central character. Calling the poem a tragedy assigns it to a particular genre, though unlike classical definitions of tragedy Chaucer uses the term to refer simply to a narrative which describes a central figure's fall from happiness and prosperity into adversity. The narrating voice instructs his poem to leave him and hopes that God will send this poem's author the capacity to compose some sort of comedy before he dies (that is, to create successfully a work with a happy ending, opposite in structure to that of *Troilus and Criseyde*).

The narrating voice also tells his book not to seek to rival any other 'makyng' (1789), that is, to seek to be valued in the same terms as other contemporary vernacular literary entertainments, but instead to be submissive and deferential to all ancient and highly revered poetry. It should do no more than meekly kiss the footsteps left behind when much more famous and authoritative classical authors pass by (as if the poem is a humble commoner watching an aristocratic or regal procession, who should not presume to attract the attention of his superiors or join in the procession as an equal). This instruction is simultaneously both modest and audacious, suggesting humility but also implying that his work, however pale in comparison, belongs with the famous poets of antiquity. Chaucer echoes the opening lines of Homer's *Iliad* and Virgil's *Aeneid* at the close of his work (see v.1765–6 and 1800–1), again associating his own poem with those of the most famous classical authors.

The narrating voice now turns to his poem's transmission once it leaves his hands. Because there is such great variety (both of dialects and of variant forms of words) within the English language, he prays that no one makes an error when copying out his poem. Before the invention of the printing press, literary works were disseminated by being copied and recopied by scribes who might, through inevitable human error, omit, miscopy or substitute words from the text from which they were copying. He also prays that none of these scribes ruin his poem's metre because of what he calls errors in their own speech. In the late fourteenth century, English did not have a standardized spelling system, so instead scribes spelled words according to their own dialect and their training. A scribe might therefore copy Chaucer's poem in accordance with a different set of spelling conventions and thus make changes. Such changes might, if they altered the number of syllables in a word, spoil the intended metrical pattern of a line of verse. The narrating voice ends his envoy by begging God that his book be understood wherever it is read or sung (a formulaic expression meaning however it is conveyed).

(iv) Lines 1799 to 1834: Troilus's death and ascension

Having digressed in order to address his readers and his book, the narrating first-person now acknowledges that he must return to the point of what he was previously describing (that is, the way in which Troilus's jealous anger inspires him on the battlefield). He repeats and exaggerates his description of how the Greeks paid dearly for Troilus's wrath, reporting that thousands died at his hands. He next describes how Troilus was cruelly slain by the Greek warrior Achilles. He exclaims in sorrow at Troilus's death but nevertheless acknowledges it was God's will that he died at that moment.

Chaucer here adds to his source the description of the ascent of Troilus's soul, drawing the details from the account of the flight of Arcita's soul after death in **Giovanni Boccaccio's** ***Teseida delle nozze d'Emilia*** ('the book of Theseus about the nuptials of Emilia'). In the medieval geocentric model of the cosmos, the stars and planets were thought to be carried around the Earth by rotating spheres of rarefied matter. The moon, sun and five then-known planets (Mercury, Venus, Mars, Jupiter and Saturn) occupy a sphere each. Moving outwards, these seven planetary spheres are followed by the eighth stellar sphere containing the fixed stars. Beyond the fixed stars was the outermost sphere moved by a fixed unmoving mover and the Empyrean, the dwelling-place of God. Following his death, Troilus's weightless soul ascends to the empty space inside the eighth sphere, leaving behind each of the planetary spheres. Troilus's soul has thus reached the sphere of the fixed stars. He has a clear view to look at the wandering stars in the seven planetary spheres below (the five then-known planets and the sun and moon were called wandering because their orbits, when viewed from Earth, appeared to wander erratically around the heavens). He also listens to the harmony of music full of heavenly melody. This is the music of the spheres, the harmonious sound produced by the motion of the spheres in rotation.

Troilus's soul has thus ascended to a position far above the ever-changing world of human concerns, giving him posthumously a new perspective on what he sees. Just as his soul ascends closer to heaven, his new perspective is closer to the divine in its atemporality, omniscience and insight. He now looks down intently at what is called this little spot of Earth, surrounded on all sides by the sea. From his great height, the whole globe appears to Troilus to be a tiny speck in the distance covered in oceans. His new perspective leads him to despise this wretched world and consider everything in it to be worthless or transitory when compared to the perfect bliss of heaven. He looks finally at the place on the battlefield outside Troy where he was slain. Rather than having sympathy for those who weep so much over his death, within himself he simply laughs at their grief. It is laughable to grieve for the loss of a single individual because such a loss is, from his new position of insight, both inevitable and insignificant.

Troilus next condemns all of our (i.e., humanity's) earthly actions which are dedicated to the pursuit of blind delights which cannot last. They are blind pleasures in the sense of being deceptive or illusory and they cannot last because everything in the sublunary world (the realm of the Earth and everything below the first planetary sphere containing the moon) is subject to change. Troilus condemns the fact that humanity pursues such actions when we should instead place all our love and trust in heaven. As readers, we are challenged to apply Troilus's sudden insights to the narrative in which we have just immersed ourselves as well as to our own behaviour. We have indeed witnessed changes of fortune and changes of heart and have seen that romantic love is not, in this case at least, the source of **felicity** and contentment that those experiencing it claimed it to be. Yet because we have been so deeply engrossed in these events it may seem difficult to dismiss them as insignificant or illusory. Was the love between Troilus and Criseyde and the happiness it brought about nothing more than an instance of the pursuit of illusory and temporary pleasure?

Finally, we are told that Troilus's soul went to where the god Mercury (in his role as the guide who escorts the souls of the newly dead to the afterlife) assigned it to dwell. This formulation allows Chaucer to leave unspecified the final destination of Troilus's soul, specifying neither heaven nor hell nor their pagan equivalents. Chaucer now translates a stanza from his source which bitterly laments how Troilo's 'ill-conceived love', 'wretched sorrow' and 'vain hope' (*Fil.* VIII.28), as well as his glorious reputation, have led to such an end, his brutal death at the hands of Achilles. In the *Filostrato*, which does not allocate Troilo any posthumous ascent, insight or immortality, these lines more straightforwardly revise the story in the light of Troilo's wretched death, seeing the events which led him there as misguided and unfortunate. In contrast, Chaucer borrows from Boccaccio the repeated *such an end had X* formula but makes its meaning and tone much less certain. We are told that Troilus had such an end for love. All of his great merit, his royal rank, his delight (whether *blynde* or not) and his nobility have such an end. Adopting Troilus's new perspective, the narrating voice says that the fragility of this deceptive world also ends in the same way. But what end is being referred to? Is it Troilus's misery and his violent and ignominious death, or the unspecified final location of his soul, or the divine insight he has been granted and his new existence beyond mutability and self-deception? And why has Troilus been granted such an end, whatever that end is? Is it that his nobility and devotion have been debased by desire and folly and ended by worldly mutability or is it that all of these things, in some strange combination, have led to his posthumous exaltation and insight?

Giovanni Boccaccio's *Teseida delle nozze d'Emilia*

The *Teseida delle nozze d'Emilia* is an Italian poem by Giovanni Boccaccio, the author of *Il filostrato*, Chaucer's main source for *Troilus and Criseyde*. Chaucer translated and adapted the *Teseida* as the source for what became his *Knight's Tale*, the first of the *Canterbury Tales*. Written probably between 1339 and 1341, the *Teseida* is an imitation of a classical epic which narrates how, having been imprisoned by Theseus, duke of Athens, two Theban noblemen, Palemone and Arcita, both fall in love with Emilia, younger sister of Hippolyta, queen of the Amazons and Theseus's wife. Arcita is exiled whilst Palemone escapes from prison, yet they meet again by chance and fight each other in a grove. They are discovered by Theseus, who decrees that the two men should battle in his amphitheatre for Emilia's hand in marriage. Although the god Mars helps Arcita to victory, the goddess Venus bids one of the Furies to frighten Arcita's horse as he rides triumphantly around the amphitheatre. As his horse startles, Arcita is injured by being thrown against the pommel of his saddle and he eventually dies from this injury. After his funeral, and as Arcita himself had wished, Theseus decrees that Palemone and Emilia should be married. As well as drawing on the description of Arcita's pagan funeral to provide some of the details of Troilus's instructions to Pandarus as regards his own funeral (V.295–315), Chaucer borrows Boccaccio's description of the ascent of Arcita's soul after his death (a passage which he omitted from the *Knight's Tale*) as the source of his description of the ascent of Troilus's soul:

'When Arcita had thus ended by calling upon her whom he loved more than any other in the world [i.e., Emilia] his free spirit flew away towards the inner surface of the eighth sphere, leaving behind it the outer bounds of the others. From there he gazed in wonder at the orderliness and supreme beauty of the moving stars and heard sounds that were full of the utmost sweetness.

'Then he turned downwards to look again at what he had left behind him. And he saw the little globe of Earth with the sea and air encircling it and the fire above, and he judged it all to be worthless by comparison with Heaven. But then, looking backwards for a while, he let his eyes linger upon the place in which his body remained. 'And he smiled to himself, thinking of all the Greeks and their lamentations, and greatly deplored the futile behaviour of earthly men whose minds are so darkened and befogged as to make them frenziedly pursue the false attractions of the world and turn away from Heaven. Then he departed to the place that Mercury allotted to him' (*Chaucer's Boccaccio*, ed. and trans. Havely, p. 144).

Chaucer, when referring to that which Troilus views anew from the eighth sphere, replaces Boccaccio's definite article ('*the* little globe', '*the* Greeks', '*the* futile behaviour') with demonstrative pronouns. The use of proximal rather than distal deixis to refer to the world at which Troilus looks (the narrating voice of *Troilus* says that it is *this* spot, implying closeness in time, rather than *that* spot, implying remoteness in time) suggests that he is looking not only down at Troy, a particular, limited moment in history, but atemporally at the whole of human history, then and now (whether that be fourteenth-century England or the here-and-now of every reader). Likewise, Chaucer's narrative describes the target of Troilus's condemnation with the first-person plural possessive *our* ('al *oure* werk', 'al *oure* herte'), thus implicating everyone, past, present and future.

(v) Lines 1835 to 1859: the narrating voice addresses his readers

The narrating voice now addresses another section of his readership, in this case young men and women. The narrator of the *Filostrato* addresses only young men at this point, warning them to distrust all women, especially youthful or snobbish ones. In contrast, the narrating voice of Chaucer's poem offers a warning not about whom to choose as your loved one but what sort of love to choose. He instructs young people to return home (in the sense of returning to their Creator and to their heavenly origin), to leave behind trivial or meaningless pleasures and to direct the attention of their hearts to God. They should echo Troilus's final thoughts and consider the temporal world to be nothing more than a fair, a temporary and short-lived entertainment which is over as quickly as the fairest flowers fade away. They should instead love Christ. Christ will not deceive or be unfaithful to anyone who devotes their heart to Him. Chaucer's choice of verb here contrasts Criseyde's betrayal with the certainty of Christian devotion. Criseyde 'falsed' Troilus (v.1053, 1056) but Christ will not *falsen* any Christian. Since Christ is therefore the best object of devotion and the most benevolent, the narrating voice asks his young audiences, what need is there to pursue loves which are a false sham when compared to Christian love?

We may find it hard to redirect our gaze as the narrating voice instructs. Are the joy and sorrow of romantic and erotic love as described in this poem to be dismissed as an inferior simulacrum of divine love and hence an exemplification of the shortcomings of false love? Is the imagined world created in this poem merely a brief distraction from larger truths? It must be, and yet however much the narrating voice condemns it, the book remains in our hands and the story remains with us. Yet if we struggle to follow the instruction to turn our eyes to heaven, how might we defend the events of the story from this criticism?

The narrating voice tells his young readers or hearers what he now sees in his work. Here can be seen what he calls the profane old rites of pagans and how little use are all of their various pagan deities. Here can be seen these wretched worldly desires ('appetites' can mean both unspecified craving and sexual desire in particular). Here can be seen what end and what reward is received for service of Jove, Apollo, Mars and other such worthless individuals (a contemptuous reference to these classical gods). Here also can be seen the 'forme' (1854), the particular literary style in which classical authors wrote their poetry (implying again that this poem is composed in imitation of classical models). Once again, we must now square the narrating first-person's final verdict on his poem with what we have previously read. We might agree that desire has led to spiritual, moral or philosophical blindness, that the appeals made to pagan deities for help have proved fruitless and that Trojan beliefs about fortune and predestination are limited or partial in comparison with revealed Christian truth. Yet if that is so, why was love also presented as supremely joyful and ennobling, aligned with the sacred ordering of the universe and with divine benevolence? The narrating voice labels his story (in terms of both its content and style) as pagan and hence contemptible (or at least inferior) from a Christian perspective, yet nonetheless presents it as an imitation of an ancient classical work (with all the cultural authority this implies). The narrating voice ridicules and condemns aspects of his narrative, yet we may be provoked to celebrate, defend and tolerate it in other ways.

Finally, the narrating voice directs the poem towards two particular named readers. He addresses 'moral Gower' and 'philosophical Strode' (1856–7), asking them to agree to correct it where necessary. John Gower was a fellow poet and friend of Chaucer whilst Ralph Strode was first an Oxford academic and later a London lawyer who also had a reputation as a poet (though none of his works survives). The adjectives which qualify their names specify their particular areas of expertise: Gower as an author of works concerning morality and Strode as an author of learned treatises on logic, part of the academic discipline of philosophy. This dedication thus proposes two ways of evaluating the poem, one moral and one philosophical. We might thus speculate on whether Gower and Strode would have responded to the poem in the same way, given their different expertise, interests and modes of enquiry, and which aspects of it they might each have chosen to amend. What might be the moral lesson of this poem and what philosophical education or consolation might it provide?

(vi) Lines 1860 to 1869: a final prayer

Boccaccio's *Filostrato* ends with an envoy attributing inspiration for the work to its narrator's love for his lady and bidding his book to tell her about his own sorrows in love by means of Troilo's suffering. The narrating voice of *Troilus and Criseyde*, in contrast, ends his work with prayers to Christ and to the Trinity. Just as he began his work by describing it as akin to a charitable act of mercy, so the narrating first-person ends by asking Christ for mercy for his own soul. Just as he urged his youthful readers, his own attention is now directed away from pagan antiquity and towards the divine. He addresses the three parts of the Trinity palindromically (that is, the same words first forwards and then in reverse), invoking the triune God as both limitless and that which encompasses everything (perhaps a hint that even the vain, pagan, worldly matters of Chaucer's own poem are ultimately within God's compass). Chaucer borrows these lines from the joyful song of praise sung three times by each of the souls gathered in two circles around Dante and Beatrice in the fourth of the circles of heaven as described in the *Paradiso*, the third and final part of the *Divina commedia*.[13] The fourth circle of heaven, that of the sun, contains the souls of the wise, including theologians, philosophers and scholars.

The regular iambic rhythms of the first two lines of the final stanza enhance their palindromic symmetry in combination with the antithesis of line 1865. Repetitions in this final stanza both of individual words (*mercy*) and of morphological elements (*-circumscri-*, *-visible*) create a feeling of harmony, yet the intricate syntax and inversions of normal word order embody the difficulty of adequately comprehending and conveying such Christian mysteries. The narrating voice asks the Trinity to defend us from visible and invisible enemies, that is, to defend us from both human and fiendish evil. His final prayer asks Jesus, by means of His mercy, to make every one of us worthy of His mercy, for the sake of His love for 'mayde and moder thyn benigne' (1869), merciful and gentle Mary who was paradoxically both virgin and mother. With this prayer and paradox, the poem ends.

[13] 'That one and two and three which lives for ever and reigns for ever in three and two and one, uncircumscribed and circumscribing all, was sung three times by each of these spirits.' Dante, *Divine Comedy*, trans. Sisson, p. 410 (*Paradiso*, XIV.28–31).

Further reading

PRIMARY SOURCES IN TRANSLATION

Alain of Lille, *Plaint of Nature*, trans. J. J. Sheridan, Mediaeval Sources in Translation 26 (Toronto: Pontifical Institute of Mediaeval Studies, 1980)

Benoît of Sainte-Maure, *Le Roman de Troie*: see *Chaucer's Boccaccio*, ed. and trans. Havely

Boccaccio, Giovanni, *Il filostrato*: see *Troilus and Criseyde*, ed. Barney, under Editions and Translations

Teseida delle nozze d'Emilia: see *Chaucer's Boccaccio*, ed. and trans. Havely

Boethius, *The Consolation of Philosophy*, trans. V. Watts, rev. edn, Penguin Classics (London: Penguin, 1999)

Chaucer's Boccaccio: Sources for 'Troilus' and the 'Knight's' and 'Franklin's Tales', ed. and trans. N. R. Havely, Chaucer Studies 3 (Cambridge: Brewer, 1980)

Cicero, *De inventione, De optimo genere oratorum, Topica*, ed. and trans. H. M. Hubbell, Loeb Classical Library 386 (London: Heinemann; Cambridge, MA: Harvard University Press, 1949)

Dante Alighieri, *The Divine Comedy*, trans. C. H. Sisson, Oxford World's Classics (Oxford University Press, 1998)

Geoffrey of Vinsauf, *Poetria nova*, trans. M. F. Nims, rev. edn, Mediaeval Sources in Translation 49 (Toronto: Pontifical Institute of Mediaeval Studies, 2010)

Guido of Colonna, *Historia destructionis Troiae: Guido delle Colonne*, trans. M. E. Meek (Bloomington: Indiana University Press, 1974)

Horace, *Satires, Epistles, Ars poetica*, ed. and trans. H. R. Fairclough, Loeb Classical Library 194 (London: Heinemann, 1952)

Joseph of Exeter, *The Iliad of Dares Phrygius*, trans. G. Roberts (Cape Town: Balkema, 1970)

Juvenal, *Satires*, in *Juvenal and Persius*, ed. and trans. S. Morton Braund, Loeb Classical Library 91 (Cambridge, MA: Harvard University Press, 2004)

Petrarch, *Canzoniere: Selected Poems*, trans. A. Mortimer, Penguin Classics (London: Penguin, 2002)

Le Roman de Thèbes (The Story of Thebes), trans. J. Smartt Coley, Garland Library of Medieval Literature 44 (New York: Garland, 1986)

Statius, *Silvae, Thebaid, Achilleid*, ed. and trans. D. R. Shackleton Bailey, 3 vols., Loeb Classical Library 206, 207, 498 (Cambridge, MA: Harvard University Press, 2003)

The Story of Troilus: As Told by Benoît de Sainte-Maure, Giovanni Boccaccio, Geoffrey Chaucer, Robert Henryson, trans. R. K. Gordon, paperback edn (New York: Dutton, 1964)

The Trojan War: The Chronicles of Dictys of Crete and Dares the Phrygian, trans. R. M. Frazer (Bloomington: Indiana University Press, 1966)

EDITIONS AND TRANSLATIONS OF *TROILUS AND CRISEYDE*

Troilus and Criseyde: A New Edition of 'The Book of Troilus', ed. B. A. Windeatt (London: Longman, 1984)

Troilus and Criseyde: A New Translation, trans. B. A. Windeatt, Oxford World's Classics (Oxford University Press, 1998)

Troilus and Criseyde, with Facing-page Il filostrato: Authoritative Texts, The Testament of Cresseid, Criticism, ed. S. A. Barney (New York: Norton, 2006)

SELECTED FURTHER READING

INTRODUCTORY BOOKS AND CHAPTERS

Benson, C. D., *Chaucer's 'Troilus and Criseyde'* (London: Unwin Hyman, 1990)

Blamires, A., 'Chaucer's *Troilus and Criseyde*', in C. Saunders (ed.), *A Companion to Medieval Poetry*, Blackwell Companions to Literature and Culture 67 (Chichester: Wiley-Blackwell, 2010), pp. 435–51

Summit, J., '*Troilus and Criseyde*', in S. Lerer (ed.), *The Yale Companion to Chaucer* (New Haven, CT: Yale University Press, 2006), pp. 213–42

Windeatt, B. A., *'Troilus and Criseyde': Oxford Guides to Chaucer* (Oxford: Clarendon Press, 1992)

COLLECTIONS OF CRITICAL ESSAYS

Barney, S. A. (ed.), *Chaucer's 'Troilus': Essays in Criticism* (London: Scolar Press, 1980)

Benson, C. D. (ed.), *Critical Essays on Chaucer's 'Troilus and Criseyde' and His Major Early Poems* (Milton Keynes: Open University Press, 1991)

Salu, M. (ed.), *Essays on 'Troilus and Criseyde'*, Chaucer Studies 3 (Cambridge: Brewer, 1979)

Shoaf, R. A. (ed.), *Chaucer's 'Troilus and Criseyde' – 'Subgit to alle Poesye': Essays in Criticism*, Medieval and Renaissance Texts and Studies 104 (State University of New York at Binghamton, 1992)

SOURCES, GENRES AND INFLUENCES

Boitani, P. (ed.), *The European Tragedy of Troilus* (Oxford: Clarendon Press, 1989)

Calabrese, M. A., *Chaucer's Ovidian Arts of Love* (Gainesville: University Press of Florida, 1994): Chapter 2, 'Love, Change and the Ovidian "Game" in the *Troilus*: Books I and II', pp. 33–50; and Chapter 3, 'Change and Remedy: Books III, IV and V of the *Troilus*', pp. 51–80

Davenport, W. A., *Chaucer: Complaint and Narrative*, Chaucer Studies 14 (Cambridge: Brewer, 1988): Chapter 6, 'Complaint in Narrative II: *Troilus and Criseyde*', pp. 129–77

Gordon, I. L., *The Double Sorrow of Troilus: A Study of Ambiguities in 'Troilus and Criseyde'* (Oxford: Clarendon Press, 1970)

Kelly, H. A., *Chaucerian Tragedy*, Chaucer Studies 24 (Cambridge: Brewer, 1997): Chapter 3, 'The Tragedy of Troilus', pp. 92–148

Lewis, C. S., 'What Chaucer Really Did to *Il Filostrato*', *Essays and Studies*, **17** (1932), 56–75

McAlpine, M. E., *The Genre of 'Troilus and Criseyde'* (Ithaca, NY: Cornell University Press, 1978)

Mieszkowski, G., 'R. K. Gordon and the *Troilus and Criseyde* Story', *Chaucer Review*, **15** (1980), 127–37

Muscatine, C., *Chaucer and the French Tradition* (Berkeley: University of California Press, 1957): Chapter 5, '*Troilus and Criseyde*', pp. 124–65

Nolan, B., *Chaucer and the Tradition of the Roman Antique* (Cambridge University Press, 1992): Chapter 6, 'Saving the Poetry: Authors, Translators, Texts and Readers in Chaucer's *Book of Troilus and Criseyde*', pp. 198–246

Wallace, D., 'Chaucer's Italian Inheritance', in P. Boitani and J. Mann (eds.), *The Cambridge Companion to Chaucer*, 2nd edn (Cambridge University Press, 2003), pp. 36–57

Wimsatt, J. I., 'Guillaume de Machaut and Chaucer's *Troilus and Criseyde*', *Medium Ævum*, **45** (1976), 277–93

GENDER

Dinshaw, C., *Chaucer's Sexual Poetics* (Madison: University of Wisconsin Press, 1989): Chapter 1, 'Reading Like a Man: The Critics, the Narrator, Troilus, and Pandarus', pp. 28–64

Mann, J., *Feminizing Chaucer*, new edn (Woodbridge: Brewer, 2002): Chapter 1, 'Women and Betrayal', pp. 5–38

Martin, P., *Chaucer's Women: Nuns, Wives and Amazons*, rev. edn (Basingstoke: Macmillan, 1996): Chapter 9, 'Criseyde', pp. 156–88

Pugh, T. and M. Smith Marzec (eds.), *Men and Masculinities in Chaucer's 'Troilus and Criseyde'*, Chaucer Studies 38 (Cambridge: Brewer, 2008)

Tuttle Hansen, E., *Chaucer and the Fictions of Gender* (Berkeley: University of California Press, 1992): Chapter 6, '*Troilus and Criseyde*: "Beth War of Men, and Herkneth What I Seye!"', pp. 141–87

Vitto, C. L. and M. Smith Marzec (eds.), *New Perspectives on Criseyde* (Asheville, NY: Pegasus Press, [2004])

NARRATION

Donaldson, E. T., *Speaking of Chaucer*, paperback edn (London: Athlone Press, 1970): Chapter 5, 'Criseide and Her Narrator', pp. 65–83; and Chapter 6, 'The Ending of *Troilus*', pp. 84–101

Lambert, M., 'Telling the Story in *Troilus and Criseyde*', in P. Boitani and J. Mann (eds.), *The Cambridge Companion to Chaucer,* 2nd edn (Cambridge University Press, 2003), pp. 78–92

Salter, E., '*Troilus and Criseyde*: Poet and Narrator', in her *English and International: Studies in the Literature, Art and Patronage of Medieval England*, ed. D. Pearsall and N. Zeeman (Cambridge University Press, 1988), pp. 231–8

Spearing, A. C., *Textual Subjectivity: The Encoding of Subjectivity in Medieval Narratives and Lyrics* (Oxford University Press, 2005): Chapter 3, '*Troilus and Criseyde*', pp. 68–100

OTHER CRITICAL STUDIES

Aers, D., *Community, Gender, and Individual Identity: English Writing 1360–1430* (London: Routledge, 1988): Chapter 3, 'Masculine Identity in the Courtly Community: The Self Loving in *Troilus and Criseyde*', pp. 117–52

Bishop, I., *Chaucer's 'Troilus and Criseyde': A Critical Study* (University of Bristol, 1981)

Giancarlo, M., 'The Structure of Fate and the Devising of History in Chaucer's *Troilus and Criseyde*', *Studies in the Age of Chaucer*, **26** (2004), 227–66

Grady, F., 'The Boethian Reader of *Troilus and Criseyde*', *Chaucer Review*, **33** (1999), 230–51

Mann, J., 'Chance and Destiny in *Troilus and Criseyde* and the *Knight's Tale*', in P. Boitani and J. Mann (eds.), *The Cambridge Companion to Chaucer*, 2nd edn (Cambridge University Press, 2003), pp. 93–111 (especially pp. 93–105)

McAlpine, M. E., 'Criseyde's Prudence', *Studies in the Age of Chaucer*, **25** (2003), 199–224

Minnis, A. J., *Chaucer and Pagan Antiquity*, Chaucer Studies 8 (Cambridge: Brewer, 1982): Chapter 3, 'Pagan Emotion and Enlightenment in *Troilus and Criseyde*', pp. 61–107

Mitchell, J. A., *Ethics and Eventfulness in Middle English Literature* (New York: Palgrave Macmillan, 2009): Chapter 2, 'Love and Ethics to Come in *Troilus and Criseyde*', pp. 27–46

Morgan, G., *The Tragic Argument of 'Troilus and Criseyde'*, 2 vols. (Lewiston, NY: Mellen, [2005])

Stokes, M., 'Wordes White: Disingenuity in *Troilus and Criseyde*', *English Studies*, **64** (1983), 18–29

Wetherbee, W., *Chaucer and the Poets: An Essay on 'Troilus and Criseyde'* (Ithaca, NY: Cornell University Press, 1984)

Index